MznLnx

Missing Links Exam Preps

Exam Prep for

Marketing: Real People, Real Choices

Solomon, et al., 5th Edition

The MznLnx Exam Prep is your link from the texbook and lecture to your exams.
The MznLnx Exam Preps are unauthorized and comprehensive reviews of your textbooks.

All material provided by MznLnx and Rico Publications (c) 2010
Textbook publishers and textbook authors do not particpate in or contribute to these reviews.

MznLnx

Rico Publications

Exam Prep for Marketing: Real People, Real Choices
5th Edition
Solomon, et al.

Publisher: Raymond Houge
Assistant Editor: Michael Rouger
Text and Cover Designer: Lisa Buckner
Marketing Manager: Sara Swagger
Project Manager, Editorial Production: Jerry Emerson
Art Director: Vernon Lowerui

Product Manager: Dave Mason
Editorial Assitant: Rachel Guzmanji
Pedagogy: Debra Long
Cover Image: Jim Reed/Getty Images
Text and Cover Printer: City Printing, Inc.
Compositor: Media Mix, Inc.

(c) 2010 Rico Publications
ALL RIGHTS RESERVED. No part of this work covered by the copyright may be reproduced or used in any form or by an means--graphic, electronic, or mechanical, including photocopying, recording, taping, Web distribution, information storage, and retrieval systems, or in any other manner--without the written permission of the publisher.

Printed in the United States
ISBN:

For more information about our products, contact us at:
Dave.Mason@RicoPublications.com

For permission to use material from this text or product, submit a request online to:
Dave.Mason@RicoPublications.com

Contents

CHAPTER 1
WELCOME TO THE WORLD OF MARKETING: Creating and Delivering Value — 1

CHAPTER 2
STRATEGIC MARKET PLANNING: Capturing the Big Picture — 13

CHAPTER 3
THRIVING IN THE MARKETING ENVIRONMENT: The World Is Flat — 22

CHAPTER 4
MARKETING RESEARCH: Gathering, Analyzing, and Using Information — 39

CHAPTER 5
CONSUMER BEHAVIOR — 50

CHAPTER 6
BUSINESS-TO-BUSINESS MARKETS: How and Why Organizations Buy — 59

CHAPTER 7
SHARPENING THE FOCUS — 64

CHAPTER 8
CREATING THE PRODUCT — 74

CHAPTER 9
MANAGING THE PRODUCT — 83

CHAPTER 10
SERVICES AND OTHER INTANGIBLES: Marketing the Product That Isn`t There — 92

CHAPTER 11
PRICING THE PRODUCT — 101

CHAPTER 12
CATCHING THE BUZZ — 115

CHAPTER 13
ADVERTISING, SALES PROMOTION, AND PUBLIC RELATIONS — 125

CHAPTER 14
PERSONAL SELLING, SALES MANAGEMENT, AND DIRECT MARKETING — 139

CHAPTER 15
DELIVERING VALUE THROUGH SUPPLY CHAIN MANAGEMENT — 146

CHAPTER 16
RETAILING: Bricks and Clicks — 156

ANSWER KEY — 173

TO THE STUDENT

COMPREHENSIVE

The *MznLnx* Exam Prep series is designed to help you pass your exams. Editors at MznLnx review your textbooks and then prepare these practice exams to help you master the textbook material. Unlike study guides, workbooks, and practice tests provided by the texbook publisher and textbook authors, *MznLnx* gives you **all** of the material in each chapter in exam form, not just samples, so you can be sure to nail your exam.

MECHANICAL

The MznLnx Exam Prep series creates exams that will help you learn the subject matter as well as test you on your understanding. Each question is designed to help you master the concept. Just working through the exams, you gain an understanding of the subject--its a simple mechanical process that produces success.

INTEGRATED STUDY GUIDE AND REVIEW

MznLnx is not just a set of exams designed to test you, its also a comprehensive review of the subject content. Each exam question is also a review of the concept, making sure that you will get the answer correct without having to go to other sources of material. You learn as you go! Its the easiest way to pass an exam.

HUMOR

Studying can be tedious and dry. MznLnx's instructional design includes moderate humor within the exam questions on occassion, to break the tedium and revitalize the brain

Chapter 1. WELCOME TO THE WORLD OF MARKETING: Creating and Delivering Value

1. _____ is a form of communication that typically attempts to persuade potential customers to purchase or to consume more of a particular brand of product or service. 'While now central to the contemporary global economy and the reproduction of global production networks, it is only quite recently that _____ has been more than a marginal influence on patterns of sales and production. The formation of modern _____ was intimately bound up with the emergence of new forms of monopoly capitalism around the end of the 19th and beginning of the 20th century as one element in corporate strategies to create, organize and where possible control markets, especially for mass produced consumer goods.
   a. ACNielsen
   b. ADTECH
   c. Advertising
   d. AMAX

2. An _____ is a series of advertisement messages that share a single idea and theme which make up an integrated marketing communication (IMC.) _____s appear in different media across a specific time frame.

   The critical part of making an _____ is determining a campaign theme, as it sets the tone for the individual advertisements and other forms of marketing communications that will be used.

   a. ADTECH
   b. AMAX
   c. ACNielsen
   d. Advertising campaign

3. _____ is a broad label that refers to any individuals or households that use goods and services generated within the economy. The concept of a _____ is used in different contexts, so that the usage and significance of the term may vary.

   A _____ is a person who uses any product or service.

   a. Power III
   b. 180SearchAssistant
   c. 6-3-5 Brainwriting
   d. Consumer

4. _____ is one of the four Ps of the marketing mix. The other three aspects are product, promotion, and place. It is also a key variable in microeconomic price allocation theory.
   a. Relationship based pricing
   b. Price
   c. Pricing
   d. Competitor indexing

5. A personal and cultural _____ is a relative ethic _____, an assumption upon which implementation can be extrapolated. A _____ system is a set of consistent _____s and measures that is soo not true. A principle _____ is a foundation upon which other _____s and measures of integrity are based.
   a. Package-on-Package
   b. Perceptual maps
   c. Value
   d. Supreme Court of the United States

6. _____ is a form of applied ethics that examines ethical principles and moral or ethical problems that arise in a business environment. It applies to all aspects of business conduct and is relevant to the conduct of individuals and business organizations as a whole. Applied ethics is a field of ethics that deals with ethical questions in many fields such as medical, technical, legal and _____.
   a. 6-3-5 Brainwriting
   b. 180SearchAssistant
   c. Power III
   d. Business ethics

Chapter 1. WELCOME TO THE WORLD OF MARKETING: Creating and Delivering Value

7. _____ is a pricing method used by companies. It is used primarily because it is easy to calculate and requires little information. There are several varieties, but the common thread in all of them is that one first calculates the cost of the product, then includes an additional amount to represent profit.

   a. Loss leader
   b. Break even analysis
   c. Relationship based pricing
   d. Cost-plus Pricing

8. _____ is a branch of philosophy which seeks to address questions about morality, such as how a moral outcome can be achieved in a specific situation (applied _____), how moral values should be determined (normative _____), what moral values people actually abide by (descriptive _____), what the fundamental semantic, ontological, and epistemic nature of _____ or morality is (meta-_____), and how moral capacity or moral agency develops and what its nature is (moral psychology.)

   Socrates was one of the first Greek philosophers to encourage both scholars and the common citizen to turn their attention from the outside world to the condition of man. In this view, Knowledge having a bearing on human life was placed highest, all other knowledge being secondary.

   a. Ethics
   b. ADTECH
   c. AMAX
   d. ACNielsen

9. _____ is the practice of influencing decisions made by government. It includes all attempts to influence legislators and officials, whether by other legislators, constituents or organized groups. A lobbyist is a person who tries to influence legislation on behalf of a special interest or a member of a lobby.

   a. AStore
   b. African Americans
   c. Albert Einstein
   d. Lobbying

10. _____ is defined by the American _____ Association as the activity, set of institutions, and processes for creating, communicating, delivering, and exchanging offerings that have value for customers, clients, partners, and society at large. The term developed from the original meaning which referred literally to going to market, as in shopping, or going to a market to sell goods or services.

    _____ practice tends to be seen as a creative industry, which includes advertising, distribution and selling.

    a. Customer acquisition management
    b. Product naming
    c. Marketing
    d. Marketing myopia

11. _____ is a term commonly used to describe commerce transactions between businesses like the one between a manufacturer and a wholesaler or a wholesaler and a retailer i.e both the buyer and the seller are business entity.This is unlike business-to-consumers (B2C) which involve a business entity and end consumer, or business-to-government (B2G) which involve a business entity and government.

    The volume of B2B transactions is much higher than the volume of B2C transactions. The primary reason for this is that in a typical supply chain there will be many B2B transactions involving subcomponent or raw materials, and only one B2C transaction, specifically sale of the finished product to the end customer.

a. Disruptive technology
b. Customer relationship management
c. Business-to-business
d. Social marketing

12. A _____ is a collection of symbols, experiences and associations connected with a product, a service, a person or any other artifact or entity.

_____s have become increasingly important components of culture and the economy, now being described as 'cultural accessories and personal philosophies'.

Some people distinguish the psychological aspect of a _____ from the experiential aspect.

a. Brand equity
b. Brandable software
c. Store brand
d. Brand

13. _____ is the application of marketing techniques to a specific product, product line, or brand. It seeks to increase the product's perceived value to the customer and thereby increase brand franchise and brand equity. Marketers see a brand as an implied promise that the level of quality people have come to expect from a brand will continue with future purchases of the same product.

a. Store brand
b. Trademark distinctiveness
c. Naming rights
d. Brand management

14. _____ is a measure of the strength of a brand, product, service relative to competitive offerings. There is often a geographic element to the competitive landscape. In defining _____, you must see to what extent a product, brand, or firm controls a product category in a given geographic area.

a. Discretionary spending
b. Market dominance
c. Productivity
d. Market system

15. _____ is an advertisement in which a particular product specifically mentions a competitor by name for the express purpose of showing why the competitor is inferior to the product naming it.

This should not be confused with parody advertisements, where a fictional product is being advertised for the purpose of poking fun at the particular advertisement, nor should it be confused with the use of a coined brand name for the purpose of comparing the product without actually naming an actual competitor. ('Wikipedia tastes better and is less filling than the Encyclopedia Galactica.')

In the 1980s, during what has been referred to as the cola wars, soft-drink manufacturer Pepsi ran a series of advertisements where people, caught on hidden camera, in a blind taste test, chose Pepsi over rival Coca-Cola.

a. Comparative advertising
b. Heavy-up
c. GL-70
d. Cost per conversion

16. _____ is marketing based on relationship and value. It may be used to market a service or a product.

Marketing a service-base business is different from marketing a goods-base business.

a. Power III	b. 6-3-5 Brainwriting
c. 180SearchAssistant	d. Services Marketing

17. In economics, _____ is the desire to own something and the ability to pay for it. The term _____ signifies the ability or the willingness to buy a particular commodity at a given point of time.

a. Discretionary spending	b. Market system
c. Market dominance	d. Demand

18. A _____ is the space, actual or metaphorical, in which a market operates. The term is also used in a trademark law context to denote the actual consumer environment, ie. the 'real world' in which products and services are provided and consumed.

a. 6-3-5 Brainwriting	b. Power III
c. 180SearchAssistant	d. Marketplace

19. In economics, _____ is a measure of the relative satisfaction from consumption of various goods and services. Given this measure, one may speak meaningfully of increasing or decreasing _____, and thereby explain economic behavior in terms of attempts to increase one's _____. For illustrative purposes, changes in _____ are sometimes expressed in units called utils.

a. AMAX	b. ADTECH
c. Utility	d. ACNielsen

20. A number of different _____s are indicated below.

- Randomized controlled trial
    - Double-blind randomized trial
    - Single-blind randomized trial
    - Non-blind trial
- Nonrandomized trial (quasi-experiment)
    - Interrupted time series design (measures on a sample or a series of samples from the same population are obtained several times before and after a manipulated event or a naturally occurring event) - considered a type of quasi-experiment

- Cohort study
    - Prospective cohort
    - Retrospective cohort
    - Time series study
- Case-control study
    - Nested case-control study
- Cross-sectional study
    - Community survey (a type of cross-sectional study)

When choosing a _____, many factors must be taken into account. Different types of studies are subject to different types of bias. For example, recall bias is likely to occur in cross-sectional or case-control studies where subjects are asked to recall exposure to risk factors.

a. 180SearchAssistant
c. Power III

b. Longitudinal studies
d. Study design

21. The _____ was a worldwide economic downturn starting in most places in 1929 and ending at different times in the 1930s or early 1940s for different countries. It was the largest and most important economic depression in the 20th century, and is used in the 21st century as an example of how far the world's economy can fall. The _____ originated in the United States; historians most often use as a starting date the stock market crash on October 29, 1929, known as Black Tuesday.

a. 6-3-5 Brainwriting
c. Power III

b. 180SearchAssistant
d. Great Depression

22. In advertising, a _____ is an advertisement or campaign that uses a more direct, forceful, and overt sales message. This approach works in opposition to a soft sell.

Theorists have examined the value of repetition for _____ versus soft sell messages to determine their relative efficacy.

a. Rack card
c. GL-70

b. Comparative advertising
d. Hard sell

23. A _____ dominated business thought from the beginning of capitalism to the mid 1950s, and some argue it still exists in some industries. Business concerned itself primarily with production, manufacturing, and efficiency issues. Say's Law encapsulated this viewpoint, stating: 'Supply creates its own demand'.

a. Marketing
c. Product differentiation

b. Production orientation
d. Blitz QFD

24. _____ consists of the processes a company uses to track and organize its contacts with its current and prospective customers. _____ software is used to support these processes; information about customers and customer interactions can be entered, stored and accessed by employees in different company departments. Typical _____ goals are to improve services provided to customers, and to use customer contact information for targeted marketing.

a. Demand generation
c. Commercialization

b. Product bundling
d. Customer relationship management

25. _____ is a business management strategy aimed at embedding awareness of quality in all organizational processes. _____ has been widely used in manufacturing, education, call centers, government, and service industries, as well as NASA space and science programs.

When used together as a phrase, the three words in this expression have the following meanings:

- Total: Involving the entire organization, supply chain, and/or product life cycle
- Quality: With its usual definitions, with all its complexities
- Management: The system of managing with steps like Plan, Organize, Control, Lead, Staff, provisioning and organizing.

6 *Chapter 1. WELCOME TO THE WORLD OF MARKETING: Creating and Delivering Value*

As defined by the International Organization for Standardization (ISO):

'_____ is a management approach for an organization, centered on quality, based on the participation of all its members and aiming at long-term success through customer satisfaction, and benefits to all members of the organization and to society.' ISO 8402:1994

One major aim is to reduce variation from every process so that greater consistency of effort is obtained. (Royse, D., Thyer, B., Padgett D., ' Logan T., 2006)

In Japan, _____ comprises four process steps, namely:

1. Kaizen - Focuses on 'Continuous Process Improvement', to make processes visible, repeatable and measurable.
2. Atarimae Hinshitsu - The idea that 'things will work as they are supposed to'.
3. Kansei - Examining the way the user applies the product leads to improvement in the product itself.
4. Miryokuteki Hinshitsu - The idea that 'things should have an aesthetic quality' (for example, a pen will write in a way that is pleasing to the writer.)

_____ requires that the company maintain this quality standard in all aspects of its business. This requires ensuring that things are done right the first time and that defects and waste are eliminated from operations.

a. 6-3-5 Brainwriting
b. Power III
c. 180SearchAssistant
d. Total quality management

26. _____ refer to a collection of facts usually collected as the result of experience, observation or experiment or a set of premises. This may consist of numbers, words particularly as measurements or observations of a set of variables. _____ are often viewed as a lowest level of abstraction from which information and knowledge are derived.
    a. Data
    b. Mean
    c. Pearson product-moment correlation coefficient
    d. Sample size

27. Customer _____ consists of the processes a company uses to track and organize its contacts with its current and prospective customers. CRelationship management software is used to support these processes; information about customers and customer interactions can be entered, stored and accessed by employees in different company departments. Typical CRelationship management goals are to improve services provided to customers, and to use customer contact information for targeted marketing.
    a. Green marketing
    b. Marketing
    c. Relationship management
    d. Product bundling

28. A _____ is a relatively new executive level position at a corporation, company, organization typically reporting directly to the CEO or board of directors. The _____ is responsible for a brand's image, experience, and promise, and propagating it throughout all aspects of the company. The brand officer oversees marketing, advertising, design, public relations and customer service departments.

Chapter 1. WELCOME TO THE WORLD OF MARKETING: Creating and Delivering Value

a. Chief brand officer
b. Power III
c. Financial analyst
d. Chief executive officer

29. _____ is the systematic application of marketing along with other concepts and techniques to achieve specific behavioral goals for a social good. _____ can be applied to promote, for example, merit goods, make the society avoid demerit goods and thus to promote that considers society's well being as a whole. This may include asking people not to smoke in public areas, for example, ask them to use seat belts, prompting to make them follow speed limits.

a. Marketing strategy
b. Social marketing
c. Psychographic
d. Market development

30. _____ is difficult to define. For example, in 1952, Alfred Kroeber and Clyde Kluckhohn compiled a list of 164 definitions of '_____' in _____: A Critical Review of Concepts and Definitions. However, the word '_____' is most commonly used in three basic senses:

- excellence of taste in the fine arts and humanities
- an integrated pattern of human knowledge, belief, and behavior that depends upon the capacity for symbolic thought and social learning
- the set of shared attitudes, values, goals, and practices that characterizes an institution, organization or group.

When the concept first emerged in eighteenth- and nineteenth-century Europe, it connoted a process of cultivation or improvement, as in agriculture or horticulture. In the nineteenth century, it came to refer first to the betterment or refinement of the individual, especially through education, and then to the fulfillment of national aspirations or ideals.

a. AStore
b. Albert Einstein
c. Culture
d. African Americans

31. _____ are final goods specifically intended for the mass market. For instance, _____ do not include investment assets, like precious antiques, even though these antiques are final goods.

Manufactured goods are goods that have been processed by way of machinery.

a. Durable good
b. Power III
c. Free good
d. Consumer goods

32. In operant conditioning, _____ occurs when an event following a response causes an increase in the probability of that response occurring in the future. Response strength can be assessed by measures such as the frequency with which the response is made (for example, a pigeon may peck a key more times in the session), or the speed with which it is made (for example, a rat may run a maze faster.) The environment change contingent upon the response is called a reinforcer.

a. Reinforcement
b. Generic brands
c. Completely randomized designs
d. Relationship Management Application

33. _____ is one of the four elements of marketing mix. An organization or set of organizations (go-betweens) involved in the process of making a product or service available for use or consumption by a consumer or business user.

The other three parts of the marketing mix are product, pricing, and promotion.

a. Distribution
b. Japan Advertising Photographers' Association
c. Better Living Through Chemistry
d. Comparison-Shopping agent

34. _____ is a business term meaning the market segment to which a particular good or service is marketed. It is mainly defined by age, gender, geography, socio-economic grouping, technographic, or any other combination of demographics. It is generally studied and mapped by an organization through lists and reports containing demographic information that may have an effect on the marketing of key products or services.

a. Category Development Index
b. Brando
c. Distribution
d. Market specialization

35. In the field of marketing, a customer _____ consists of the sum total of benefits which a vendor promises that a customer will receive in return for the customer's associated payment (or other value-transfer.)

Put simply, the _____ is what the customer gets for his money.

Accordingly, a customer can evaluate a company's value-proposition on two broad dimensions with multiple subsets:

1. relative performance: what the customer gets from the vendor relative to a competitor's offering;
2. price: which consists of the payment the customer makes to acquire the product or service; plus the access cost

The vendor-company's marketing and sales efforts offer a customer _____; the vendor-company's delivery and customer-service processes then fulfill that value-proposition.

A value-proposition can assist in a firm's marketing strategy, and may guide a business to target a particular market segment.

a. Relationship management
b. DefCom Australia
c. Marketing performance measurement and management
d. Value proposition

36. In economic models, the _____ time frame assumes no fixed factors of production. Firms can enter or leave the marketplace, and the cost (and availability) of land, labor, raw materials, and capital goods can be assumed to vary. In contrast, in the short-run time frame, certain factors are assumed to be fixed, because there is not sufficient time for them to change.

a. Power III
b. Long-run
c. 6-3-5 Brainwriting
d. 180SearchAssistant

37. Competitiveness is a comparative concept of the ability and performance of a firm, sub-sector or country to sell and supply goods and/or services in a given market. Although widely used in economics and business management, the usefulness of the concept, particularly in the context of national competitiveness, is vigorously disputed by economists, such as Paul Krugman .

The term may also be applied to markets, where it is used to refer to the extent to which the market structure may be regarded as perfectly _____.

a. Customs union
b. Geographical pricing
c. Free trade zone
d. Competitive

38. _____ is, in very basic words, a position a firm occupies against its competitors.

According to Michael Porter, the three methods for creating a sustainable _____ are through:

1. Cost leadership - Cost advantage occurs when a firm delivers the same services as its competitors but at a lower cost;

2.

a. 6-3-5 Brainwriting
b. Power III
c. Competitive advantage
d. 180SearchAssistant

39. In marketing, customer _____, lifetime customer value (LCV), or _____ (LTV) and a new concept of 'customer life cycle management' is the present value of the future cash flows attributed to the customer relationship. Use of customer _____ as a marketing metric tends to place greater emphasis on customer service and long-term customer satisfaction, rather than on maximizing short-term sales.

Customer _____ has intuitive appeal as a marketing concept, because in theory it represents exactly how much each customer is worth in monetary terms, and therefore exactly how much a marketing department should be willing to spend to acquire each customer.

a. Sweepstakes
b. Lifetime value
c. Brand infiltration
d. Value chain

40. The _____ is a concept from business management that was first described and popularized by Michael Porter in his 1985 best-seller, Competitive Advantage: Creating and Sustaining Superior Performance.

A _____ is a chain of activities. Products pass through all activities of the chain in order and at each activity the product gains some value.

a. Relationship management
b. Value chain
c. Mass marketing
d. Business-to-business

41. A _____ is a process that can allow an organization to concentrate its limited resources on the greatest opportunities to increase sales and achieve a sustainable competitive advantage. A _____ should be centered around the key concept that customer satisfaction is the main goal.

A _____ is most effective when it is an integral component of corporate strategy, defining how the organization will successfully engage customers, prospects, and competitors in the market arena.

a. Societal marketing
b. Psychographic
c. Marketing strategy
d. Cyberdoc

42. _____ is a reference to the passing of information from person to person. Originally the term referred specifically to oral communication (literally words from the mouth), but now includes any type of human communication, such as face to face, telephone, email, and text messaging.

Word-of-mouth marketing, which encompasses a variety of subcategories, including buzz, blog, viral, grassroots, cause influencers and social media marketing, as well as ambassador programs, work with consumer-generated media and more, can be highly valued by product marketers.

a. New Media Strategies
b. Merchandise
c. Marketing communication
d. Word of mouth

43. The U.S. _____ is an agency of the United States Department of Health and Human Services and is responsible for regulating and supervising the safety of foods, dietary supplements, drugs, vaccines, biological medical products, blood products, medical devices, radiation-emitting devices, veterinary products, and cosmetics. The FDA also enforces section 361 of the Public Health Service Act and the associated regulations, including sanitation requirements on interstate travel as well as specific rules for control of disease on products ranging from pet turtles to semen donations for assisted reproductive medicine techniques.

The FDA is an agency within the United States Department of Health and Human Services responsible for protecting and promoting the nation's public health.

a. Power III
b. 180SearchAssistant
c. Food and Drug Administration
d. 6-3-5 Brainwriting

44. _____ is the study of when, why, how, where and what people do or do not buy products. It blends elements from psychology, sociology, social psychology, anthropology and economics. It attempts to understand the buyer decision making process, both individually and in groups. It studies characteristics of individual consumers such as demographics and behavioural variables in an attempt to understand people's wants. It also tries to assess influences on the consumer from groups such as family, friends, reference groups, and society in general.

a. Consumer behavior
b. Consumer confidence
c. Communal marketing
d. Multidimensional scaling

45. _____ (or citizen-to-citizen) electronic commerce involves the electronically-facilitated transactions between consumers through some third party. A common example is the online auction, in which a consumer posts an item for sale and other consumers bid to purchase it; the third party generally charges a flat fee or commission. The sites are only intermediaries, just there to match consumers.

a. Locator software
b. Business-to-government
c. Web banner
d. Consumer-to-consumer

Chapter 1. WELCOME TO THE WORLD OF MARKETING: Creating and Delivering Value

46. Electronic commerce, commonly known as _____ or eCommerce, consists of the buying and selling of products or services over electronic systems such as the Internet and other computer networks. The amount of trade conducted electronically has grown extraordinarily with wide-spread Internet usage. A wide variety of commerce is conducted in this way, spurring and drawing on innovations in electronic funds transfer, supply chain management, Internet marketing, online transaction processing, electronic data interchange (EDI), inventory management systems, and automated data collection systems.
    a. AMAX
    b. ACNielsen
    c. ADTECH
    d. E-commerce

47. _____ in organizations and public policy is both the organizational process of creating and maintaining a plan; and the psychological process of thinking about the activities required to create a desired goal on some scale. As such, it is a fundamental property of intelligent behavior. This thought process is essential to the creation and refinement of a plan, or integration of it with other plans, that is, it combines forecasting of developments with the preparation of scenarios of how to react to them.
    a. Power III
    b. Planning
    c. 6-3-5 Brainwriting
    d. 180SearchAssistant

48. A _____ is a subgroup of people or organizations sharing one or more characteristics that cause them to have similar product and/or service needs. A true _____ meets all of the following criteria: it is distinct from other segments (different segments have different needs), it is homogeneous within the segment (exhibits common needs); it responds similarly to a market stimulus, and it can be reached by a market intervention. The term is also used when consumers with identical product and/or service needs are divided up into groups so they can be charged different amounts.
    a. Commercial planning
    b. Customer insight
    c. Production orientation
    d. Market segment

49. The _____ is generally accepted as the use and specification of the four p's describing the strategic position of a product in the marketplace. One version of the origins of the _____ starts in 1948 when James Culliton said that a marketing decision should be a result of something similar to a recipe. This version continued in 1953 when Neil Borden, in his American Marketing Association presidential address, took the recipe idea one step further and coined the term 'Marketing-Mix'.
    a. 180SearchAssistant
    b. Power III
    c. 6-3-5 Brainwriting
    d. Marketing mix

50. A _____ is a written document that details the necessary actions to achieve one or more marketing objectives. It can be for a product or service, a brand, or a product line. _____s cover between one and five years.
    a. Disruptive technology
    b. Marketing strategy
    c. Prosumer
    d. Marketing plan

51. _____ is a market coverage strategy in which a firm decides to ignore market segment differences and go after the whole market with one offer.it is type of marketing (or attempting to sell through persuasion) of a product to a wide audience. The idea is to broadcast a message that will reach the largest number of people possible. Traditionally _____ has focused on radio, television and newspapers as the medium used to reach this broad audience.
    a. Marketspace
    b. Cyberdoc
    c. Business-to-consumer
    d. Mass marketing

Chapter 1. WELCOME TO THE WORLD OF MARKETING: Creating and Delivering Value

52. The _____ is a general business term describing the largest group of consumers for a specified industry product. It is the opposite extreme of the term niche market.

The _____ is the group of consumers who occupy the overwhelming mass of a bell curve for common household products, i.e. they could be tagged as being 'average'.

a. Service-profit chain
c. Whole product
b. Tacit collusion
d. Mass market

53. _____ in economics and business is the result of an exchange and from that trade we assign a numerical monetary value to a good, service or asset. If I trade 4 apples for an orange, the _____ of an orange is 4 - apples. Inversely, the _____ of an apple is 1/4 oranges.

a. Pricing
c. Contribution margin-based pricing
b. Discounts and allowances
d. Price

Chapter 2. STRATEGIC MARKET PLANNING: Capturing the Big Picture

1. A _____ is a formal statement of a set of business goals, the reasons why they are believed attainable, and the plan for reaching those goals. It may also contain background information about the organization or team attempting to reach those goals.

The business goals may be defined for for-profit or for non-profit organizations.

a. Logistics management
b. Product marketing
c. Digital strategy
d. Business plan

2. _____ is defined by the American _____ Association as the activity, set of institutions, and processes for creating, communicating, delivering, and exchanging offerings that have value for customers, clients, partners, and society at large. The term developed from the original meaning which referred literally to going to market, as in shopping, or going to a market to sell goods or services.

_____ practice tends to be seen as a creative industry, which includes advertising, distribution and selling.

a. Marketing
b. Product naming
c. Marketing myopia
d. Customer acquisition management

3. A _____ is a written document that details the necessary actions to achieve one or more marketing objectives. It can be for a product or service, a brand, or a product line. _____ s cover between one and five years.

a. Disruptive technology
b. Marketing plan
c. Prosumer
d. Marketing strategy

4. _____ in organizations and public policy is both the organizational process of creating and maintaining a plan; and the psychological process of thinking about the activities required to create a desired goal on some scale. As such, it is a fundamental property of intelligent behavior. This thought process is essential to the creation and refinement of a plan, or integration of it with other plans, that is, it combines forecasting of developments with the preparation of scenarios of how to react to them.

a. Planning
b. 6-3-5 Brainwriting
c. 180SearchAssistant
d. Power III

5. _____ in economics and business is the result of an exchange and from that trade we assign a numerical monetary value to a good, service or asset. If I trade 4 apples for an orange, the _____ of an orange is 4 - apples. Inversely, the _____ of an apple is 1/4 oranges.

a. Pricing
b. Contribution margin-based pricing
c. Discounts and allowances
d. Price

6. _____ is an organization's process of defining its strategy and making decisions on allocating its resources to pursue this strategy, including its capital and people. Various business analysis techniques can be used in _____, including SWOT analysis (Strengths, Weaknesses, Opportunities, and Threats) and PEST analysis (Political, Economic, Social, and Technological analysis) or STEER analysis involving Socio-cultural, Technological, Economic, Ecological, and Regulatory factors and EPISTEL (Environment, Political, Informatic, Social, Technological, Economic and Legal)

_____ is the formal consideration of an organization's future course. All _____ deals with at least one of three key questions:

1. 'What do we do?'
2. 'For whom do we do it?'
3. 'How do we excel?'

In business _____, the third question is better phrased 'How can we beat or avoid competition?'. (Bradford and Duncan, page 1.)

a. 6-3-5 Brainwriting
c. Power III

b. 180SearchAssistant
d. Strategic planning

7. A _____ is a brief statement of the purpose of a company, organization. It is ideally used to guide the actions of the organization.

_____s often contain the following:

- Purpose of the organization
- The organization's primary stakeholders: clients, stockholders, etc.
- Responsibilities of the organization towards these stockholders
- Products and services offered

Generally shorter _____s are more effective than longer ones.

In developing a _____:

- Encourage input as feasible from employees, volunteers, and other stakeholders
- Publicize it broadly

The _____ can be used to resolve differences between business stakeholders. Stakeholders include: employees including managers and executives, stockholders, board of directors, customers, suppliers, distributors, creditors, governments (local, state, federal, etc.), unions, competitors, NGO's, and the general public.

a. Power III
c. 6-3-5 Brainwriting

b. 180SearchAssistant
d. Mission statement

8. An _____ is a subset of strategic work plan. It describes short-term ways of achieving milestones and explains how, or what portion of, a strategic plan will be put into operation during a given operational period, in the case of commercial application, a fiscal year or another given budgetary term. An operational plan is the basis for, and justification of an annual operating budget request.

Chapter 2. STRATEGIC MARKET PLANNING: Capturing the Big Picture 15

a. ADTECH
c. AMAX
b. ACNielsen
d. Operational planning

9. _____ is understood as a business unit within the overall corporate identity which is distinguishable from other business because it serves a defined external market where management can conduct strategic planning in relation to products and markets. When companies become really large, they are best thought of as being composed of a number of businesses (or _____s.)

In the broader domain of strategic management, the phrase '_____' came into use in the 1960s, largely as a result of General Electric's many units.

a. Cost leadership
c. Corporate strategy
b. Business strategy
d. Strategic business unit

10. _____ is a marketing term, and involves evaluating the situation and trends in a particular company's market. _____ is often called the 'three c's', which refers to the three major elements that must be studied:

- Customers
- Costs
- Competition

The number of 'c's' is sometimes extended to four, five, or even six, with 'Collaboration', 'Company', and 'Competitive advantage'.

- Marketing mix
- SWOT analysis

a. Power III
c. 6-3-5 Brainwriting
b. Situation analysis
d. 180SearchAssistant

11. In economics, an externality or spillover of an economic transaction is an impact on a party that is not directly involved in the transaction. In such a case, prices do not reflect the full costs or benefits in production or consumption of a product or service. A positive impact is called an _____ benefit, while a negative impact is called an _____ cost.
a. ADTECH
c. AMAX
b. External
d. ACNielsen

12. _____ is a strategic planning method used to evaluate the Strengths, Weaknesses, Opportunities, and Threats involved in a project or in a business venture. It involves specifying the objective of the business venture or project and identifying the internal and external factors that are favorable and unfavorable to achieving that objective. The technique is credited to Albert Humphrey, who led a research project at Stanford University in the 1960s and 1970s using data from Fortune 500 companies.
a. Market environment
c. Product differentiation
b. Lead scoring
d. SWOT analysis

Chapter 2. STRATEGIC MARKET PLANNING: Capturing the Big Picture

13. In business, a _____ is a product or a business unit that generates unusually high profit margins: so high that it is responsible for a large amount of a company's operating profit. This profit far exceeds the amount necessary to maintain the _____ business, and the excess is used by the business for other purposes.

A firm is said to be acting as a _____ when its earnings per share (EPS) is equal to its dividends per share (DPS), or in other words, when a firm pays out 100% of its free cash flow (FCF) to its shareholders as dividends at the end of each accounting term.

a. Crisis management
c. Goal setting
b. Corporate transparency
d. Cash cow

14. _____, in strategic management and marketing, is the percentage or proportion of the total available market or market segment that is being serviced by a company. It can be expressed as a company's sales revenue (from that market) divided by the total sales revenue available in that market. It can also be expressed as a company's unit sales volume (in a market) divided by the total volume of units sold in that market.

a. Demand generation
c. Customer relationship management
b. Cyberdoc
d. Market share

15. A _____ strategy targets non-buying customers in currently targeted segments. It also targets new customers in new segments. (Winer)

A marketing manager has to think about the following questions before implementing a _____ strategy: Is it profitable? Will it require the introduction of new or modified products? Is the customer and channel well enough researched and understood?

The marketing manager uses these four groups to give more focus to the market segment decision: existing customers, competitor customers, non-buying in current segments, new segments.

a. Commercial planning
c. Perceptual mapping
b. Kano model
d. Market development

16. _____ is one of the four growth strategies of the Product-Market Growth Matrix defined by Ansoff. _____ occurs when a company enters/penetrates a market with current products. The best way to achieve this is by gaining competitors' customers (part of their market share.)

a. Marketization
c. Pasar pagi
b. Horizontal market
d. Market penetration

17. _____ is an organizational lifecycle function within a company dealing with the planning or marketing of a product or products at all stages of the product lifecycle.

_____ and product marketing (outbound focused) are different yet complementary efforts with the objective of maximizing sales revenues, market share, and profit margins. The role of _____ spans many activities from strategic to tactical and varies based on the organizational structure of the company.

Chapter 2. STRATEGIC MARKET PLANNING: Capturing the Big Picture

a. Service product management
b. Product information management
c. Requirement prioritization
d. Product management

18. The Ansoff _____ is a marketing tool created by Igor Ansoff and first published in his article 'Strategies for Diversification' in the Harvard Business Review (1957.) The matrix allows marketers to consider ways to grow the business via existing and/or new products, in existing and/or new markets - there are four possible product/market combinations. This matrix helps companies decide what course of action should be taken given current performance.
   a. Market penetration
   b. Partial equilibrium
   c. Market system
   d. Product-market growth matrix

19. In business and engineering, new _____ is the term used to describe the complete process of bringing a new product or service to market. There are two parallel paths involved in the Nproduct development process: one involves the idea generation, product design, and detail engineering; the other involves market research and marketing analysis. Companies typically see new _____ as the first stage in generating and commercializing new products within the overall strategic process of product life cycle management used to maintain or grow their market share.
   a. New product development
   b. Specification tree
   c. New product screening
   d. Product development

20. _____ commonly refers to the electronic retailing / _____ channels industry, which includes such billion dollar companies as Home shoppingN, QVC, eBay, ShopNBC, Buy.com, and Amazon.com. _____ allows consumers to shop for goods while in the privacy of their own home, as opposed to traditional shopping, which requires you to visit brick and mortar stores and shopping malls.

The _____ / electronic retailing industry was created in 1977 when small market radio talk show host Bob Circosta was asked to sell avocado-green-colored can openers live on the air by station owner Bud Paxson when an advertiser traded 112 units of product instead of paying his advertising bill.

   a. 180SearchAssistant
   b. 6-3-5 Brainwriting
   c. Power III
   d. Home shopping

21. The _____ is generally accepted as the use and specification of the four p's describing the strategic position of a product in the marketplace. One version of the origins of the _____ starts in 1948 when James Culliton said that a marketing decision should be a result of something similar to a recipe. This version continued in 1953 when Neil Borden, in his American Marketing Association presidential address, took the recipe idea one step further and coined the term 'Marketing-Mix'.
   a. 180SearchAssistant
   b. Power III
   c. 6-3-5 Brainwriting
   d. Marketing mix

22. _____ is the examining of goods or services from retailers with the intent to purchase at that time. _____ is an activity of selection and/or purchase. In some contexts it is considered a leisure activity as well as an economic one.
   a. Khodebshchik
   b. Discount store
   c. Hawkers
   d. Shopping

23. _____ is a broad label that refers to any individuals or households that use goods and services generated within the economy. The concept of a _____ is used in different contexts, so that the usage and significance of the term may vary.

Chapter 2. STRATEGIC MARKET PLANNING: Capturing the Big Picture

A _____ is a person who uses any product or service.

a. Power III
b. 180SearchAssistant
c. 6-3-5 Brainwriting
d. Consumer

24. A _____ is a process that can allow an organization to concentrate its limited resources on the greatest opportunities to increase sales and achieve a sustainable competitive advantage. A _____ should be centered around the key concept that customer satisfaction is the main goal.

A _____ is most effective when it is an integral component of corporate strategy, defining how the organization will successfully engage customers, prospects, and competitors in the market arena.

a. Cyberdoc
b. Psychographic
c. Societal marketing
d. Marketing strategy

25. _____ is one of the four Ps of the marketing mix. The other three aspects are product, promotion, and place. It is also a key variable in microeconomic price allocation theory.

a. Competitor indexing
b. Price
c. Pricing
d. Relationship based pricing

26. A _____ is a plan of action designed to achieve a particular goal.

_____ is different from tactics. In military terms, tactics is concerned with the conduct of an engagement while _____ is concerned with how different engagements are linked.

a. Strategy
b. 6-3-5 Brainwriting
c. Power III
d. 180SearchAssistant

27. _____ is a business term meaning the market segment to which a particular good or service is marketed. It is mainly defined by age, gender, geography, socio-economic grouping, technographic, or any other combination of demographics. It is generally studied and mapped by an organization through lists and reports containing demographic information that may have an effect on the marketing of key products or services.

a. Distribution
b. Brando
c. Category Development Index
d. Market specialization

28. _____ is a term commonly used to describe commerce transactions between businesses like the one between a manufacturer and a wholesaler or a wholesaler and a retailer i.e both the buyer and the seller are business entity.This is unlike business-to-consumers (B2C) which involve a business entity and end consumer, or business-to-government (B2G) which involve a business entity and government.

The volume of B2B transactions is much higher than the volume of B2C transactions. The primary reason for this is that in a typical supply chain there will be many B2B transactions involving subcomponent or raw materials, and only one B2C transaction, specifically sale of the finished product to the end customer.

Chapter 2. STRATEGIC MARKET PLANNING: Capturing the Big Picture

a. Disruptive technology
b. Customer relationship management
c. Social marketing
d. Business-to-business

29. _____ is a pricing method used by companies. It is used primarily because it is easy to calculate and requires little information. There are several varieties, but the common thread in all of them is that one first calculates the cost of the product, then includes an additional amount to represent profit.
   a. Loss leader
   b. Break even analysis
   c. Relationship based pricing
   d. Cost-plus Pricing

30. A _____ is a subgroup of people or organizations sharing one or more characteristics that cause them to have similar product and/or service needs. A true _____ meets all of the following criteria: it is distinct from other segments (different segments have different needs), it is homogeneous within the segment (exhibits common needs); it responds similarly to a market stimulus, and it can be reached by a market intervention. The term is also used when consumers with identical product and/or service needs are divided up into groups so they can be charged different amounts.
   a. Commercial planning
   b. Production orientation
   c. Customer insight
   d. Market segment

31. _____ is one of the four elements of marketing mix. An organization or set of organizations (go-betweens) involved in the process of making a product or service available for use or consumption by a consumer or business user.

The other three parts of the marketing mix are product, pricing, and promotion.

   a. Comparison-Shopping agent
   b. Better Living Through Chemistry
   c. Japan Advertising Photographers' Association
   d. Distribution

32. In operant conditioning, _____ occurs when an event following a response causes an increase in the probability of that response occurring in the future. Response strength can be assessed by measures such as the frequency with which the response is made (for example, a pigeon may peck a key more times in the session), or the speed with which it is made (for example, a rat may run a maze faster.) The environment change contingent upon the response is called a reinforcer.
   a. Completely randomized designs
   b. Reinforcement
   c. Generic brands
   d. Relationship Management Application

33. _____ is the realization of an application idea, model, design, specification, standard, algorithm an _____ is a realization of a technical specification or algorithm as a program, software component, or other computer system. Many _____ s may exist for a given specification or standard.
   a. AMAX
   b. ADTECH
   c. ACNielsen
   d. Implementation

34. _____ generally refers to a list of all planned expenses and revenues. It is a plan for saving and spending. A _____ is an important concept in microeconomics, which uses a _____ line to illustrate the trade-offs between two or more goods.
   a. Power III
   b. 180SearchAssistant
   c. 6-3-5 Brainwriting
   d. Budget

35. Organizational culture is not the same as _____. It is wider and deeper concepts, something that an organization 'is' rather than what it 'has' (according to Buchanan and Huczynski.)

_____ is the total sum of the values, customs, traditions and meanings that make a company unique.

a. Cross-functional team
c. 180SearchAssistant
b. Power III
d. Corporate culture

36. A personal and cultural _____ is a relative ethic _____, an assumption upon which implementation can be extrapolated. A _____ system is a set of consistent _____s and measures that is soo not true. A principle _____ is a foundation upon which other _____s and measures of integrity are based.

a. Package-on-Package
c. Perceptual maps
b. Value
d. Supreme Court of the United States

37. _____ is a form of applied ethics that examines ethical principles and moral or ethical problems that arise in a business environment. It applies to all aspects of business conduct and is relevant to the conduct of individuals and business organizations as a whole. Applied ethics is a field of ethics that deals with ethical questions in many fields such as medical, technical, legal and _____.

a. Power III
c. 6-3-5 Brainwriting
b. Business ethics
d. 180SearchAssistant

38. _____ is difficult to define. For example, in 1952, Alfred Kroeber and Clyde Kluckhohn compiled a list of 164 definitions of '_____' in _____: A Critical Review of Concepts and Definitions. However, the word '_____' is most commonly used in three basic senses:

- excellence of taste in the fine arts and humanities
- an integrated pattern of human knowledge, belief, and behavior that depends upon the capacity for symbolic thought and social learning
- the set of shared attitudes, values, goals, and practices that characterizes an institution, organization or group.

When the concept first emerged in eighteenth- and nineteenth-century Europe, it connoted a process of cultivation or improvement, as in agriculture or horticulture. In the nineteenth century, it came to refer first to the betterment or refinement of the individual, especially through education, and then to the fulfillment of national aspirations or ideals.

a. AStore
c. Albert Einstein
b. Culture
d. African Americans

39. _____ is a branch of philosophy which seeks to address questions about morality, such as how a moral outcome can be achieved in a specific situation (applied _____), how moral values should be determined (normative _____), what moral values people actually abide by (descriptive _____), what the fundamental semantic, ontological, and epistemic nature of _____ or morality is (meta-_____), and how moral capacity or moral agency develops and what its nature is (moral psychology.)

Socrates was one of the first Greek philosophers to encourage both scholars and the common citizen to turn their attention from the outside world to the condition of man. In this view, Knowledge having a bearing on human life was placed highest, all other knowledge being secondary.

a. Ethics
b. AMAX
c. ACNielsen
d. ADTECH

40. _____ in survey research refers to the ratio of number of people who answered the survey divided by the number of people in the sample. It is usually expressed in the form of a percentage.

Example: if 1,000 surveys were sent by mail, and 257 were successfully completed and returned, then the _____ would be 25.7 %.

a. Sentence completion tests
b. Response rate
c. Power III
d. Reference value

Chapter 3. THRIVING IN THE MARKETING ENVIRONMENT: The World Is Flat

1. _____ is a branch of philosophy which seeks to address questions about morality, such as how a moral outcome can be achieved in a specific situation (applied _____), how moral values should be determined (normative _____), what moral values people actually abide by (descriptive _____), what the fundamental semantic, ontological, and epistemic nature of _____ or morality is (meta-_____), and how moral capacity or moral agency develops and what its nature is (moral psychology.)

Socrates was one of the first Greek philosophers to encourage both scholars and the common citizen to turn their attention from the outside world to the condition of man. In this view, Knowledge having a bearing on human life was placed highest, all other knowledge being secondary.

    a. AMAX   b. Ethics
    c. ADTECH   d. ACNielsen

2. The break-even point for a product is the point where total revenue received equals the total costs associated with the sale of the product (TR=TC.) A break-even point is typically calculated in order for businesses to determine if it would be profitable to sell a proposed product, as opposed to attempting to modify an existing product instead so it can be made lucrative. _____ can also be used to analyse the potential profitability of an expenditure in a sales-based business.

In _____, margin of safety is how much output or sales level can fall before a business reaches its break-even point (BEP).

    a. Price skimming   b. Pay Per Sale
    c. Contribution margin-based pricing   d. Break even analysis

3. _____ is a form of applied ethics that examines ethical principles and moral or ethical problems that arise in a business environment. It applies to all aspects of business conduct and is relevant to the conduct of individuals and business organizations as a whole. Applied ethics is a field of ethics that deals with ethical questions in many fields such as medical, technical, legal and _____.
    a. Power III   b. 180SearchAssistant
    c. 6-3-5 Brainwriting   d. Business ethics

4. A _____ is the space, actual or metaphorical, in which a market operates. The term is also used in a trademark law context to denote the actual consumer environment, ie. the 'real world' in which products and services are provided and consumed.
    a. Marketplace   b. Power III
    c. 6-3-5 Brainwriting   d. 180SearchAssistant

5. _____ is an advertisement in which a particular product specifically mentions a competitor by name for the express purpose of showing why the competitor is inferior to the product naming it.

This should not be confused with parody advertisements, where a fictional product is being advertised for the purpose of poking fun at the particular advertisement, nor should it be confused with the use of a coined brand name for the purpose of comparing the product without actually naming an actual competitor. ('Wikipedia tastes better and is less filling than the Encyclopedia Galactica.')

In the 1980s, during what has been referred to as the cola wars, soft-drink manufacturer Pepsi ran a series of advertisements where people, caught on hidden camera, in a blind taste test, chose Pepsi over rival Coca-Cola.

Chapter 3. THRIVING IN THE MARKETING ENVIRONMENT: The World Is Flat

a. Heavy-up
b. Cost per conversion
c. Comparative advertising
d. GL-70

6. A personal and cultural _____ is a relative ethic _____, an assumption upon which implementation can be extrapolated. A _____ system is a set of consistent _____s and measures that is soo not true. A principle _____ is a foundation upon which other _____s and measures of integrity are based.

a. Package-on-Package
b. Perceptual maps
c. Supreme Court of the United States
d. Value

7. _____ is a broad label that refers to any individuals or households that use goods and services generated within the economy. The concept of a _____ is used in different contexts, so that the usage and significance of the term may vary.

A _____ is a person who uses any product or service.

a. 180SearchAssistant
b. Power III
c. 6-3-5 Brainwriting
d. Consumer

8. In 1962, President John F. Kennedy presented a speech to the United States Congress in which he extolled four basic consumer rights, later called The _____.

While later expanded, the original six basic beliefs of consumer protection are the most widely recognized.

In 1985, the concept of consumer rights was endorsed by the United Nations and expanded to included eight basic rights.

a. Power III
b. Consumer Bill of Rights
c. 6-3-5 Brainwriting
d. 180SearchAssistant

9. _____ is the equation of personal happiness with consumption and the purchase of material possessions.

The term is often associated with criticisms of consumption starting with Thorstein Veblen.

Veblen's subject of examination, the newly emergent middle class arising at the turn of the twentieth century, comes to full fruition by the end of the twentieth century through the process of globalization.

In economics, _____ refers to economic policies placing emphasis on consumption.

a. Power III
b. 180SearchAssistant
c. 6-3-5 Brainwriting
d. Consumerism

10. The _____ of 1977 (15 U.S.C. §§ 78dd-1, et seq.) is a United States federal law known primarily for two of its main provisions, one that addresses accounting transparency requirements under the Securities Exchange Act of 1934 and another concerning bribery of foreign officials.

a. Trademark dilution
b. Copyright
c. Tenth Amendment
d. Foreign Corrupt Practices Act

11. _____ is defined by the American _____ Association as the activity, set of institutions, and processes for creating, communicating, delivering, and exchanging offerings that have value for customers, clients, partners, and society at large. The term developed from the original meaning which referred literally to going to market, as in shopping, or going to a market to sell goods or services.

_____ practice tends to be seen as a creative industry, which includes advertising, distribution and selling.

a. Customer acquisition management
b. Product naming
c. Marketing myopia
d. Marketing

12. _____ is a form of communication that typically attempts to persuade potential customers to purchase or to consume more of a particular brand of product or service. 'While now central to the contemporary global economy and the reproduction of global production networks, it is only quite recently that _____ has been more than a marginal influence on patterns of sales and production. The formation of modern _____ was intimately bound up with the emergence of new forms of monopoly capitalism around the end of the 19th and beginning of the 20th century as one element in corporate strategies to create, organize and where possible control markets, especially for mass produced consumer goods.

a. Advertising
b. ADTECH
c. AMAX
d. ACNielsen

13. False advertising or _____ is the use of false or misleading statements in advertising. As advertising has the potential to persuade people into commercial transactions that they might otherwise avoid, many governments around the world use regulations to control false, deceptive or misleading advertising. Truth in labeling refers to essentially the same concept, that customers have the right to know what they are buying, and that all necessary information should be on the label.

a. Deceptive advertising
b. Misleading advertising
c. Power III
d. Fine print

14. The _____ is an independent agency of the United States government, established in 1914 by the _____ Act. Its principal mission is the promotion of 'consumer protection' and the elimination and prevention of what regulators perceive to be harmfully 'anti-competitive' business practices, such as coercive monopoly.

The _____ Act was one of President Wilson's major acts against trusts.

a. Federal Trade Commission
b. 6-3-5 Brainwriting
c. Power III
d. 180SearchAssistant

15. The _____ of 1914 (15 U.S.C §§ 41-58, as amended) established the Federal Trade Commission (FTC), a bipartisan body of five members appointed by the President of the United States for seven year terms. This Commission was authorized to issue Cease and Desist orders to large corporations to curb unfair trade practices. This Act also gave more flexibility to the US congress for judicial matters.

a. Product liability
b. Gripe site
c. Comparative negligence
d. Federal Trade Commission Act

16. The U.S. _____ is an agency of the United States Department of Health and Human Services and is responsible for regulating and supervising the safety of foods, dietary supplements, drugs, vaccines, biological medical products, blood products, medical devices, radiation-emitting devices, veterinary products, and cosmetics. The FDA also enforces section 361 of the Public Health Service Act and the associated regulations, including sanitation requirements on interstate travel as well as specific rules for control of disease on products ranging from pet turtles to semen donations for assisted reproductive medicine techniques.

The FDA is an agency within the United States Department of Health and Human Services responsible for protecting and promoting the nation's public health.

a. 180SearchAssistant
b. Food and Drug Administration
c. 6-3-5 Brainwriting
d. Power III

17. The _____ is generally accepted as the use and specification of the four p's describing the strategic position of a product in the marketplace. One version of the origins of the _____ starts in 1948 when James Culliton said that a marketing decision should be a result of something similar to a recipe. This version continued in 1953 when Neil Borden, in his American Marketing Association presidential address, took the recipe idea one step further and coined the term 'Marketing-Mix'.

a. Marketing mix
b. Power III
c. 6-3-5 Brainwriting
d. 180SearchAssistant

18. In operant conditioning, _____ occurs when an event following a response causes an increase in the probability of that response occurring in the future. Response strength can be assessed by measures such as the frequency with which the response is made (for example, a pigeon may peck a key more times in the session), or the speed with which it is made (for example, a rat may run a maze faster.) The environment change contingent upon the response is called a reinforcer.

a. Completely randomized designs
b. Relationship Management Application
c. Reinforcement
d. Generic brands

19. _____ is one of the four Ps of the marketing mix. The other three aspects are product, promotion, and place. It is also a key variable in microeconomic price allocation theory.

a. Relationship based pricing
b. Competitor indexing
c. Pricing
d. Price

20. _____ as a legal term refers to promotional statements and claims that express subjective rather than objective views, such that no reasonable person would take literally. _____ is especially featured in testimonials.

In a legal context, the term originated in the English Court of Appeal case Carlill v Carbolic Smoke Ball Company, which centred on whether a monetary reimbursement should be paid when an influenza preventative device failed to work.

a. Conquesting
b. Custom media
c. Puffery
d. Heinz pickle pin

21. According to the American Marketing Association, _____ is the marketing of products that are presumed to be environmentally safe. Thus _____ incorporates a broad range of activities, including product modification, changes to the production process, packaging changes, as well as modifying advertising. Yet defining _____ is not a simple task where several meanings intersect and contradict each other; an example of this will be the existence of varying social, environmental and retail definitions attached to this term.
   a. Value proposition
   b. Commercialization
   c. Green marketing
   d. Customer Interaction Tracker

22. A _____ is a process that can allow an organization to concentrate its limited resources on the greatest opportunities to increase sales and achieve a sustainable competitive advantage. A _____ should be centered around the key concept that customer satisfaction is the main goal.

   A _____ is most effective when it is an integral component of corporate strategy, defining how the organization will successfully engage customers, prospects, and competitors in the market arena.

   a. Psychographic
   b. Cyberdoc
   c. Marketing strategy
   d. Societal marketing

23. A _____ is a plan of action designed to achieve a particular goal.

   _____ is different from tactics. In military terms, tactics is concerned with the conduct of an engagement while _____ is concerned with how different engagements are linked.

   a. 6-3-5 Brainwriting
   b. Power III
   c. Strategy
   d. 180SearchAssistant

24. _____ or cause-related marketing refers to a type of marketing involving the cooperative efforts of a 'for profit' business and a non-profit organization for mutual benefit. The term is sometimes used more broadly and generally to refer to any type of marketing effort for social and other charitable causes, including in-house marketing efforts by non-profit organizations. _____ differs from corporate giving (philanthropy) as the latter generally involves a specific donation that is tax deductible, while _____ is a marketing relationship generally not based on a donation.
   a. Cause marketing
   b. Digital marketing
   c. Global marketing
   d. Cause-related Marketing

25. _____ is the variety of human societies or cultures in a specific region, or in the world as a whole. (The term is also sometimes used to refer to multiculturalism within an organisation)
   a. Cultural diversity
   b. 6-3-5 Brainwriting
   c. Power III
   d. 180SearchAssistant

26. _____ is a term commonly used to describe commerce transactions between businesses like the one between a manufacturer and a wholesaler or a wholesaler and a retailer i.e both the buyer and the seller are business entity. This is unlike business-to-consumers (B2C) which involve a business entity and end consumer, or business-to-government (B2G) which involve a business entity and government.

Chapter 3. THRIVING IN THE MARKETING ENVIRONMENT: The World Is Flat

The volume of B2B transactions is much higher than the volume of B2C transactions. The primary reason for this is that in a typical supply chain there will be many B2B transactions involving subcomponent or raw materials, and only one B2C transaction, specifically sale of the finished product to the end customer.

a. Disruptive technology
b. Business-to-business
c. Social marketing
d. Customer relationship management

27. The Oxford University Press defines _____ as 'marketing on a worldwide scale reconciling or taking commercial advantage of global operational differences, similarities and opportunities in order to meet global objectives.' Oxford University Press' Glossary of Marketing Terms.

Here are three reasons for the shift from domestic to _____ as given by the authors of the textbook, _____ Management--3rd Edition by Masaaki Kotabe and Kristiaan Helsen, 2004.

One of the product categories in which global competition has been easy to track is in U.S. automotive sales.

a. Digital marketing
b. Guerrilla Marketing
c. Diversity marketing
d. Global marketing

28. Merchandising refers to the methods, practices and operations conducted to promote and sustain certain categories of commercial activity. The term is understood to have different specific meanings depending on the context. _____ is a sale goods at a store

In marketing, one of the definitions of merchandising is the practice in which the brand or image from one product or service is used to sell another.

a. New Media Strategies
b. Merchandise
c. Merchandising
d. Sales promotion

29. _____ is exchanging goods or services that are paid for, in whole or part, with other goods or services.

There are five main variants of _____:

- Barter: Exchange of goods or services directly for other goods or services without the use of money as means of purchase or payment.
- Switch trading: Practice in which one company sells to another its obligation to make a purchase in a given country.
- Counter purchase: Sale of goods and services to a country by a company that promises to make a future purchase of a specific product from the country.
- Buyback: occurs when a firm builds a plant in a country - or supplies technology, equipment, training, or other services to the country and agrees to take a certain percentage of the plant's output as partial payment for the contract.
- Offset: Agreement that a company will offset a hard - currency purchase of an unspecified product from that nation in the future. Agreement by one nation to buy a product from another, subject to the purchase of some or all of the components and raw materials from the buyer of the finished product, or the assembly of such product in the buyer nation.

a. Retail loss prevention
c. Merchant
b. RFM
d. Countertrade

30. _____ can be regarded as an outcome of mental processes (cognitive process) leading to the selection of a course of action among several alternatives. Every _____ process produces a final choice. The output can be an action or an opinion of choice.
   a. Power III
   c. 6-3-5 Brainwriting
   b. 180SearchAssistant
   d. Decision making

31. In economics, _____ is the desire to own something and the ability to pay for it. The term _____ signifies the ability or the willingness to buy a particular commodity at a given point of time.

   a. Discretionary spending
   c. Demand
   b. Market dominance
   d. Market system

32. Competitiveness is a comparative concept of the ability and performance of a firm, sub-sector or country to sell and supply goods and/or services in a given market. Although widely used in economics and business management, the usefulness of the concept, particularly in the context of national competitiveness, is vigorously disputed by economists, such as Paul Krugman.

The term may also be applied to markets, where it is used to refer to the extent to which the market structure may be regarded as perfectly _____.

   a. Competitive
   c. Free trade zone
   b. Geographical pricing
   d. Customs union

33. _____ is, in very basic words, a position a firm occupies against its competitors.

Chapter 3. THRIVING IN THE MARKETING ENVIRONMENT: The World Is Flat

According to Michael Porter, the three methods for creating a sustainable _____ are through:

1. Cost leadership - Cost advantage occurs when a firm delivers the same services as its competitors but at a lower cost;

2.

   a. 6-3-5 Brainwriting   b. Competitive advantage
   c. 180SearchAssistant   d. Power III

34. _____ is a form of intellectual property which gives the creator of an original work exclusive rights for a certain time period in relation to that work, including its publication, distribution and adaptation; after which time the work is said to enter the public domain. _____ applies to any expressible form of an idea or information that is substantive and discrete. Some jurisdictions also recognize 'moral rights' of the creator of a work, such as the right to be credited for the work.
   a. Copyright   b. Reasonable person standard
   c. Collective mark   d. Celler-Kefauver Act

35. _____s is the social science that studies the production, distribution, and consumption of goods and services. The term _____s comes from the Ancient Greek οἰκονομία from οἶκος (oikos, 'house') + νόμος (nomos, 'custom' or 'law'), hence 'rules of the house(hold)'. Current _____ models developed out of the broader field of political economy in the late 19th century, owing to a desire to use an empirical approach more akin to the physical sciences.
   a. Industrial organization   b. ACNielsen
   c. ADTECH   d. Economic

36. The _____ was the outcome of the failure of negotiating governments to create the International Trade Organization (ITO.) GATT was formed in 1947 and lasted until 1994, when it was replaced by the World Trade Organization. The Bretton Woods Conference had introduced the idea for an organization to regulate trade as part of a larger plan for economic recovery after World War II.
   a. Power III   b. General Agreement on Trade in Services
   c. Trade pact   d. General Agreement on Tariffs and Trade

37. A _____ is a set of exclusive rights granted by a State to an inventor or his assignee for a limited period of time in exchange for a disclosure of an invention.

The procedure for granting _____s, the requirements placed on the _____ee and the extent of the exclusive rights vary widely between countries according to national laws and international agreements. Typically, however, a _____ application must include one or more claims defining the invention which must be new, inventive, and useful or industrially applicable.

   a. Reasonable person standard   b. Product liability
   c. Foreign Corrupt Practices Act   d. Patent

38. _____ is the economic policy of restraining trade between nations, through methods such as tariffs on imported goods, restrictive quotas, and a variety of other restrictive government regulations designed to discourage imports, and prevent foreign take-over of local markets and companies. This policy is closely aligned with anti-globalization, and contrasts with free trade, where government barriers to trade are kept to a minimum. The term is mostly used in the context of economics, where _____ refers to policies or doctrines which 'protect' businesses and workers within a country by restricting or regulating trade with foreign nations.
   a. Market economy
   b. Black market
   c. Gift economy
   d. Protectionism

39. _____ refers to 'controlling human or societal behaviour by rules or restrictions.' _____ can take many forms: legal restrictions promulgated by a government authority, self-_____, social _____, co-_____ and market _____. One can consider _____ as actions of conduct imposing sanctions (such as a fine.) This action of administrative law, or implementing regulatory law, may be contrasted with statutory or case law.
   a. Non-conventional trademark
   b. Rule of four
   c. CAN-SPAM
   d. Regulation

40. A _____ is a tax imposed on goods when they are moved across a political boundary. They are usually associated with protectionism, the economic policy of restraining trade between nations. For political reasons, _____s are usually imposed on imported goods, although they may also be imposed on exported goods.
   a. Fiscal policy
   b. Power III
   c. Tariff
   d. Monetary policy

41. The _____ is an international organization whose stated aims are to facilitate cooperation in international law, international security, economic development, social progress, human rights and achieving world peace. The _____ was founded in 1945 after World War II to replace the League of Nations, to stop wars between countries and to provide a platform for dialogue.

There are currently 192 member states, including nearly every recognized independent state in the world.

   a. United Nations
   b. AMAX
   c. ACNielsen
   d. ADTECH

42. The _____ is an international organization designed to supervise and liberalize international trade. The _____ came into being on 1 January 1995, and is the successor to the General Agreement on Tariffs and Trade (GATT), which was created in 1947, and continued to operate for almost five decades as a de facto international organization.

The _____ deals with the rules of trade between nations at a near-global level; it is responsible for negotiating and implementing new trade agreements, and is in charge of policing member countries' adherence to all the _____ agreements, signed by the majority of the world's trading nations and ratified in their parliaments.

   a. Merchandise Mart
   b. Population Reference Bureau
   c. BSI Group
   d. World Trade Organization

Chapter 3. THRIVING IN THE MARKETING ENVIRONMENT: The World Is Flat

43. The _____ is an economic and political union of 27 member states, located primarily in Europe. It was established by the Treaty of Maastricht on 1 November 1993 upon the foundations of the pre-existing European Economic Community. With almost 500 million citizens, the _____ combined generates an estimated 30% share (US$16.8 trillion in 2007) of the nominal gross world product.

  a. Eurozone
  b. European Union
  c. ADTECH
  d. ACNielsen

44. _____ is a designated group of countries that have agreed to eliminate tariffs, quotas and preferences on most (if not all) goods and services traded between them. It can be considered the second stage of economic integration. Countries choose this kind of economic integration form if their economical structures are complementary.

  a. Power III
  b. 6-3-5 Brainwriting
  c. 180SearchAssistant
  d. Free Trade Area

45. The _____ or gross domestic income (GDI) is one of the measures of national income and output for a given country's economy. It is the total value of all final goods and services produced in a particular economy; the dollar value of all goods and services produced within a country's borders in a given year. _____ can be defined in three ways, all of which are conceptually identical.

  a. Microeconomics
  b. Macroeconomics
  c. Gross domestic product
  d. Leading indicator

46. A variety of measures of national income and output are used in economics to estimate total economic activity in a country or region, including gross domestic product (GDP), _____ , and net national income (NNI).

_____ is defined as the 'value of all goods and services produced in a country in one year, plus income earned by its citizens abroad, minus income earned by foreigners in the country'.

  a. Consumer Expenditure Survey
  b. Power III
  c. Bureau of Labor Statistics
  d. Gross national product

47. The _____ is a trilateral trade bloc in North America created by the governments of the United States, Canada, and Mexico. It superseded the Canada-United States Free Trade Agreement between the US and Canada.

Following diplomatic negotiations dating back to 1990 between the three nations, the leaders met in San Antonio, Texas on December 17, 1992 to sign _____ .

  a. North American Free Trade Agreement
  b. 180SearchAssistant
  c. 6-3-5 Brainwriting
  d. Power III

48. The _____ is a marketing term and refers to all of the forces outside of marketing that affect marketing management's ability to build and maintain successful relationships with target customers. The _____ consists of both the macroenvironment and the microenvironment.

The microenvironment refers to the forces that are close to the company and affect its ability to serve its customers.

a. Psychographic	b. Customer franchise
c. Market environment	d. Business-to-consumer

49. The term _____ is used to describe countries that have a high level of development according to some criteria. Which criteria, and which countries are classified as being developed, is a contentious issue and there is fierce debate about this. Economic criteria have tended to dominate discussions.

a. Brando	b. Bringin' Home the Oil
c. Developed country	d. Completely randomized designs

50. The term _____ refers to economy-wide fluctuations in production or economic activity over several months or years. These fluctuations occur around a long-term growth trend, and typically involve shifts over time between periods of relatively rapid economic growth (expansion or boom), and periods of relative stagnation or decline (contraction or recession.)

These fluctuations are often measured using the growth rate of real gross domestic product.

a. Business cycle	b. Monopolistic competition
c. Perfect competition	d. Market structure

51. In economics, the term _____ describes the reduction of a country's gross domestic product (GDP) for at least two quarters. The usual dictionary definition is 'a period of reduced economic activity', a business cycle contraction.

The United States-based National Bureau of Economic Research (NBER) defines economic _____ as: 'a significant decline in [the] economic activity spread across the country, lasting more than a few months, normally visible in real GDP growth, real personal income, employment (non-farm payrolls), industrial production, and wholesale-retail sales.' The NBER's Business Cycle Dating Committee is generally seen as the authority for dating US _____s.

a. Leading indicator	b. Law of demand
c. Macroeconomics	d. Recession

52. A _____ is a collection of symbols, experiences and associations connected with a product, a service, a person or any other artifact or entity.

_____s have become increasingly important components of culture and the economy, now being described as 'cultural accessories and personal philosophies'.

Some people distinguish the psychological aspect of a _____ from the experiential aspect.

a. Brand	b. Store brand
c. Brand equity	d. Brandable software

53. _____ is a rivalry between individuals, groups, nations for territory, a niche, or allocation of resources. It arises whenever two or more parties strive for a goal which cannot be shared. _____ occurs naturally between living organisms which co-exist in the same environment.

a. Competition
b. Non-price competition
c. Price fixing
d. Price competition

54. _____ is income after subtracting taxes and normal expenses (such as rent or mortgage and food) to maintain a certain standard of living. It is the amount of an individual's income available for spending after the essentials (such as food, clothing, and shelter) have been taken care of:

_____ = Gross income - taxes - necessities

Despite the formal definitions above, disposable income is commonly used to denote _____. The meaning should therefore be interpreted from context.

a. 6-3-5 Brainwriting
b. 180SearchAssistant
c. Power III
d. Discretionary income

55. In economics, a _____ exists when a specific individual or enterprise has sufficient control over a particular product or service to determine significantly the terms on which other individuals shall have access to it. Monopolies are thus characterized by a lack of economic competition for the good or service that they provide and a lack of viable substitute goods. The verb 'monopolize' refers to the process by which a firm gains persistently greater market share than what is expected under perfect competition.

a. 180SearchAssistant
b. 6-3-5 Brainwriting
c. Power III
d. Monopoly

56. _____ is a common market form. Many markets can be considered monopolistically competitive, often including the markets for restaurants, cereal, clothing, shoes and service industries in large cities. Short-run equilibrium of the firm under _____

Monopolistically competitive markets have the following characteristics:

- There are many producers and many consumers in a given market, and no business has total control over the market price.
- Consumers perceive that there are non-price differences among the competitors' products.
- There are few barriers to entry and exit.
- Producers have a degree of control over price.

Long-run equilibrium of the firm under _____

The characteristics of a monopolistically competitive market are almost the same as in perfect competition, with the exception of heterogeneous products, and that _____ involves a great deal of non-price competition (based on subtle product differentiation.) A firm making profits in the short run will break even in the long run because demand will decrease and average total cost will increase.

a. Macroeconomics
b. Gross domestic product
c. Recession
d. Monopolistic competition

57. An _____ is a market form in which a market or industry is dominated by a small number of sellers (oligopolists.) Because there are few participants in this type of market, each oligopolist is aware of the actions of the others. The decisions of one firm influence, and are influenced by, the decisions of other firms.
   a. ACNielsen
   b. ADTECH
   c. AMAX
   d. Oligopoly

58. In neoclassical economics and microeconomics, _____ describes a market in which there are many small firms, all producing homogeneous goods. In the short term, such markets are productively inefficient as output will not occur where mc is equal to ac, but allocatively efficient, as output under _____ will always occur where mc is equal to mr, and therefore where mc equals ar. However, in the long term, such markets are both allocatively and productively efficient.
   a. Perfect competition
   b. Gross domestic product
   c. Market structure
   d. Money

59. Regulation refers to 'controlling human or societal behaviour by rules or restrictions.' Regulation can take many forms: legal restrictions promulgated by a government authority, self-regulation, social regulation (e.g. norms), co-regulation and market regulation. One can consider regulation as actions of conduct imposing sanctions (such as a fine.) This action of administrative law, or implementing _____ law, may be contrasted with statutory or case law.
   a. Regulatory
   b. Right to Financial Privacy Act
   c. Privacy law
   d. Robinson-Patman Act

60. The United States federal wage garnishment law, widely known as the _____ guards employees from discharge by their employers because their wages have been garnished in any one week. It was approved by the government in 1968. The Wage and Hour Division of the United States Department of Labor includes the Employment Standards Administration, who administers the act.
   a. Power III
   b. 180SearchAssistant
   c. 6-3-5 Brainwriting
   d. Consumer Credit Protection Act

61. The _____ requires the Federal government to investigate and pursue trusts, companies and organizations suspected of violating the Act. It was the first United States Federal statute to limit cartels and monopolies, and today still forms the basis for most antitrust litigation by the federal government.
   a. Sherman Antitrust Act
   b. Power III
   c. 6-3-5 Brainwriting
   d. 180SearchAssistant

62. The United States _____ is an independent agency of the United States government created in 1972 through the Consumer Product Safety Act to protect 'against unreasonable risks of injuries associated with consumer products.' As of 2006 its acting chairman is Nancy Nord, a Republican. The other commissioner is Thomas Hill Moore, a Democrat. Normally the board has three commissioners.
   a. 6-3-5 Brainwriting
   b. Power III
   c. Consumer Product Safety Commission
   d. 180SearchAssistant

63. _____, is the act of taking an industry or assets into the public ownership of a national government or state. _____ usually refers to private assets, but may also mean assets owned by lower levels of government, such as municipalities, being state operated or owned by the state. The opposite of _____ is usually privatization or de-nationalisation, but may also be municipalization.

a. Power III
b. 6-3-5 Brainwriting
c. 180SearchAssistant
d. Nationalization

64. _____ is a foundational element of logic and human reasoning. _____ posits the existence of a domain or set of elements, as well as one or more common characteristics shared by those elements. As such, it is the essential basis of all valid deductive inference.
a. 6-3-5 Brainwriting
b. 180SearchAssistant
c. Generalization
d. Power III

65. _____ or _____ data refers to selected population characteristics as used in government, marketing or opinion research, or the _____ profiles used in such research. Note the distinction from the term 'demography' Commonly-used _____ include race, age, income, disabilities, mobility (in terms of travel time to work or number of vehicles available), educational attainment, home ownership, employment status, and even location.
a. African Americans
b. AStore
c. Albert Einstein
d. Demographic

66. _____ is difficult to define. For example, in 1952, Alfred Kroeber and Clyde Kluckhohn compiled a list of 164 definitions of '_____' in _____: A Critical Review of Concepts and Definitions. However, the word '_____' is most commonly used in three basic senses:

- excellence of taste in the fine arts and humanities
- an integrated pattern of human knowledge, belief, and behavior that depends upon the capacity for symbolic thought and social learning
- the set of shared attitudes, values, goals, and practices that characterizes an institution, organization or group.

When the concept first emerged in eighteenth- and nineteenth-century Europe, it connoted a process of cultivation or improvement, as in agriculture or horticulture. In the nineteenth century, it came to refer first to the betterment or refinement of the individual, especially through education, and then to the fulfillment of national aspirations or ideals.

a. African Americans
b. Culture
c. Albert Einstein
d. AStore

67. _____ is the tendency to believe that one's own race or ethnic group is the most important and that some or all aspects of its culture are superior to those of other groups. Since within this ideology, individuals will judge other groups in relation to their own particular ethnic group or culture, especially with concern to language, behavior, customs, and religion. These ethnic distinctions and sub-divisions serve to define each ethnicity's unique cultural identity.
a. African Americans
b. Ethnocentrism
c. Albert Einstein
d. AStore

68. In economics, an _____ is any good or commodity, transported from one country to another country in a legitimate fashion, typically for use in trade. _____ goods or services are provided to foreign consumers by domestic producers. _____ is an important part of international trade.
a. ADTECH
b. ACNielsen
c. AMAX
d. Export

69. _____ is exchange of capital, goods, and services across international borders or territories. In most countries, it represents a significant share of gross domestic product (GDP.) While _____ has been present throughout much of history, its economic, social, and political importance has been on the rise in recent centuries.
   a. ACNielsen
   b. ADTECH
   c. International trade
   d. Incoterms

70. _____s function as professionals who deal with trade, dealing in commodities that they do not produce themselves, in order to produce profit.

_____s can be of two types:

1. A wholesale _____ operates in the chain between producer and retail _____. Some wholesale _____s only organize the movement of goods rather than move the goods themselves.
2. A retail _____ or retailer, sells commodities to consumers (including businesses.) A shop owner is a retail _____.

A _____ class characterizes many pre-modern societies. Its status can range from high (even achieving titles like that of _____ prince or nabob) to low, such as in Chinese culture, due to the soiling capabilities of profiting from 'mere' trade, rather than from the labor of others reflected in agricultural produce, craftsmanship, and tribute.

In the United States, '_____' is defined (under the Uniform Commercial Code) as any person while engaged in a business or profession or a seller who deals regularly in the type of goods sold.

   a. RFM
   b. Trade credit
   c. Retail loss prevention
   d. Merchant

71. The most important feature of a contract is that one party makes an _____ for an arrangement that another accepts. This can be called a 'concurrence of wills' or 'ad idem' (meeting of the minds) of two or more parties. The concept is somewhat contested.
   a. Offer
   b. AMAX
   c. ACNielsen
   d. ADTECH

72. Foreign _____ in its classic form is defined as a company from one country making a physical investment into building a factory in another country. It is the establishment of an enterprise by a foreigner. Its definition can be extended to include investments made to acquire lasting interest in enterprises operating outside of the economy of the investor.
   a. VideoJug
   b. Fountain Fresh International
   c. Brash Brands
   d. Direct investment

73. _____ refers to the methods of practicing and using another person's philosophy of business. The franchisor grants the independent operator the right to distribute its products, techniques, and trademarks for a percentage of gross monthly sales and a royalty fee. Various tangibles and intangibles such as national or international advertising, training, and other support services are commonly made available by the franchisor.
   a. Franchise fee
   b. Power III
   c. 180SearchAssistant
   d. Franchising

Chapter 3. THRIVING IN THE MARKETING ENVIRONMENT: The World Is Flat

74. A _____ is an entity formed between two or more parties to undertake economic activity together. The parties agree to create a new entity by both contributing equity, and they then share in the revenues, expenses, and control of the enterprise. The venture can be for one specific project only, or a continuing business relationship such as the Fuji Xerox _____.
   a. Consumer protection
   b. Gripe site
   c. Trademark attorney
   d. Joint venture

75. The verb _____ or grant _____ means to give permission. The noun _____ refers to that permission as well as to the document memorializing that permission. _____ may be granted by a party to another party as an element of an agreement between those parties.
   a. License
   b. 6-3-5 Brainwriting
   c. Power III
   d. 180SearchAssistant

76. _____ is a measure of the strength of a brand, product, service relative to competitive offerings. There is often a geographic element to the competitive landscape. In defining _____, you must see to what extent a product, brand, or firm controls a product category in a given geographic area.
   a. Productivity
   b. Discretionary spending
   c. Market system
   d. Market dominance

77. _____ in economics and business is the result of an exchange and from that trade we assign a numerical monetary value to a good, service or asset. If I trade 4 apples for an orange, the _____ of an orange is 4 - apples. Inversely, the _____ of an apple is 1/4 oranges.
   a. Discounts and allowances
   b. Contribution margin-based pricing
   c. Pricing
   d. Price

78. _____ refers to messages and related media used to communicate with a market. Those who practice advertising, branding, direct marketing, graphic design, marketing, packaging, promotion, publicity, public relations, sales, sales promotion and online marketing are termed marketing communicators, _____ managers, or more briefly as marcom managers.
   a. Sales promotion
   b. Merchandise
   c. Merchandising
   d. Marketing Communication

79. _____ is one of the four elements of marketing mix. An organization or set of organizations (go-betweens) involved in the process of making a product or service available for use or consumption by a consumer or business user.

The other three parts of the marketing mix are product, pricing, and promotion.

   a. Better Living Through Chemistry
   b. Comparison-Shopping agent
   c. Distribution
   d. Japan Advertising Photographers' Association

80. In economics, '_____' can refer to any kind of predatory pricing. However, the word is now generally used only in the context of international trade law, where _____ is defined as the act of a manufacturer in one country exporting a product to another country at a price which is either below the price it charges in its home market or is below its costs of production. The term has a negative connotation, but advocates of free markets see '_____' as beneficial for consumers and believe that protectionism to prevent it would have net negative consequences.

a. Hawkers
b. Gold Key Matching Service
c. Sample sales
d. Dumping

81. A grey market or _____ is the trade of a commodity through distribution channels which, while legal, are unofficial, unauthorized, or unintended by the original manufacturer. In contrast, a black market is the trade of goods and services that are illegal in themselves and/or distributed through illegal channels, such as the selling of stolen goods or illegal items such as heroin or unregistered handguns.

The two main types of grey market are imported manufactured goods that would be normally unavailable or more expensive in a certain country and unissued securities that are not yet traded in official markets.

a. Green market
b. Zone pricing
c. Customs union
d. Gray market

82. In psychology, philosophy, and the cognitive sciences, _____ is the process of attaining awareness or understanding of sensory information. It is a task far more complex than was imagined in the 1950s and 1960s, when it was predicted that building perceiving machines would take about a decade, a goal which is still very far from fruition. The word _____ comes from the Latin words _____, percepio, meaning 'receiving, collecting, action of taking possession, apprehension with the mind or senses.'

_____ is one of the oldest fields in psychology.

a. Power III
b. 180SearchAssistant
c. Groupthink
d. Perception

Chapter 4. MARKETING RESEARCH: Gathering, Analyzing, and Using Information

1. _____ is defined by the American _____ Association as the activity, set of institutions, and processes for creating, communicating, delivering, and exchanging offerings that have value for customers, clients, partners, and society at large. The term developed from the original meaning which referred literally to going to market, as in shopping, or going to a market to sell goods or services.

_____ practice tends to be seen as a creative industry, which includes advertising, distribution and selling.

a. Marketing
b. Product naming
c. Customer acquisition management
d. Marketing myopia

2. Consumer market research is a form of applied sociology that concentrates on understanding the behaviours, whims and preferences, of consumers in a market-based economy, and aims to understand the effects and comparative success of marketing campaigns. The field of consumer _____ as a statistical science was pioneered by Arthur Nielsen with the founding of the ACNielsen Company in 1923.

Thus _____ is the systematic and objective identification, collection, analysis, and dissemination of information for the purpose of assisting management in decision making related to the identification and solution of problems and opportunities in marketing.

a. Marketing research process
b. Marketing research
c. Logit analysis
d. Focus group

3. _____ refer to a collection of facts usually collected as the result of experience, observation or experiment or a set of premises. This may consist of numbers, words particularly as measurements or observations of a set of variables. _____ are often viewed as a lowest level of abstraction from which information and knowledge are derived.

a. Pearson product-moment correlation coefficient
b. Sample size
c. Mean
d. Data

4. Competitiveness is a comparative concept of the ability and performance of a firm, sub-sector or country to sell and supply goods and/or services in a given market. Although widely used in economics and business management, the usefulness of the concept, particularly in the context of national competitiveness, is vigorously disputed by economists, such as Paul Krugman.

The term may also be applied to markets, where it is used to refer to the extent to which the market structure may be regarded as perfectly _____.

a. Geographical pricing
b. Customs union
c. Competitive
d. Free trade zone

5. _____, according to Cornish, 'the process of acquiring and analyzing information in order to understand the market (both existing and potential customers); to determine the current and future needs and preferences, attitudes and behavior of the market; and to assess changes in the business environment that may affect the size and nature of the market in the future.' ('Product', 1997, p147.)

This figure shows how the interaction between variables from producers, communication channels, and consumers vary the effectiveness of _____ which affects the performance of the sales of a new product. The product is central in a circle because it helps to direct what information is gathered and how.

Chapter 4. MARKETING RESEARCH: Gathering, Analyzing, and Using Information

a. Brand parity
c. Line extension
b. Co-branding
d. Market intelligence

6. Mystery shopping or Mystery Consumer is a tool used by market research companies to measure quality of retail service or gather specific information about products and services. _____ posing as normal customers perform specific tasks-- such as purchasing a product, asking questions, registering complaints or behaving in a certain way - and then provide detailed reports or feedback about their experiences.

Mystery shopping began in the 1940s as a way to measure employee integrity.

a. Market research
c. Mystery shopping
b. Mystery shoppers
d. Questionnaire

7. A _____ is a structured collection of records or data that is stored in a computer system. The structure is achieved by organizing the data according to a _____ model. The model in most common use today is the relational model.
a. Power III
c. 180SearchAssistant
b. 6-3-5 Brainwriting
d. Database

8. _____ is a broad label that refers to any individuals or households that use goods and services generated within the economy. The concept of a _____ is used in different contexts, so that the usage and significance of the term may vary.

A _____ is a person who uses any product or service.

a. 180SearchAssistant
c. Consumer
b. 6-3-5 Brainwriting
d. Power III

9. _____ can be regarded as an outcome of mental processes (cognitive process) leading to the selection of a course of action among several alternatives. Every _____ process produces a final choice. The output can be an action or an opinion of choice.
a. Decision making
c. 180SearchAssistant
b. 6-3-5 Brainwriting
d. Power III

10. Perceptual mapping is a graphics technique used by asset marketers that attempts to visually display the perceptions of customers or potential customers. Typically the position of a product, product line, brand, or company is displayed relative to their competition.

_____ can have any number of dimensions but the most common is two dimensions.

a. Comparison-Shopping agent
c. Developed country
b. Retail floor planning
d. Perceptual maps

11. _____ constitute a class of computer-based information systems including knowledge-based systems that support decision-making activities.

Chapter 4. MARKETING RESEARCH: Gathering, Analyzing, and Using Information

_____ are a specific class of computerized information system that supports business and organizational decision-making activities. A properly-designed _____ is an interactive software-based system intended to help decision makers compile useful information from raw data, documents, personal knowledge, and/or business models to identify and solve problems and make decisions.

a. Power III
b. Decision support systems
c. 6-3-5 Brainwriting
d. 180SearchAssistant

12. _____ is an information system that helps with decision-making in the formation of a marketing plan. The reason for using an MKDSS is because it helps to support the software vendors' planning strategy for marketing products; it can help to identify advantageous levels of pricing, advertising spending, and advertising copy for the firm's products (Arinze, 1990.) This helps determines the firms marketing mix for product software.

a. Marketing decision support systems
b. Power III
c. 6-3-5 Brainwriting
d. 180SearchAssistant

13. _____ is the activity that the selling organization undertakes to reduce customer account defections. The success of this activity is when the customer account places an additional order before a 12-month period has expired. Note that ideally these orders will need to contribute similar financial amounts to the previous 12 months.

a. First-mover advantage
b. Customer centricity
c. Customer base
d. Customer retention

14. _____ is the process of extracting hidden patterns from data. As more data is gathered, with the amount of data doubling every three years, _____ is becoming an increasingly important tool to transform this data into information. It is commonly used in a wide range of profiling practices, such as marketing, surveillance, fraud detection and scientific discovery.

a. 180SearchAssistant
b. Power III
c. Structure mining
d. Data mining

15. _____ describes the situation when output from (or information about the result of) an event or phenomenon in the past will influence the same event/phenomenon in the present or future. When an event is part of a chain of cause-and-effect that forms a circuit or loop, then the event is said to 'feed back' into itself.

_____ is also a synonym for:

- _____ Signal; the information about the initial event that is the basis for subsequent modification of the event.
- _____ Loop; the causal path that leads from the initial generation of the _____ signal to the subsequent modification of the event.

_____ is a mechanism, process or signal that is looped back to control a system within itself. Such a loop is called a _____ loop.

a. 6-3-5 Brainwriting
b. 180SearchAssistant
c. Power III
d. Feedback

Chapter 4. MARKETING RESEARCH: Gathering, Analyzing, and Using Information

16. A number of different _____s are indicated below.

- Randomized controlled trial
    - Double-blind randomized trial
    - Single-blind randomized trial
    - Non-blind trial
- Nonrandomized trial (quasi-experiment)
    - Interrupted time series design (measures on a sample or a series of samples from the same population are obtained several times before and after a manipulated event or a naturally occurring event) - considered a type of quasi-experiment

- Cohort study
    - Prospective cohort
    - Retrospective cohort
    - Time series study
- Case-control study
    - Nested case-control study
- Cross-sectional study
    - Community survey (a type of cross-sectional study)

When choosing a _____, many factors must be taken into account. Different types of studies are subject to different types of bias. For example, recall bias is likely to occur in cross-sectional or case-control studies where subjects are asked to recall exposure to risk factors.

a. Longitudinal studies
b. Power III
c. Study design
d. 180SearchAssistant

17. _____ involves the summary, collation and/or synthesis of existing research rather than primary research, where data is collected from, for example, research subjects or experiments.

The term is widely used in market research and in medical research. The principal methodology in medical _____ is the systematic review, commonly using meta-analytic statistical techniques, although other methods of synthesis, like realist reviews and meta-narrative reviews, have been developed in recent years.

a. 6-3-5 Brainwriting
b. Power III
c. 180SearchAssistant
d. Secondary research

18. _____ is a type of research conducted because a problem has not been clearly defined. _____ helps determine the best research design, data collection method and selection of subjects. Given its fundamental nature, _____ often concludes that a perceived problem does not actually exist.

a. Intent scale translation
b. ACNielsen
c. IDDEA
d. Exploratory research

19. _____ is a term for unprocessed data, it is also known as primary data. It is a relative term _____ can be input to a computer program or used in manual analysis procedures such as gathering statistics from a survey.

Chapter 4. MARKETING RESEARCH: Gathering, Analyzing, and Using Information

a. Chief marketing officer
c. Shoppers Food ' Pharmacy
b. Product manager
d. Raw data

20. _____ involves the collection of data that does not already exist. This can be through numerous forms, including questionnaires and telephone interviews amongst others. This information may be collected in things like questionnaires, magazines, and Interviews

The term is widely used in market research and competitive intelligence.

a. Blitz QFD
c. Bitcom
b. Brand infiltration
d. Primary research

21. _____ is a field of inquiry that crosscuts disciplines and subject matters . _____ers aim to gather an in-depth understanding of human behavior and the reasons that govern such behavior. The discipline investigates the why and how of decision making, not just what, where, when.

a. Power III
c. Qualitative research
b. 6-3-5 Brainwriting
d. 180SearchAssistant

22. Combining Existing _____ Sources with New Primary Data Sources

Imagine that we could get hold of a good collection of surveys taken in earlier years, such as detailed studies about changes going on in this phase and hopefully additional studies in the years to come. Analyzing this data base over time could give us a good picture of what changes actually have taken place in the orientation of the population and of the extent to which new technical concepts did have an impact on subgroups of the population. Furthermore, data archives can help to prepare studies on change over time by monitoring what questions have been asked in earlier years and alerting principal investigators to important questions which should be repeated in planned research projects.

a. 180SearchAssistant
c. 6-3-5 Brainwriting
b. Power III
d. Secondary data

23. A _____ is a form of qualitative research in which a group of people are asked about their attitude towards a product, service, concept, advertisement, idea, or packaging. Questions are asked in an interactive group setting where participants are free to talk with other group members.

Ernest Dichter originated the idea of having a 'group therapy' for products and this process is what became known as a _____.

a. Cross tabulation
c. Focus group
b. Marketing research process
d. Logit analysis

24. _____ is a cohort which consists of those people born after the Generation X cohort. Its name is controversial and is synonymous with several alternative names including The Net Generation, Millennials, Echo Boomers, and iGeneration. _____ consists primarily of the offspring of the Generation Jones and Baby Boomers cohorts.

44 *Chapter 4. MARKETING RESEARCH: Gathering, Analyzing, and Using Information*

a. AStore
b. Generation Y
c. Generation X
d. Greatest Generation

25. _____ is a genre of writing that uses fieldwork to provide a descriptive study of human societies. _____ presents the results of a holistic research method founded on the idea that a system's properties cannot necessarily be accurately understood independently of each other. The genre has both formal and historical connections to travel writing and colonial office reports.
a. ACNielsen
b. ADTECH
c. AMAX
d. Ethnography

26. The terms '_____' and 'independent variable' are used in similar but subtly different ways in mathematics and statistics as part of the standard terminology in those subjects. They are used to distinguish between two types of quantities being considered, separating them into those available at the start of a process and those being created by it, where the latter (_____s) are dependent on the former (independent variables.)

In traditional calculus, a function is defined as a relation between two terms called variables because their values vary.

a. Field experiment
b. 180SearchAssistant
c. Dependent variable
d. Power III

27. _____ describes data and characteristics about the population or phenomenon being studied. _____ answers the questions who, what, where, when and how.

Although the data description is factual, accurate and systematic, the research cannot describe what caused a situation.

a. Sampling error
b. Two-tailed test
c. Power III
d. Descriptive research

28. A _____ attribute is one that exists in a range of magnitudes, and can therefore be measured. Measurements of any particular _____ property are expressed as a specific quantity, referred to as a unit, multiplied by a number. Examples of physical quantities are distance, mass, and time.
a. Dolly Dimples
b. BeyondROI
c. Lifestyle city
d. Quantitative

29. _____s are used in open sentences. For instance, in the formula x + 1 = 5, x is a _____ which represents an 'unknown' number. _____s are often represented by letters of the Roman alphabet, or those of other alphabets, such as Greek, and use other special symbols.
a. Book of business
b. Quantitative
c. Personalization
d. Variable

30. A _____ is a research instrument consisting of a series of questions and other prompts for the purpose of gathering information from respondents. Although they are often designed for statistical analysis of the responses, this is not always the case. The _____ was invented by Sir Francis Galton.

Chapter 4. MARKETING RESEARCH: Gathering, Analyzing, and Using Information

a. Mystery shopping
c. Mystery shoppers
b. Market research
d. Questionnaire

31. _____ is a method of direct marketing in which a salesperson solicits to prospective customers to buy products or services, either over the phone or through a subsequent face to face or Web conferencing appointment scheduled during the call.

_____ can also include recorded sales pitches programmed to be played over the phone via automatic dialing. _____ has come under fire in recent years, being viewed as an annoyance by many.

a. Joe job
c. Directory Harvest Attack
b. Phishing
d. Telemarketing

32. _____ is either an activity of a living being (such as a human), consisting of receiving knowledge of the outside world through the senses, or the recording of data using scientific instruments. The term may also refer to any datum collected during this activity.

The scientific method requires _____s of nature to formulate and test hypotheses.

a. AMAX
c. ACNielsen
b. ADTECH
d. Observation

33. A _____ is a tool used to measure the viewing habits of TV and cable audiences.

The _____ is a 'box', about the size of a paperback book. The box is hooked up to each television set and is accompanied by a remote control unit.

a. 180SearchAssistant
c. Power III
b. 6-3-5 Brainwriting
d. People meter

34. _____ is that part of statistical practice concerned with the selection of individual observations intended to yield some knowledge about a population of concern, especially for the purposes of statistical inference. Each observation measures one or more properties (weight, location, etc.) of an observable entity enumerated to distinguish objects or individuals.
a. Sports Marketing Group
c. Richard Buckminster 'Bucky' Fuller
b. AStore
d. Sampling

35. In 1962, President John F. Kennedy presented a speech to the United States Congress in which he extolled four basic consumer rights, later called The _____.

While later expanded, the original six basic beliefs of consumer protection are the most widely recognized.

In 1985, the concept of consumer rights was endorsed by the United Nations and expanded to included eight basic rights.

a. 180SearchAssistant
c. 6-3-5 Brainwriting
b. Power III
d. Consumer Bill of Rights

36. The _____ is an independent agency of the United States government, established in 1914 by the _____ Act. Its principal mission is the promotion of 'consumer protection' and the elimination and prevention of what regulators perceive to be harmfully 'anti-competitive' business practices, such as coercive monopoly.

The _____ Act was one of President Wilson's major acts against trusts.

a. 6-3-5 Brainwriting
c. 180SearchAssistant
b. Power III
d. Federal Trade Commission

37. The _____ of 1914 (15 U.S.C §§ 41-58, as amended) established the Federal Trade Commission (FTC), a bipartisan body of five members appointed by the President of the United States for seven year terms. This Commission was authorized to issue Cease and Desist orders to large corporations to curb unfair trade practices. This Act also gave more flexibility to the US congress for judicial matters.

a. Product liability
c. Comparative negligence
b. Gripe site
d. Federal Trade Commission Act

38. _____ is the ability of an individual or group to seclude themselves or information about themselves and thereby reveal themselves selectively. The boundaries and content of what is considered private differ among cultures and individuals, but share basic common themes. _____ is sometimes related to anonymity, the wish to remain unnoticed or unidentified in the public realm.

a. 180SearchAssistant
c. Power III
b. 6-3-5 Brainwriting
d. Privacy

39. _____ in organizations and public policy is both the organizational process of creating and maintaining a plan; and the psychological process of thinking about the activities required to create a desired goal on some scale. As such, it is a fundamental property of intelligent behavior. This thought process is essential to the creation and refinement of a plan, or integration of it with other plans, that is, it combines forecasting of developments with the preparation of scenarios of how to react to them.

a. Power III
c. 6-3-5 Brainwriting
b. Planning
d. 180SearchAssistant

40. _____ is the ongoing process of identifying and articulating market requirements that define a product's feature set.

a. Targeted advertising
c. Brand parity
b. Product planning
d. Market intelligence

41. _____ is a standard point of view or personal prejudice. especially when the tendency interferes with the ability to be impartial, unprejudiced, or objective. The term _____ed is used to describe an action, judgment, or other outcome influenced by a prejudged perspective.

a. Bias
c. 180SearchAssistant
b. 6-3-5 Brainwriting
d. Power III

Chapter 4. MARKETING RESEARCH: Gathering, Analyzing, and Using Information

42. _____ is a way of expressing knowledge or belief that an event will occur or has occurred. In mathematics the concept has been given an exact meaning in _____ theory, that is used extensively in such areas of study as mathematics, statistics, finance, gambling, science, and philosophy to draw conclusions about the likelihood of potential events and the underlying mechanics of complex systems.
  a. Linear regression
  b. Probability
  c. Data
  d. Heteroskedastic

43. A sample is a subject chosen from a population for investigation. A _____ is one chosen by a method involving an unpredictable component. Random sampling can also refer to taking a number of independent observations from the same probability distribution, without involving any real population.
  a. Selection bias
  b. 180SearchAssistant
  c. Power III
  d. Random sample

44. In statistics, a simple random sample is a subset of individuals (a sample) chosen from a larger set (a population.) Each individual is chosen randomly and entirely by chance, such that each individual has the same probability of being chosen at any stage during the sampling process, and each subset of k individuals has the same probability of being chosen for the sample as any other subset of k individuals (.) This process and technique is known as _____, and should not be confused with Random Sampling.
  a. Market analysis
  b. Focus group
  c. Logit analysis
  d. Simple random sampling

45. _____ is a statistical method involving the selection of elements from an ordered sampling frame. The most common form of _____ is an equal-probability method, in which every k^{th} element in the frame is selected, where k, the sampling interval (sometimes known as the 'skip'), is calculated as:

sample size (n) = population size (N) /k

Using this procedure each element in the population has a known and equal probability of selection. This makes _____ functionally similar to simple random sampling.

  a. Systematic sampling
  b. Power III
  c. Selection bias
  d. 180SearchAssistant

46. _____ is anything that is intended to save time, energy or frustration. A _____ store at a petrol station, for example, sells items that have nothing to do with gasoline/petrol, but it saves the consumer from having to go to a grocery store. '_____' is a very relative term and its meaning tends to change over time.
  a. Demographic profile
  b. MaxDiff
  c. Marketing buzz
  d. Convenience

47. _____ is an authority or agency in a country responsible for collecting and safeguarding _____ duties and for controlling the flow of goods including animals, personal effects and hazardous items in and out of a country. Depending on local legislation and regulations, the import or export of some goods may be restricted or forbidden, and the _____ agency enforces these rules. The _____ agency may be different from the immigration authority, which monitors persons who leave or enter the country, checking for appropriate documentation, apprehending people wanted by international arrest warrants, and impeding the entry of others deemed dangerous to the country.

48 Chapter 4. MARKETING RESEARCH: Gathering, Analyzing, and Using Information

a. Madrid system for the international registration of marks
b. Customs
c. Registered trademark symbol
d. Specific Performance

48. The Oxford University Press defines _____ as 'marketing on a worldwide scale reconciling or taking commercial advantage of global operational differences, similarities and opportunities in order to meet global objectives.' Oxford University Press' Glossary of Marketing Terms.

Here are three reasons for the shift from domestic to _____ as given by the authors of the textbook, _____ Management--3rd Edition by Masaaki Kotabe and Kristiaan Helsen, 2004.

One of the product categories in which global competition has been easy to track is in U.S. automotive sales.

a. Guerrilla Marketing
b. Diversity marketing
c. Digital marketing
d. Global marketing

49. _____ is a term used to describe a process of preparing and collecting data - for example as part of a process improvement or similar project.

_____ usually takes place early on in an improvement project, and is often formalised through a _____ Plan which often contains the following activity.

1. Pre collection activity - Agree goals, target data, definitions, methods
2. Collection - _____
3. Present Findings - usually involves some form of sorting analysis and/or presentation.

A formal _____ process is necessary as it ensures that data gathered is both defined and accurate and that subsequent decisions based on arguments embodied in the findings are valid . The process provides both a baseline from which to measure from and in certain cases a target on what to improve. Types of _____ 1-By mail questionnaires 2-By personal interview

- Six sigma
- Sampling (statistics)

a. Power III
b. 180SearchAssistant
c. 6-3-5 Brainwriting
d. Data collection

50. _____ is the identity of a group or culture, or of an individual as far as one is influenced by one's belonging to a group or culture. _____ is similar to and has overlaps with, but is not synonymous with, identity politics.

There are modern questions of culture that are transferred into questions of identity.

Chapter 4. MARKETING RESEARCH: Gathering, Analyzing, and Using Information

a. 180SearchAssistant
b. Power III
c. Cultural identity
d. 6-3-5 Brainwriting

51. _____ is a term used in business for a short document that summarises a longer report, proposal or group of related reports in such a way that readers can rapidly become acquainted with a large body of material without having to read it all. It will usually contain a brief statement of the problem or proposal covered in the major document(s), background information, concise analysis and main conclusions. It is intended as an aid to decision making by business managers.
a. ACNielsen
b. AMAX
c. ADTECH
d. Executive Summary

Chapter 5. CONSUMER BEHAVIOR

1. _____ is a broad label that refers to any individuals or households that use goods and services generated within the economy. The concept of a _____ is used in different contexts, so that the usage and significance of the term may vary.

   A _____ is a person who uses any product or service.

   a. 180SearchAssistant
   b. 6-3-5 Brainwriting
   c. Power III
   d. Consumer

2. _____ is the study of when, why, how, where and what people do or do not buy products. It blends elements from psychology, sociology, social psychology, anthropology and economics. It attempts to understand the buyer decision making process, both individually and in groups. It studies characteristics of individual consumers such as demographics and behavioural variables in an attempt to understand people's wants. It also tries to assess influences on the consumer from groups such as family, friends, reference groups, and society in general.

   a. Consumer confidence
   b. Multidimensional scaling
   c. Communal marketing
   d. Consumer behavior

3. _____ can be regarded as an outcome of mental processes (cognitive process) leading to the selection of a course of action among several alternatives. Every _____ process produces a final choice. The output can be an action or an opinion of choice.

   a. Power III
   b. 180SearchAssistant
   c. 6-3-5 Brainwriting
   d. Decision making

4. _____ is the subjective judgment that people make about the characteristics and severity of a risk. The phrase is most commonly used in reference to natural hazards and threats to the environment or health, such as nuclear power. Several theories have been proposed to explain why different people make different estimates of the dangerousness of risks.

   a. 6-3-5 Brainwriting
   b. Risk perception
   c. 180SearchAssistant
   d. Power III

5. _____ is a concept that denotes the precise probability of specific eventualities. Technically, the notion of _____ is independent from the notion of value and, as such, eventualities may have both beneficial and adverse consequences. However, in general usage the convention is to focus only on potential negative impact to some characteristic of value that may arise from a future event.

   a. 6-3-5 Brainwriting
   b. Power III
   c. Risk
   d. 180SearchAssistant

6. _____ is systematic determination of merit, worth, and significance of something or someone using criteria against a set of standards. _____ often is used to characterize and appraise subjects of interest in a wide range of human enterprises, including the arts, criminal justice, foundations and non-profit organizations, government, health care, and other human services.

   Depending on the topic of interest, there are professional groups which look to the quality and rigor of the _____ process.

Chapter 5. CONSUMER BEHAVIOR

a. AMAX
b. Evaluation
c. ADTECH
d. ACNielsen

7. In environmental modeling and especially in hydrology, a _____ model means a model that is acceptably consistent with observed natural processes, i.e. that simulates well, for example, observed river discharge. It is a key concept of the so-called Generalized Likelihood Uncertainty Estimation (GLUE) methodology to quantify how uncertain environmental predictions are.

a. Power III
b. 6-3-5 Brainwriting
c. 180SearchAssistant
d. Behavioral

8. _____ or behavioural targeting is a technique used by online publishers and advertisers to increase the effectiveness of their campaigns.

_____ uses information collected on an individual's web-browsing behavior, such as the pages they have visited or the searches they have made, to select which advertisements to display to that individual. Practitioners believe this helps them deliver their online advertisements to the users who are most likely to be influenced by them.

a. Hit inflation attack
b. Search engine image protection
c. Contextual advertising
d. Behavioral targeting

9. _____s are Web-based intelligent software applications that can help online shoppers find lower price for commodities or services. Price comparison services was the earliest service a _____ provides. To search the price of a particular item, a _____ would search multiple online stores based on the keyword the online shopper provides.

a. Net Promoter^R score
b. Book of business
c. Comparison-Shopping agent
d. Distribution

10. _____ is the examining of goods or services from retailers with the intent to purchase at that time. _____ is an activity of selection and/or purchase. In some contexts it is considered a leisure activity as well as an economic one.

a. Khodebshchik
b. Shopping
c. Hawkers
d. Discount store

11. A _____ is a collection of symbols, experiences and associations connected with a product, a service, a person or any other artifact or entity.

_____s have become increasingly important components of culture and the economy, now being described as 'cultural accessories and personal philosophies'.

Some people distinguish the psychological aspect of a _____ from the experiential aspect.

a. Brand
b. Brand equity
c. Brandable software
d. Store brand

Chapter 5. CONSUMER BEHAVIOR

12. _____, in marketing, consists of a consumer's commitment to repurchase the brand and can be demonstrated by repeated buying of a product or service or other positive behaviors such as word of mouth advocacy. True _____ implies that the consumer is willing, at least on occasion, to put aside their own desires in the interest of the brand. _____ has been proclaimed by some to be the ultimate goal of marketing.

   a. Brand awareness
   c. Trade Symbols
   b. Brand implementation
   d. Brand loyalty

13. Cognition is the scientific term for 'the process of thought.' Its usage varies in different ways in accord with different disciplines: For example, in psychology and _____ science it refers to an information processing view of an individual's psychological functions. Other interpretations of the meaning of cognition link it to the development of concepts; individual minds, groups, organizations, and even larger coalitions of entities, can be modelled as 'societies' (Society of Mind), which cooperate to form concepts.

The autonomous elements of each 'society' would have the opportunity to demonstrate emergent behavior in the face of some crisis or opportunity.

   a. Power III
   c. 6-3-5 Brainwriting
   b. 180SearchAssistant
   d. Cognitive

14. _____ is an uncomfortable feeling caused by holding two contradictory ideas simultaneously. The 'ideas' or 'cognitions' in question may include attitudes and beliefs, and also the awareness of one's behavior. The theory of _____ proposes that people have a motivational drive to reduce dissonance by changing their attitudes, beliefs, and behaviors, or by justifying or rationalizing their attitudes, beliefs, and behaviors.

   a. Perception
   c. Power III
   b. 180SearchAssistant
   d. Cognitive dissonance

15. _____, a business term, is a measure of how products and services supplied by a company meet or surpass customer expectation. It is seen as a key performance indicator within business and is part of the four perspectives of a Balanced Scorecard.

In a competitive marketplace where businesses compete for customers, _____ is seen as a key differentiator and increasingly has become a key element of business strategy.

   a. Customer base
   c. Supplier diversity
   b. Customer satisfaction
   d. Psychological pricing

16. _____ is one of the four Ps of the marketing mix. The other three aspects are product, promotion, and place. It is also a key variable in microeconomic price allocation theory.

   a. Competitor indexing
   c. Relationship based pricing
   b. Price
   d. Pricing

17. In psychology, philosophy, and the cognitive sciences, _____ is the process of attaining awareness or understanding of sensory information. It is a task far more complex than was imagined in the 1950s and 1960s, when it was predicted that building perceiving machines would take about a decade, a goal which is still very far from fruition. The word _____ comes from the Latin words _____, percepio, meaning 'receiving, collecting, action of taking possession, apprehension with the mind or senses.'

Chapter 5. CONSUMER BEHAVIOR

_____ is one of the oldest fields in psychology.

- a. Groupthink
- b. Power III
- c. Perception
- d. 180SearchAssistant

18. _____ is a form of communication that typically attempts to persuade potential customers to purchase or to consume more of a particular brand of product or service. 'While now central to the contemporary global economy and the reproduction of global production networks, it is only quite recently that _____ has been more than a marginal influence on patterns of sales and production. The formation of modern _____ was intimately bound up with the emergence of new forms of monopoly capitalism around the end of the 19th and beginning of the 20th century as one element in corporate strategies to create, organize and where possible control markets, especially for mass produced consumer goods.

- a. ACNielsen
- b. ADTECH
- c. AMAX
- d. Advertising

19. Maslow's _____ is a theory in psychology, proposed by Abraham Maslow in his 1943 paper A Theory of Human Motivation, which he subsequently extended to include his observations of humans' innate curiosity.

Maslow studied what he called exemplary people such as Albert Einstein, Jane Addams, Eleanor Roosevelt, and Frederick Douglass rather than mentally ill or neurotic people, writing that 'the study of crippled, stunted, immature, and unhealthy specimens can yield only a cripple psychology and a cripple philosophy.' Maslow also studied the healthiest one percent of the college student population. In his book, The Farther Reaches of Human Nature, Maslow writes, 'By ordinary standards of this kind of laboratory research...

- a. Hierarchy of needs
- b. 6-3-5 Brainwriting
- c. Power III
- d. 180SearchAssistant

20. _____ is the set of reasons that determines one to engage in a particular behavior. The term is generally used for human _____ but, theoretically, it can be used to describe the causes for animal behavior as well

- a. Power III
- b. 180SearchAssistant
- c. Role playing
- d. Motivation

21. _____ is a form of associative learning that was first demonstrated by Ivan Pavlov. The typical procedure for inducing _____ involves presentations of a neutral stimulus along with a stimulus of some significance. The neutral stimulus could be any event that does not result in an overt behavioral response from the organism under investigation. Pavlov referred to this as a conditioned stimulus (CS.)

- a. Power III
- b. 6-3-5 Brainwriting
- c. Classical conditioning
- d. 180SearchAssistant

22. _____ is the use of consequences to modify the occurrence and form of behavior. _____ is distinguished from classical conditioning (also called respondent conditioning, or Pavlovian conditioning) in that _____ deals with the modification of 'voluntary behavior' or operant behavior. Operant behavior 'operates' on the environment and is maintained by its consequences, while classical conditioning deals with the conditioning of respondent behaviors which are elicited by antecedent conditions.

a. ADTECH
b. ACNielsen
c. Operant conditioning
d. AMAX

23. In psychology and education, a common definition of learning is a process that brings together cognitive, emotional, and environmental influences and experiences for acquiring, enhancing skills, values, and world views (Illeris,2000; Ormorod, 1995.) Learning as a process focuses on what happens when the learning takes place. Explanations of what happens constitute _____.

a. 180SearchAssistant
b. Learning theories
c. Self-concept
d. Power III

24. There are many important decisions about product and service development and marketing. In the process of product development and marketing we should focus on strategic decisions about product attributes, product branding, product packaging, product labeling and product support services. But product strategy also calls for building a _____.

a. Macromarketing
b. Product line
c. Technology acceptance model
d. Pinstorm

25. A _____ is the use of an established product's brand name for a new item in the same product category. _____s occur when a company introduces additional items in the same product category under the same brand name such as new flavors, forms, colors, added ingredients, package sizes.

a. Retail floor planning
b. Pearson's chi-square
c. Product line extension
d. Comparison-Shopping agent

26. A product _____ is the use of an established product's brand name for a new item in the same product category. _____s occur when a company introduces additional items in the same product category under the same brand name such as new flavors, forms, colors, added ingredients, package sizes.Examples includei) Zen LXI, Zen VXIii) Surf, Surf Excel, Surf Excel Blueiii) Splendour, Splendour Plusiv) Coke, Diet Coke, Vanilla Cokev) Clinic All Clear, Clinic Plus

- brand
- brand management
- marketing
- product management
- Product lining

a. Perishability
b. Line extension
c. Brand Development Index
d. Targeted advertising

27. The philosophy of _____ holds that the only thing that exists is matter, and is considered a form of physicalism. Fundamentally, all things are composed of material and all phenomena (including consciousness) are the result of material interactions; therefore, matter is the only substance. As a theory, _____ belongs to the class of monist ontology.

a. Power III
b. 180SearchAssistant
c. 6-3-5 Brainwriting
d. Materialism

28. The _____, in psychology, is a personality variable reflecting the extent to which people engage in and enjoy effortful cognitive activities.

Chapter 5. CONSUMER BEHAVIOR

People high in the _____ are more likely to form their attitudes by paying close attention to relevant arguments (i.e., via the central route to persuasion), whereas people low in the _____ are more likely to rely on peripheral cues, such as how attractive or credible a speaker is. Psychological research on the _____ has been conducted using self-report tests, where research participants answered a series of statements such as 'I prefer my life to be filled with puzzles that I must solve' and were scored on how much they felt the statements represented them.

a. Self-concept
c. 180SearchAssistant
b. Need for cognition
d. Power III

29. _____ or self identity refers to the global understanding a sentient being has of him or herself. It presupposes but can be distinguished from self-consciousness, which is simply an awareness of one's self. It is also more general than self-esteem, which is the purely evaluative element of the _____.

a. Power III
c. Self-concept
b. 180SearchAssistant
d. Need for cognition

30. _____ or _____ data refers to selected population characteristics as used in government, marketing or opinion research, or the _____ profiles used in such research. Note the distinction from the term 'demography' Commonly-used _____ include race, age, income, disabilities, mobility (in terms of travel time to work or number of vehicles available), educational attainment, home ownership, employment status, and even location.

a. AStore
c. Albert Einstein
b. African Americans
d. Demographic

31. _____ was originally coined by Austrian psychologist Alfred Adler in 1929. The current broader sense of the word dates from 1961.

In sociology, a _____ is the way a person lives.

a. 180SearchAssistant
c. 6-3-5 Brainwriting
b. Power III
d. Lifestyle

32. In the field of marketing, demographics, opinion research, and social research in general, _____ variables are any attributes relating to personality, values, attitudes, interests, or lifestyles. They are also called IAO variables . They can be contrasted with demographic variables (such as age and gender), behavioral variables (such as usage rate or loyalty), and bizographic variables (such as industry, seniority and functional area.)

a. Lifetime value
c. Marketing myopia
b. Business-to-business
d. Psychographic

33. _____ is a fee paid on borrowed assets. It is the price paid for the use of borrowed money , or, money earned by deposited funds . Assets that are sometimes lent with _____ include money, shares, consumer goods through hire purchase, major assets such as aircraft, and even entire factories in finance lease arrangements.

a. AMAX
c. ACNielsen
b. ADTECH
d. Interest

Chapter 5. CONSUMER BEHAVIOR

34. _____ is difficult to define. For example, in 1952, Alfred Kroeber and Clyde Kluckhohn compiled a list of 164 definitions of '_____' in _____: A Critical Review of Concepts and Definitions. However, the word '_____' is most commonly used in three basic senses:

- excellence of taste in the fine arts and humanities
- an integrated pattern of human knowledge, belief, and behavior that depends upon the capacity for symbolic thought and social learning
- the set of shared attitudes, values, goals, and practices that characterizes an institution, organization or group.

When the concept first emerged in eighteenth- and nineteenth-century Europe, it connoted a process of cultivation or improvement, as in agriculture or horticulture. In the nineteenth century, it came to refer first to the betterment or refinement of the individual, especially through education, and then to the fulfillment of national aspirations or ideals.

a. Culture
c. African Americans
b. Albert Einstein
d. AStore

35. A personal and cultural _____ is a relative ethic _____, an assumption upon which implementation can be extrapolated. A _____ system is a set of consistent _____s and measures that is soo not true. A principle _____ is a foundation upon which other _____s and measures of integrity are based.

a. Package-on-Package
c. Value
b. Supreme Court of the United States
d. Perceptual maps

36. _____ is a form of applied ethics that examines ethical principles and moral or ethical problems that arise in a business environment. It applies to all aspects of business conduct and is relevant to the conduct of individuals and business organizations as a whole. Applied ethics is a field of ethics that deals with ethical questions in many fields such as medical, technical, legal and _____.

a. Power III
c. Business ethics
b. 180SearchAssistant
d. 6-3-5 Brainwriting

37. _____ is a branch of philosophy which seeks to address questions about morality, such as how a moral outcome can be achieved in a specific situation (applied _____), how moral values should be determined (normative _____), what moral values people actually abide by (descriptive _____), what the fundamental semantic, ontological, and epistemic nature of _____ or morality is (meta-_____), and how moral capacity or moral agency develops and what its nature is (moral psychology.)

Socrates was one of the first Greek philosophers to encourage both scholars and the common citizen to turn their attention from the outside world to the condition of man. In this view, Knowledge having a bearing on human life was placed highest, all other knowledge being secondary.

a. Ethics
c. AMAX
b. ACNielsen
d. ADTECH

Chapter 5. CONSUMER BEHAVIOR

38. In sociology, anthropology and cultural studies, a _____ is a group of people with a culture (whether distinct or hidden) which differentiates them from the larger culture to which they belong. If a particular _____ is characterized by a systematic opposition to the dominant culture, it may be described as a counterculture. As Ken Gelder notes, _____s are social, with their own shared conventions, values and rituals, but they can also seem 'immersed' or self-absorbed--another feature that distinguishes them from countercultures.

a. 6-3-5 Brainwriting
b. Subculture
c. Power III
d. 180SearchAssistant

39. A _____ is a sociological concept referring to a group to which an individual or another group is compared.

_____s are used in order to evaluate and determine the nature of a given individual or other group's characteristics and sociological attributes. It is the group to which the individual relates or aspires relate himself or self psychologically.

a. Minority
b. Power III
c. Mociology
d. Reference group

40. _____ is a concept that arose out of the theory of two-step flow of communication propounded by Paul Lazarsfeld and Elihu Katz. This theory is one of several models that try to explain the diffusion of innovations, ideas, or commercial products.

The opinion leader is the agent who is an active media user and who interprets the meaning of media messages or content for lower-end media users.

a. Elasticity
b. ACNielsen
c. Opinion leadership
d. Intellectual property

41. _____ (or citizen-to-citizen) electronic commerce involves the electronically-facilitated transactions between consumers through some third party. A common example is the online auction, in which a consumer posts an item for sale and other consumers bid to purchase it; the third party generally charges a flat fee or commission. The sites are only intermediaries, just there to match consumers.

a. Locator software
b. Web banner
c. Business-to-government
d. Consumer-to-consumer

42. _____ are used for a variety of social and professional groups interacting via the Internet. It does not necessarily mean that there is a strong bond among the members, although Howard Rheingold, author of the book of the same name, mentions that _____ form 'when people carry on public discussions long enough, with sufficient human feeling, to form webs of personal relationships'. An email distribution list may have hundreds of members and the communication which takes place may be merely informational (questions and answers are posted), but members may remain relative strangers and the membership turnover rate could be high.

a. 6-3-5 Brainwriting
b. Power III
c. 180SearchAssistant
d. Virtual communities

43. Electronic commerce, commonly known as _____ or eCommerce, consists of the buying and selling of products or services over electronic systems such as the Internet and other computer networks. The amount of trade conducted electronically has grown extraordinarily with wide-spread Internet usage. A wide variety of commerce is conducted in this way, spurring and drawing on innovations in electronic funds transfer, supply chain management, Internet marketing, online transaction processing, electronic data interchange (EDI), inventory management systems, and automated data collection systems.

   a. AMAX   b. ADTECH
   c. E-commerce   d. ACNielsen

44. A _____ is a type of website, usually maintained by an individual with regular entries of commentary, descriptions of events, or other material such as graphics or video. Entries are commonly displayed in reverse-chronological order. '_____' can also be used as a verb, meaning to maintain or add content to a _____.

   a. 6-3-5 Brainwriting   b. 180SearchAssistant
   c. Power III   d. Blog

45. _____ is defined by the American _____ Association as the activity, set of institutions, and processes for creating, communicating, delivering, and exchanging offerings that have value for customers, clients, partners, and society at large. The term developed from the original meaning which referred literally to going to market, as in shopping, or going to a market to sell goods or services.

_____ practice tends to be seen as a creative industry, which includes advertising, distribution and selling.

   a. Marketing myopia   b. Product naming
   c. Marketing   d. Customer acquisition management

Chapter 6. BUSINESS-TO-BUSINESS MARKETS: How and Why Organizations Buy

1. _____ is a term commonly used to describe commerce transactions between businesses like the one between a manufacturer and a wholesaler or a wholesaler and a retailer i.e both the buyer and the seller are business entity.This is unlike business-to-consumers (B2C) which involve a business entity and end consumer, or business-to-government (B2G) which involve a business entity and government.

The volume of B2B transactions is much higher than the volume of B2C transactions. The primary reason for this is that in a typical supply chain there will be many B2B transactions involving subcomponent or raw materials, and only one B2C transaction, specifically sale of the finished product to the end customer.

   a. Disruptive technology
   b. Social marketing
   c. Customer relationship management
   d. Business-to-business

2. _____ is a broad label that refers to any individuals or households that use goods and services generated within the economy. The concept of a _____ is used in different contexts, so that the usage and significance of the term may vary.

A _____ is a person who uses any product or service.

   a. 6-3-5 Brainwriting
   b. 180SearchAssistant
   c. Power III
   d. Consumer

3. _____ is defined by the American _____ Association as the activity, set of institutions, and processes for creating, communicating, delivering, and exchanging offerings that have value for customers, clients, partners, and society at large. The term developed from the original meaning which referred literally to going to market, as in shopping, or going to a market to sell goods or services.

_____ practice tends to be seen as a creative industry, which includes advertising, distribution and selling.

   a. Product naming
   b. Customer acquisition management
   c. Marketing myopia
   d. Marketing

4. _____ is the study of the Earth and its lands, features, inhabitants, and phenomena. A literal translation would be 'to describe or write about the Earth'. The first person to use the word '_____' was Eratosthenes .
   a. 6-3-5 Brainwriting
   b. 180SearchAssistant
   c. Power III
   d. Geography

5. In economic models, the _____ time frame assumes no fixed factors of production. Firms can enter or leave the marketplace, and the cost (and availability) of land, labor, raw materials, and capital goods can be assumed to vary. In contrast, in the short-run time frame, certain factors are assumed to be fixed, because there is not sufficient time for them to change.
   a. 180SearchAssistant
   b. 6-3-5 Brainwriting
   c. Power III
   d. Long-run

6. In economics, _____ is the desire to own something and the ability to pay for it. The term _____ signifies the ability or the willingness to buy a particular commodity at a given point of time .

Chapter 6. BUSINESS-TO-BUSINESS MARKETS: How and Why Organizations Buy

a. Market system
b. Demand
c. Discretionary spending
d. Market dominance

7. _____ is a term in economics, where demand for one good or service occurs as a result of demand for another. This may occur as the former is a part of production of the second. For example, demand for coal leads to _____ for mining, as coal must be mined for coal to be consumed.
a. 180SearchAssistant
b. 6-3-5 Brainwriting
c. Power III
d. Derived demand

8. In economics, _____ describes demand that is not very sensitive to a change in price.
a. AMAX
b. ACNielsen
c. ADTECH
d. Inelastic

9. _____ is the practice of individuals including commercial businesses, governments and institutions, facilitating the sale of their products or services to other companies or organizations that in turn resell them, use them as components in products or services they offer _____ is also called business-to-_____ for short. (Note that while marketing to government entities shares some of the same dynamics of organizational marketing, B2G Marketing is meaningfully different.)
a. Disruptive technology
b. Business marketing
c. Law of disruption
d. Mass marketing

10. A _____ is a company or individual that purchases goods or services with the intention of reselling them rather than consuming or using them. This is usually done for profit (but could be resold at a loss.) One example can be found in the industry of telecommunications, where companies buy excess amounts of transmission capacity or call time from other carriers and resell it to smaller carriers.
a. Discontinuation
b. Value-based pricing
c. Jobbing house
d. Reseller

11. A _____ is the space, actual or metaphorical, in which a market operates. The term is also used in a trademark law context to denote the actual consumer environment, ie. the 'real world' in which products and services are provided and consumed.
a. 180SearchAssistant
b. 6-3-5 Brainwriting
c. Marketplace
d. Power III

12. An _____ is the manufacturing of a good or service within a category. Although _____ is a broad term for any kind of economic production, in economics and urban planning _____ is a synonym for the secondary sector, which is a type of economic activity involved in the manufacturing of raw materials into goods and products.

There are four key industrial economic sectors: the primary sector, largely raw material extraction industries such as mining and farming; the secondary sector, involving refining, construction, and manufacturing; the tertiary sector, which deals with services (such as law and medicine) and distribution of manufactured goods; and the quaternary sector, a relatively new type of knowledge _____ focusing on technological research, design and development such as computer programming, and biochemistry.

Chapter 6. BUSINESS-TO-BUSINESS MARKETS: How and Why Organizations Buy

a. ACNielsen
b. ADTECH
c. AMAX
d. Industry

13. The _____ is a trilateral trade bloc in North America created by the governments of the United States, Canada, and Mexico. It superseded the Canada-United States Free Trade Agreement between the US and Canada.

Following diplomatic negotiations dating back to 1990 between the three nations, the leaders met in San Antonio, Texas on December 17, 1992 to sign _____.

a. 6-3-5 Brainwriting
b. 180SearchAssistant
c. Power III
d. North American Free Trade Agreement

14. The _____ or _____ is used by business and government to classify and measure economic activity in Canada, Mexico and the United States. It has largely replaced the older Standard Industrial Classification system; however, certain government departments and agencies, such as the U.S. Securities and Exchange Commission (SEC), still use the SIC codes.

The _____ numbering system is a six-digit code.

a. 6-3-5 Brainwriting
b. 180SearchAssistant
c. North American Industry Classification System
d. Power III

15. A _____, in marketing, procurement, and organizational studies, is a group of employees, family members, or members of any type of organization responsible for purchasing an item for the organization. In a business setting, major purchases typically require input from various parts of the organization, including finance, accounting, purchasing, information technology management, and senior management. Highly technical purchases, such as information systems or production equipment, also require the expertise of technical specialists.

a. Marketing myopia
b. Buying center
c. Commercialization
d. Packshot

16. _____ is a sub-discipline and type of marketing. There are two main definitional characteristics which distinguish it from other types of marketing. The first is that it attempts to send its messages directly to consumers, without the use of intervening media.

a. Direct marketing
b. Power III
c. Direct Marketing Associations
d. Database marketing

17. _____ refers to a business or organization attempting to acquire goods or services to accomplish the goals of the enterprise. Though there are several organizations that attempt to set standards in the _____ process, processes can vary greatly between organizations. Typically the word '_____' is not used interchangeably with the word 'procurement', since procurement typically includes Expediting, Supplier Quality, and Traffic and Logistics (T'L) in addition to _____.

a. Drop shipping
b. Supply network
c. Supply chain
d. Purchasing

18. _____ is the branch of logistics that deals with the tangible components of a supply chain. Specifically, this covers the acquisition of spare parts and replacements, quality control of purchasing and ordering such parts, and the standards involved in ordering, shipping, and warehousing the said parts.

A large component of _____ is ensuring that parts and materials used in the supply chain meet minimum requirements by performing quality assurance (QA.)

a. Vendor Managed Inventory
c. Reverse auction
b. Customer driven supply chain
d. Materials management

19. _____ can be regarded as an outcome of mental processes (cognitive process) leading to the selection of a course of action among several alternatives. Every _____ process produces a final choice. The output can be an action or an opinion of choice.

a. 180SearchAssistant
c. Power III
b. 6-3-5 Brainwriting
d. Decision making

20. A supply chain is the system of organizations, people, technology, activities, information and resources involved in moving a product or service from _____ to customer. Supply chain activities transform natural resources, raw materials and components into a finished product that is delivered to the end customer. In sophisticated supply chain systems, used products may re-enter the supply chain at any point where residual value is recyclable.

a. Bringin' Home the Oil
c. Product line extension
b. Rebate
d. Supplier

21. _____ is systematic determination of merit, worth, and significance of something or someone using criteria against a set of standards. _____ often is used to characterize and appraise subjects of interest in a wide range of human enterprises, including the arts, criminal justice, foundations and non-profit organizations, government, health care, and other human services.

Depending on the topic of interest, there are professional groups which look to the quality and rigor of the _____ process.

a. AMAX
c. ACNielsen
b. ADTECH
d. Evaluation

22. A _____ is an explicit set of requirements to be satisfied by a material, product, or service.

In engineering, manufacturing, and business, it is vital for suppliers, purchasers, and users of materials, products, or services to understand and agree upon all requirements. A _____ is a type of a standard which is often referenced by a contract or procurement document.

a. New product development
c. Product optimization
b. Specification
d. Product development

23. _____ is subcontracting a process, such as product design or manufacturing, to a third-party company. The decision to outsource is often made in the interest of lowering cost or making better use of time and energy costs, redirecting or conserving energy directed at the competencies of a particular business, or to make more efficient use of land, labor, capital, (information) technology and resources. _____ became part of the business lexicon during the 1980s.

Chapter 6. BUSINESS-TO-BUSINESS MARKETS: How and Why Organizations Buy

a. ACNielsen
b. In-house
c. Outsourcing
d. Intangible assets

24. _____ allows the same content to be used in different documents or in various formats. The labour-intensive and expensive work of editing need only be carried out once, on one document. Further transformations are carried out mechanically, by automated tools.
a. 180SearchAssistant
b. 6-3-5 Brainwriting
c. Power III
d. Single source publishing

25. Electronic commerce, commonly known as _____ or eCommerce, consists of the buying and selling of products or services over electronic systems such as the Internet and other computer networks. The amount of trade conducted electronically has grown extraordinarily with wide-spread Internet usage. A wide variety of commerce is conducted in this way, spurring and drawing on innovations in electronic funds transfer, supply chain management, Internet marketing, online transaction processing, electronic data interchange (EDI), inventory management systems, and automated data collection systems.
a. ADTECH
b. AMAX
c. E-commerce
d. ACNielsen

26. An _____ is a private network that uses Internet protocols, network connectivity, and possibly the public telecommunication system to securely share part of an organization's information or operations with suppliers, vendors, partners, customers or other businesses. An _____ can be viewed as part of a company's intranet that is extended to users outside the company (e.g.: normally over the Internet.) It has also been described as a 'state of mind' in which the Internet is perceived as a way to do business with a preapproved set of other companies business-to-business (B2B), in isolation from all other Internet users.
a. ADTECH
b. ACNielsen
c. AMAX
d. Extranet

27. In cryptography, _____ is the process of transforming information (referred to as plaintext) using an algorithm (called cipher) to make it unreadable to anyone except those possessing special knowledge, usually referred to as a key. The result of the process is encrypted information (in cryptography, referred to as ciphertext.) In many contexts, the word _____ also implicitly refers to the reverse process, decryption (e.g. 'software for _____' can typically also perform decryption), to make the encrypted information readable again (i.e. to make it unencrypted.)
a. ACNielsen
b. ADTECH
c. AMAX
d. Encryption

28. _____ refer to a collection of facts usually collected as the result of experience, observation or experiment or a set of premises. This may consist of numbers, words particularly as measurements or observations of a set of variables. _____ are often viewed as a lowest level of abstraction from which information and knowledge are derived.
a. Data
b. Sample size
c. Pearson product-moment correlation coefficient
d. Mean

Chapter 7. SHARPENING THE FOCUS

1. _____ is a broad label that refers to any individuals or households that use goods and services generated within the economy. The concept of a _____ is used in different contexts, so that the usage and significance of the term may vary.

A _____ is a person who uses any product or service.

   a. 180SearchAssistant
   b. Consumer
   c. 6-3-5 Brainwriting
   d. Power III

2. _____ is defined by the American _____ Association as the activity, set of institutions, and processes for creating, communicating, delivering, and exchanging offerings that have value for customers, clients, partners, and society at large. The term developed from the original meaning which referred literally to going to market, as in shopping, or going to a market to sell goods or services.

_____ practice tends to be seen as a creative industry, which includes advertising, distribution and selling.

   a. Customer acquisition management
   b. Marketing myopia
   c. Product naming
   d. Marketing

3. A _____ is a process that can allow an organization to concentrate its limited resources on the greatest opportunities to increase sales and achieve a sustainable competitive advantage. A _____ should be centered around the key concept that customer satisfaction is the main goal.

A _____ is most effective when it is an integral component of corporate strategy, defining how the organization will successfully engage customers, prospects, and competitors in the market arena.

   a. Psychographic
   b. Societal marketing
   c. Cyberdoc
   d. Marketing strategy

4. A _____ is a plan of action designed to achieve a particular goal.

_____ is different from tactics. In military terms, tactics is concerned with the conduct of an engagement while _____ is concerned with how different engagements are linked.

   a. Power III
   b. 6-3-5 Brainwriting
   c. Strategy
   d. 180SearchAssistant

5. _____ or _____ data refers to selected population characteristics as used in government, marketing or opinion research, or the _____ profiles used in such research. Note the distinction from the term 'demography' Commonly-used _____ include race, age, income, disabilities, mobility (in terms of travel time to work or number of vehicles available), educational attainment, home ownership, employment status, and even location.

   a. African Americans
   b. Albert Einstein
   c. AStore
   d. Demographic

6. _____ is a cohort which consists of those people born after the Generation X cohort. Its name is controversial and is synonymous with several alternative names including The Net Generation, Millennials, Echo Boomers, and iGeneration. _____ consists primarily of the offspring of the Generation Jones and Baby Boomers cohorts.

Chapter 7. SHARPENING THE FOCUS

a. Greatest Generation
c. AStore
b. Generation X
d. Generation Y

7. _____s are used in open sentences. For instance, in the formula x + 1 = 5, x is a _____ which represents an 'unknown' number. _____s are often represented by letters of the Roman alphabet, or those of other alphabets, such as Greek, and use other special symbols.
a. Variable
c. Personalization
b. Book of business
d. Quantitative

8. _____ is a term commonly used to describe commerce transactions between businesses like the one between a manufacturer and a wholesaler or a wholesaler and a retailer i.e both the buyer and the seller are business entity.This is unlike business-to-consumers (B2C) which involve a business entity and end consumer, or business-to-government (B2G) which involve a business entity and government.

The volume of B2B transactions is much higher than the volume of B2C transactions. The primary reason for this is that in a typical supply chain there will be many B2B transactions involving subcomponent or raw materials, and only one B2C transaction, specifically sale of the finished product to the end customer.

a. Social marketing
c. Business-to-business
b. Customer relationship management
d. Disruptive technology

9. A _____ is a subgroup of people or organizations sharing one or more characteristics that cause them to have similar product and/or service needs. A true _____ meets all of the following criteria: it is distinct from other segments (different segments have different needs), it is homogeneous within the segment (exhibits common needs); it responds similarly to a market stimulus, and it can be reached by a market intervention. The term is also used when consumers with identical product and/or service needs are divided up into groups so they can be charged different amounts.
a. Commercial planning
c. Production orientation
b. Customer insight
d. Market segment

10. In sociology, anthropology and cultural studies, a _____ is a group of people with a culture (whether distinct or hidden) which differentiates them from the larger culture to which they belong. If a particular _____ is characterized by a systematic opposition to the dominant culture, it may be described as a counterculture. As Ken Gelder notes, _____s are social, with their own shared conventions, values and rituals, but they can also seem 'immersed' or self-absorbed--another feature that distinguishes them from countercultures.
a. 180SearchAssistant
c. Subculture
b. 6-3-5 Brainwriting
d. Power III

11. _____ is a term used to describe a person who was born during the demographic Post-World War II baby boom. Many analysts now believe that two distinct cultural generations were born during this baby boom; the older generation is often called the Baby Boom Generation and the younger generation is often called Generation Jones. The term '_____' is sometimes used in a cultural context, and sometimes used to describe someone who was born during the post-WWII baby boom.
a. Greatest Generation
c. AStore
b. Generation X
d. Baby boomer

Chapter 7. SHARPENING THE FOCUS

12. _____ is a term used to identify people born after the post-World War II increase in birth rates (the baby boom) The term has been used in demography, the social sciences, and marketing, though it is most often used in popular culture.

In the U.S. _____ was originally referred to as the 'baby bust' generation because of the drop in the birth rate following the baby boom.

In the UK the term was first used in a 1964 study of British youth by Jane Deverson.

a. Generation X
b. AStore
c. Generation Y
d. Greatest Generation

13. _____ was originally coined by Austrian psychologist Alfred Adler in 1929. The current broader sense of the word dates from 1961.

In sociology, a _____ is the way a person lives.

a. Power III
b. 180SearchAssistant
c. 6-3-5 Brainwriting
d. Lifestyle

14. A _____ or digger group is a sociological group that does not constitute a politically dominant voting majority of the total population of a given society. A sociological _____ is not necessarily a numerical _____ -- it may include any group that is subnormal with respect to a dominant group in terms of social status, education, employment, wealth and political power. To avoid confusion, some writers prefer the terms 'subordinate group' and 'dominant group' rather than '_____' and 'majority', respectively.

a. Mociology
b. Power III
c. Reference group
d. Minority

15. _____ is the process of finding associated geographic coordinates (often expressed as latitude and longitude) from other geographic data, such as street addresses or the coordinates can be embedded into media such as digital photographs via geotagging.

Reverse _____ is the opposite: finding an associated textual location such as a street address, from geographic coordinates.

a. 180SearchAssistant
b. 6-3-5 Brainwriting
c. Power III
d. Geocoding

16. _____ is the study of the Earth and its lands, features, inhabitants, and phenomena. A literal translation would be 'to describe or write about the Earth'. The first person to use the word '_____' was Eratosthenes .

a. Geography
b. 6-3-5 Brainwriting
c. Power III
d. 180SearchAssistant

Chapter 7. SHARPENING THE FOCUS

17. _____ is difficult to define. For example, in 1952, Alfred Kroeber and Clyde Kluckhohn compiled a list of 164 definitions of '_____' in _____: A Critical Review of Concepts and Definitions. However, the word '_____' is most commonly used in three basic senses:

- excellence of taste in the fine arts and humanities
- an integrated pattern of human knowledge, belief, and behavior that depends upon the capacity for symbolic thought and social learning
- the set of shared attitudes, values, goals, and practices that characterizes an institution, organization or group.

When the concept first emerged in eighteenth- and nineteenth-century Europe, it connoted a process of cultivation or improvement, as in agriculture or horticulture. In the nineteenth century, it came to refer first to the betterment or refinement of the individual, especially through education, and then to the fulfillment of national aspirations or ideals.

a. AStore
c. African Americans
b. Albert Einstein
d. Culture

18. A personal and cultural _____ is a relative ethic _____, an assumption upon which implementation can be extrapolated. A _____ system is a set of consistent _____s and measures that is soo not true. A principle _____ is a foundation upon which other _____s and measures of integrity are based.

a. Perceptual maps
c. Package-on-Package
b. Supreme Court of the United States
d. Value

19. The _____ is a concept from business management that was first described and popularized by Michael Porter in his 1985 best-seller, Competitive Advantage: Creating and Sustaining Superior Performance.

A _____ is a chain of activities. Products pass through all activities of the chain in order and at each activity the product gains some value.

a. Relationship management
c. Mass marketing
b. Business-to-business
d. Value chain

20. In the field of marketing, demographics, opinion research, and social research in general, _____ variables are any attributes relating to personality, values, attitudes, interests, or lifestyles. They are also called IAO variables. They can be contrasted with demographic variables (such as age and gender), behavioral variables (such as usage rate or loyalty), and bizographic variables (such as industry, seniority and functional area.)

a. Psychographic
c. Marketing myopia
b. Business-to-business
d. Lifetime value

21. The acronym _____, is a psychographic segmentation. It was developed in the 1970s to explain changing U.S. values and lifestyles. It has since been reworked to enhance its ability to predict consumer behavior.

According to the _____ Framework, groups of people are arranged in a rectangle and are based on two dimensions. The vertical dimension segments people based on the degree to which they are innovative and have resources such as income, education, self-confidence, intelligence, leadership skills, and energy.

a. 6-3-5 Brainwriting
b. VALS
c. Power III
d. 180SearchAssistant

22. _____ is a fee paid on borrowed assets. It is the price paid for the use of borrowed money, or, money earned by deposited funds. Assets that are sometimes lent with _____ include money, shares, consumer goods through hire purchase, major assets such as aircraft, and even entire factories in finance lease arrangements.
   a. Interest
   b. ACNielsen
   c. ADTECH
   d. AMAX

23. _____ is the set of reasons that determines one to engage in a particular behavior. The term is generally used for human _____ but, theoretically, it can be used to describe the causes for animal behavior as well
   a. Power III
   b. Role playing
   c. 180SearchAssistant
   d. Motivation

24. In environmental modeling and especially in hydrology, a _____ model means a model that is acceptably consistent with observed natural processes, i.e. that simulates well, for example, observed river discharge. It is a key concept of the so-called Generalized Likelihood Uncertainty Estimation (GLUE) methodology to quantify how uncertain environmental predictions are.
   a. Behavioral
   b. 6-3-5 Brainwriting
   c. Power III
   d. 180SearchAssistant

25. _____ is one of the four elements of marketing mix. An organization or set of organizations (go-betweens) involved in the process of making a product or service available for use or consumption by a consumer or business user.

The other three parts of the marketing mix are product, pricing, and promotion.

   a. Better Living Through Chemistry
   b. Comparison-Shopping agent
   c. Japan Advertising Photographers' Association
   d. Distribution

26. An _____ is the manufacturing of a good or service within a category. Although _____ is a broad term for any kind of economic production, in economics and urban planning _____ is a synonym for the secondary sector, which is a type of economic activity involved in the manufacturing of raw materials into goods and products.

There are four key industrial economic sectors: the primary sector, largely raw material extraction industries such as mining and farming; the secondary sector, involving refining, construction, and manufacturing; the tertiary sector, which deals with services (such as law and medicine) and distribution of manufactured goods; and the quaternary sector, a relatively new type of knowledge _____ focusing on technological research, design and development such as computer programming, and biochemistry.

   a. ADTECH
   b. ACNielsen
   c. AMAX
   d. Industry

27. The _____ or _____ is used by business and government to classify and measure economic activity in Canada, Mexico and the United States. It has largely replaced the older Standard Industrial Classification system; however, certain government departments and agencies, such as the U.S. Securities and Exchange Commission (SEC), still use the SIC codes.

The _____ numbering system is a six-digit code.

a. 6-3-5 Brainwriting
b. 180SearchAssistant
c. Power III
d. North American Industry Classification System

28. _____ is a business term meaning the market segment to which a particular good or service is marketed. It is mainly defined by age, gender, geography, socio-economic grouping, technographic, or any other combination of demographics. It is generally studied and mapped by an organization through lists and reports containing demographic information that may have an effect on the marketing of key products or services.
a. Category Development Index
b. Distribution
c. Brando
d. Market specialization

29. On an intranet or B2E Enterprise Web portals, personalization is often based on user attributes such as department, functional area, or role. The term _____ in this context refers to the ability of users to modify the page layout or specify what content should be displayed.

There are two categories of personalizations:

1. Rule-based
2. Content-based

Web personalization models include rules-based filtering, based on 'if this, then that' rules processing, and collaborative filtering, which serves relevant material to customers by combining their own personal preferences with the preferences of like-minded others. Collaborative filtering works well for books, music, video, etc.

a. Self branding
b. Movin'
c. Cashmere Agency
d. Customization

30. _____ is a market coverage strategy in which a firm decides to ignore market segment differences and go after the whole market with one offer.it is type of marketing (or attempting to sell through persuasion) of a product to a wide audience. The idea is to broadcast a message that will reach the largest number of people possible. Traditionally _____ has focused on radio, television and newspapers as the medium used to reach this broad audience.
a. Mass marketing
b. Cyberdoc
c. Business-to-consumer
d. Marketspace

31. _____, in marketing, manufacturing, and management, is the use of flexible computer-aided manufacturing systems to produce custom output. Those systems combine the low unit costs of mass production processes with the flexibility of individual customization.

'_____' is the new frontier in business competition for both manufacturing and service industries.

a. Flanking marketing warfare strategies
b. Power III
c. Vertical integration
d. Mass customization

Chapter 7. SHARPENING THE FOCUS

32. In marketing, _____ has come to mean the process by which marketers try to create an image or identity in the minds of their target market for its product, brand, or organization. It is the 'relative competitive comparison' their product occupies in a given market as perceived by the target market.

Re-_____ involves changing the identity of a product, relative to the identity of competing products, in the collective minds of the target market.

a. Positioning
c. GE matrix

b. Moratorium
d. Containerization

33. _____ is a rivalry between individuals, groups, nations for territory, a niche, or allocation of resources. It arises whenever two or more parties strive for a goal which cannot be shared. _____ occurs naturally between living organisms which co-exist in the same environment.

a. Price fixing
c. Price competition

b. Non-price competition
d. Competition

34. Competitiveness is a comparative concept of the ability and performance of a firm, sub-sector or country to sell and supply goods and/or services in a given market. Although widely used in economics and business management, the usefulness of the concept, particularly in the context of national competitiveness, is vigorously disputed by economists, such as Paul Krugman .

The term may also be applied to markets, where it is used to refer to the extent to which the market structure may be regarded as perfectly _____.

a. Customs union
c. Geographical pricing

b. Competitive
d. Free trade zone

35. _____ is, in very basic words, a position a firm occupies against its competitors.

According to Michael Porter, the three methods for creating a sustainable _____ are through:

1. Cost leadership - Cost advantage occurs when a firm delivers the same services as its competitors but at a lower cost;

2.

a. 180SearchAssistant
c. 6-3-5 Brainwriting

b. Competitive advantage
d. Power III

36. The _____ is generally accepted as the use and specification of the four p's describing the strategic position of a product in the marketplace. One version of the origins of the _____ starts in 1948 when James Culliton said that a marketing decision should be a result of something similar to a recipe. This version continued in 1953 when Neil Borden, in his American Marketing Association presidential address, took the recipe idea one step further and coined the term 'Marketing-Mix'.

Chapter 7. SHARPENING THE FOCUS

a. 180SearchAssistant
c. Power III
b. 6-3-5 Brainwriting
d. Marketing mix

37. A _____ is a collection of symbols, experiences and associations connected with a product, a service, a person or any other artifact or entity.

_____s have become increasingly important components of culture and the economy, now being described as 'cultural accessories and personal philosophies'.

Some people distinguish the psychological aspect of a _____ from the experiential aspect.

a. Store brand
c. Brand equity
b. Brandable software
d. Brand

38. Perceptual mapping is a graphics technique used by asset marketers that attempts to visually display the perceptions of customers or potential customers. Typically the position of a product, product line, brand, or company is displayed relative to their competition.

_____ can have any number of dimensions but the most common is two dimensions.

a. Comparison-Shopping agent
c. Developed country
b. Perceptual maps
d. Retail floor planning

39. _____ consists of the processes a company uses to track and organize its contacts with its current and prospective customers. _____ software is used to support these processes; information about customers and customer interactions can be entered, stored and accessed by employees in different company departments. Typical _____ goals are to improve services provided to customers, and to use customer contact information for targeted marketing.

a. Commercialization
c. Demand generation
b. Product bundling
d. Customer relationship management

40. _____ refers to marketing strategies applied directly to a specific consumer.

Having the knowledge on the consumer preferences, there are suggested personalized products and promotions to each consumer.

The _____ is based in four main steps in order to fulfill its goals: Those stages are identify, differentiate, interact, and customize.

a. ADTECH
c. ACNielsen
b. AMAX
d. One-to-one marketing

Chapter 7. SHARPENING THE FOCUS

41. Customer _____ consists of the processes a company uses to track and organize its contacts with its current and prospective customers. CRelationship management software is used to support these processes; information about customers and customer interactions can be entered, stored and accessed by employees in different company departments. Typical CRelationship management goals are to improve services provided to customers, and to use customer contact information for targeted marketing.

a. Product bundling
c. Green marketing
b. Marketing
d. Relationship management

42. _____ is an advertisement in which a particular product specifically mentions a competitor by name for the express purpose of showing why the competitor is inferior to the product naming it.

This should not be confused with parody advertisements, where a fictional product is being advertised for the purpose of poking fun at the particular advertisement, nor should it be confused with the use of a coined brand name for the purpose of comparing the product without actually naming an actual competitor. ('Wikipedia tastes better and is less filling than the Encyclopedia Galactica.')

In the 1980s, during what has been referred to as the cola wars, soft-drink manufacturer Pepsi ran a series of advertisements where people, caught on hidden camera, in a blind taste test, chose Pepsi over rival Coca-Cola.

a. Heavy-up
c. Cost per conversion
b. GL-70
d. Comparative advertising

43. In economic models, the _____ time frame assumes no fixed factors of production. Firms can enter or leave the marketplace, and the cost (and availability) of land, labor, raw materials, and capital goods can be assumed to vary. In contrast, in the short-run time frame, certain factors are assumed to be fixed, because there is not sufficient time for them to change.

a. Power III
c. 6-3-5 Brainwriting
b. 180SearchAssistant
d. Long-run

44.

The net present value (NPV) of all of a company's customers in terms of customer loyalty and indirectly, the revenue that the company can obtain from them.

In deciding the value of a company, it is important to know of how much value its customer base is in terms of future revenues. The greater the _____ , the more future revenue in the lifetime of its clients; this means that a company with a higher _____ can get more money from its customers on average than another company that is identical in all other characteristics.

a. Marginal revenue
c. Product proliferation
b. Total cost
d. Customer equity

45. In marketing, customer _____, lifetime customer value (LCV), or _____ (LTV) and a new concept of 'customer life cycle management' is the present value of the future cash flows attributed to the customer relationship. Use of customer _____ as a marketing metric tends to place greater emphasis on customer service and long-term customer satisfaction, rather than on maximizing short-term sales.

Customer _____ has intuitive appeal as a marketing concept, because in theory it represents exactly how much each customer is worth in monetary terms, and therefore exactly how much a marketing department should be willing to spend to acquire each customer.

a. Sweepstakes
c. Brand infiltration
b. Lifetime value
d. Value chain

46. _____ is a form of applied ethics that examines ethical principles and moral or ethical problems that arise in a business environment. It applies to all aspects of business conduct and is relevant to the conduct of individuals and business organizations as a whole. Applied ethics is a field of ethics that deals with ethical questions in many fields such as medical, technical, legal and _____.

a. Business ethics
c. 180SearchAssistant
b. Power III
d. 6-3-5 Brainwriting

47. _____ is a branch of philosophy which seeks to address questions about morality, such as how a moral outcome can be achieved in a specific situation (applied _____), how moral values should be determined (normative _____), what moral values people actually abide by (descriptive _____), what the fundamental semantic, ontological, and epistemic nature of _____ or morality is (meta-_____), and how moral capacity or moral agency develops and what its nature is (moral psychology.)

Socrates was one of the first Greek philosophers to encourage both scholars and the common citizen to turn their attention from the outside world to the condition of man. In this view, Knowledge having a bearing on human life was placed highest, all other knowledge being secondary.

a. AMAX
c. Ethics
b. ADTECH
d. ACNielsen

Chapter 8. CREATING THE PRODUCT

1. A personal and cultural _____ is a relative ethic _____, an assumption upon which implementation can be extrapolated. A _____ system is a set of consistent _____s and measures that is soo not true. A principle _____ is a foundation upon which other _____s and measures of integrity are based.

   a. Value
   b. Supreme Court of the United States
   c. Perceptual maps
   d. Package-on-Package

2. In the field of marketing, a customer _____ consists of the sum total of benefits which a vendor promises that a customer will receive in return for the customer's associated payment (or other value-transfer.)

   Put simply, the _____ is what the customer gets for his money.

   Accordingly, a customer can evaluate a company's value-proposition on two broad dimensions with multiple subsets:

   1. relative performance: what the customer gets from the vendor relative to a competitor's offering;
   2. price: which consists of the payment the customer makes to acquire the product or service; plus the access cost

   The vendor-company's marketing and sales efforts offer a customer _____; the vendor-company's delivery and customer-service processes then fulfill that value-proposition.

   A value-proposition can assist in a firm's marketing strategy, and may guide a business to target a particular market segment.

   a. Marketing performance measurement and management
   b. Value proposition
   c. DefCom Australia
   d. Relationship management

3. _____ is a term commonly used to describe commerce transactions between businesses like the one between a manufacturer and a wholesaler or a wholesaler and a retailer i.e both the buyer and the seller are business entity. This is unlike business-to-consumers (B2C) which involve a business entity and end consumer, or business-to-government (B2G) which involve a business entity and government.

   The volume of B2B transactions is much higher than the volume of B2C transactions. The primary reason for this is that in a typical supply chain there will be many B2B transactions involving subcomponent or raw materials, and only one B2C transaction, specifically sale of the finished product to the end customer.

   a. Customer relationship management
   b. Business-to-business
   c. Social marketing
   d. Disruptive technology

4. On an intranet or B2E Enterprise Web portals, personalization is often based on user attributes such as department, functional area, or role. The term _____ in this context refers to the ability of users to modify the page layout or specify what content should be displayed.

Chapter 8. CREATING THE PRODUCT

There are two categories of personalizations:

1. Rule-based
2. Content-based

Web personalization models include rules-based filtering, based on 'if this, then that' rules processing, and collaborative filtering, which serves relevant material to customers by combining their own personal preferences with the preferences of like-minded others. Collaborative filtering works well for books, music, video, etc.

a. Self branding
b. Movin'
c. Cashmere Agency
d. Customization

5. In marketing, a _____ is a generic product augmented by everything that is needed for the customer to have a compelling reason to buy. The generic product is what is usually shipped to the customer. The _____ typically augments the generic product with training and support, manuals, cables, additional software or hardware, installation instructions, professional services, etc.

a. Jobbing house
b. Mass market
c. Teaser rate
d. Whole product

6. _____ is a broad label that refers to any individuals or households that use goods and services generated within the economy. The concept of a _____ is used in different contexts, so that the usage and significance of the term may vary.

A _____ is a person who uses any product or service.

a. Consumer
b. 6-3-5 Brainwriting
c. Power III
d. 180SearchAssistant

7. _____ is anything that is intended to save time, energy or frustration. A _____ store at a petrol station, for example, sells items that have nothing to do with gasoline/petrol, but it saves the consumer from having to go to a grocery store. '_____' is a very relative term and its meaning tends to change over time.

a. Demographic profile
b. MaxDiff
c. Marketing buzz
d. Convenience

8. In economics, a _____ or a hard good is a good which does not quickly wear out it yields services or utility over time rather than being completely used up when used once. Most goods are therefore _____s to a certain degree. These are goods that can last for a relatively long time, such as refrigerators, cars, and DVD players.

a. Power III
b. Luxury good
c. Free good
d. Durable good

9. _____ , are products that are sold quickly at relatively low cost. Though the absolute profit made on _____ products is relatively small, they generally sell in large quantities, so the cumulative profit on such products can be large. Examples of _____ generally include a wide range of frequently purchased consumer products such as toiletries, soap, cosmetics, teeth cleaning products, shaving products and detergents, as well as other non-durables such as glassware, light bulbs, batteries, paper products and plastic goods.

Chapter 8. CREATING THE PRODUCT

a. Marketing management
b. Performance-based advertising
c. Door-to-door
d. Fast moving consumer goods

10. An _____ is an unplanned or otherwise spontaneous purchase. One who tends to make such purchases is referred to as an impulse purchaser or impulse buyer.

Marketers and retailers tend to exploit these impulses which are tied to the basic want for instant gratification.

a. ADTECH
b. AMAX
c. ACNielsen
d. Impulse purchase

11. _____ is the examining of goods or services from retailers with the intent to purchase at that time. _____ is an activity of selection and/or purchase. In some contexts it is considered a leisure activity as well as an economic one.

a. Shopping
b. Hawkers
c. Discount store
d. Khodebshchik

12. _____ are final goods specifically intended for the mass market. For instance, _____ do not include investment assets, like precious antiques, even though these antiques are final goods.

Manufactured goods are goods that have been processed by way of machinery.

a. Free good
b. Durable good
c. Power III
d. Consumer goods

13. _____s are Web-based intelligent software applications that can help online shoppers find lower price for commodities or services. Price comparison services was the earliest service a _____ provides. To search the price of a particular item, a _____ would search multiple online stores based on the keyword the online shopper provides.

a. Book of business
b. Net Promoter^R score
c. Distribution
d. Comparison-Shopping agent

14. The _____ is an independent agency of the United States government, established in 1914 by the _____ Act. Its principal mission is the promotion of 'consumer protection' and the elimination and prevention of what regulators perceive to be harmfully 'anti-competitive' business practices, such as coercive monopoly.

The _____ Act was one of President Wilson's major acts against trusts.

a. Power III
b. 180SearchAssistant
c. 6-3-5 Brainwriting
d. Federal Trade Commission

15. The _____ of 1914 (15 U.S.C §§ 41-58, as amended) established the Federal Trade Commission (FTC), a bipartisan body of five members appointed by the President of the United States for seven year terms. This Commission was authorized to issue Cease and Desist orders to large corporations to curb unfair trade practices. This Act also gave more flexibility to the US congress for judicial matters.

a. Gripe site
b. Product liability
c. Federal Trade Commission Act
d. Comparative negligence

Chapter 8. CREATING THE PRODUCT

16. A _____ is something that is acted upon or used by or by human labour or industry, for use as a building material to create some product or structure. Often the term is used to denote material that came from nature and is in an unprocessed or minimally processed state. Iron ore, logs, and crude oil, would be examples.
   a. Raw material
   b. Power III
   c. 6-3-5 Brainwriting
   d. 180SearchAssistant

17. _____ is an advertisement in which a particular product specifically mentions a competitor by name for the express purpose of showing why the competitor is inferior to the product naming it.

This should not be confused with parody advertisements, where a fictional product is being advertised for the purpose of poking fun at the particular advertisement, nor should it be confused with the use of a coined brand name for the purpose of comparing the product without actually naming an actual competitor. ('Wikipedia tastes better and is less filling than the Encyclopedia Galactica.')

In the 1980s, during what has been referred to as the cola wars, soft-drink manufacturer Pepsi ran a series of advertisements where people, caught on hidden camera, in a blind taste test, chose Pepsi over rival Coca-Cola.

   a. Comparative advertising
   b. GL-70
   c. Heavy-up
   d. Cost per conversion

18. _____ in organizations and public policy is both the organizational process of creating and maintaining a plan; and the psychological process of thinking about the activities required to create a desired goal on some scale. As such, it is a fundamental property of intelligent behavior. This thought process is essential to the creation and refinement of a plan, or integration of it with other plans, that is, it combines forecasting of developments with the preparation of scenarios of how to react to them.
   a. Power III
   b. Planning
   c. 180SearchAssistant
   d. 6-3-5 Brainwriting

19. _____ is the ongoing process of identifying and articulating market requirements that define a product's feature set.
   a. Market intelligence
   b. Brand parity
   c. Targeted advertising
   d. Product planning

20. An _____ is a person who creates or discovers a new method, form, device or other useful means. The word _____ comes form the latin verb invenire, invent-, to find. The system of patents was established to encourage _____s by granting limited-term, limited monopoly on inventions determined to be sufficiently novel, non-obvious, and useful.
   a. Inventor
   b. ACNielsen
   c. AMAX
   d. ADTECH

21. _____ is systematic determination of merit, worth, and significance of something or someone using criteria against a set of standards. _____ often is used to characterize and appraise subjects of interest in a wide range of human enterprises, including the arts, criminal justice, foundations and non-profit organizations, government, health care, and other human services.

Chapter 8. CREATING THE PRODUCT

Depending on the topic of interest, there are professional groups which look to the quality and rigor of the _____ process.

a. AMAX
c. ADTECH
b. ACNielsen
d. Evaluation

22. A _____ is the price one pays as remuneration for services, especially the honorarium paid to a doctor, lawyer, consultant, or other member of a learned profession. _____s usually allow for overhead, wages, costs, and markup.

Traditionally, professionals in Great Britain received a _____ in contradistinction to a payment, salary, or wage, and would often use guineas rather than pounds as units of account.

a. Transfer pricing
c. Price shading
b. Price war
d. Fee

23. A _____ is a form of qualitative research in which a group of people are asked about their attitude towards a product, service, concept, advertisement, idea, or packaging. Questions are asked in an interactive group setting where participants are free to talk with other group members.

Ernest Dichter originated the idea of having a 'group therapy' for products and this process is what became known as a _____.

a. Focus group
c. Marketing research process
b. Cross tabulation
d. Logit analysis

24. _____ is the set of tasks, knowledge, and techniques required to identify business needs and determine solutions to business problems. Solutions often include a systems development component, but may also consist of process improvement or organizational change. The person who carries out this task is called a business analyst or _____.

a. Fast moving consumer goods
c. Marketing management
b. Door-to-door
d. Business analysis

25. _____ is defined by the American _____ Association as the activity, set of institutions, and processes for creating, communicating, delivering, and exchanging offerings that have value for customers, clients, partners, and society at large. The term developed from the original meaning which referred literally to going to market, as in shopping, or going to a market to sell goods or services.

_____ practice tends to be seen as a creative industry, which includes advertising, distribution and selling.

a. Product naming
c. Customer acquisition management
b. Marketing myopia
d. Marketing

26. A _____ is a process that can allow an organization to concentrate its limited resources on the greatest opportunities to increase sales and achieve a sustainable competitive advantage. A _____ should be centered around the key concept that customer satisfaction is the main goal.

Chapter 8. CREATING THE PRODUCT

A _____ is most effective when it is an integral component of corporate strategy, defining how the organization will successfully engage customers, prospects, and competitors in the market arena.

a. Marketing strategy
b. Psychographic
c. Cyberdoc
d. Societal marketing

27. In business and engineering, _____ is the term used to describe the complete process of bringing a new product or service to market. There are two parallel paths involved in the _____ process: one involves the idea generation, product design, and detail engineering; the other involves market research and marketing analysis. Companies typically see _____ as the first stage in generating and commercializing new products within the overall strategic process of product life cycle management used to maintain or grow their market share.

a. Product development
b. New product development
c. Product optimization
d. Specification

28. In business and engineering, new _____ is the term used to describe the complete process of bringing a new product or service to market. There are two parallel paths involved in the Nproduct development process: one involves the idea generation, product design, and detail engineering; the other involves market research and marketing analysis. Companies typically see new _____ as the first stage in generating and commercializing new products within the overall strategic process of product life cycle management used to maintain or grow their market share.

a. New product screening
b. Product development
c. Specification tree
d. New product development

29. A _____ is a set of exclusive rights granted by a State to an inventor or his assignee for a limited period of time in exchange for a disclosure of an invention.

The procedure for granting _____s, the requirements placed on the _____ee and the extent of the exclusive rights vary widely between countries according to national laws and international agreements. Typically, however, a _____ application must include one or more claims defining the invention which must be new, inventive, and useful or industrially applicable.

a. Reasonable person standard
b. Foreign Corrupt Practices Act
c. Product liability
d. Patent

30. Proof-of-Principle _____ This type of _____ is used to test some aspect of the intended design without attempting to exactly simulate the visual appearance, choice of materials or intended manufacturing process. Such _____s can be used to 'prove' out a potential design approach such as range of motion, mechanics, sensors, architecture, etc.

a. 6-3-5 Brainwriting
b. 180SearchAssistant
c. Power III
d. Prototype

Chapter 8. CREATING THE PRODUCT

31. A _____, in the field of business and marketing, is a geographic region or demographic group used to gauge the viability of a product or service in the mass market prior to a wide scale roll-out. The criteria used to judge the acceptability of a _____ region or group include:

1. a population that is demographically similar to the proposed target market; and
2. relative isolation from densely populated media markets so that advertising to the test audience can be efficient and economical.

The _____ ideally aims to duplicate 'everything' - promotion and distribution as well as `product' - on a smaller scale. The technique replicates, typically in one area, what is planned to occur in a national launch; and the results are very carefully monitored, so that they can be extrapolated to projected national results. The `area' may be any one of the following:

- Television area
- Test town
- Residential neighborhood
- Test site

A number of decisions have to be taken about any _____:

- Which _____?
- What is to be tested?
- How long a test?
- What are the success criteria?

The simple go or no-go decision, together with the related reduction of risk, is normally the main justification for the expense of _____s. At the same time, however, such _____s can be used to test specific elements of a new product's marketing mix; possibly the version of the product itself, the promotional message and media spend, the distribution channels and the price.

a. Test market
b. 180SearchAssistant
c. Preadolescence
d. Power III

32. _____ is the process or cycle of introducing a new product into the market. The actual launch of a new product is the final stage of new product development, and the one where the most money will have to be spent for advertising, sales promotion, and other marketing efforts. In the case of a new consumer packaged good, costs will be at least $ 10 million, but can reach up to $ 200 million.

a. Customer Interaction Tracker
b. Commercialization
c. Confusion marketing
d. Sweepstakes

33. _____ is the process by which a new idea or new product is accepted by the market. The rate of _____ is the speed that the new idea spreads from one consumer to the next. Adoption is similar to _____ except that it deals with the psychological processes an individual goes through, rather than an aggregate market process.

Chapter 8. CREATING THE PRODUCT

a. Market development
b. Diffusion
c. Perceptual maps
d. Kano model

34. The U.S. _____ is an agency of the United States Department of Health and Human Services and is responsible for regulating and supervising the safety of foods, dietary supplements, drugs, vaccines, biological medical products, blood products, medical devices, radiation-emitting devices, veterinary products, and cosmetics. The FDA also enforces section 361 of the Public Health Service Act and the associated regulations, including sanitation requirements on interstate travel as well as specific rules for control of disease on products ranging from pet turtles to semen donations for assisted reproductive medicine techniques.

The FDA is an agency within the United States Department of Health and Human Services responsible for protecting and promoting the nation's public health.

a. 180SearchAssistant
b. 6-3-5 Brainwriting
c. Power III
d. Food and Drug Administration

35. _____ is a fee paid on borrowed assets. It is the price paid for the use of borrowed money , or, money earned by deposited funds . Assets that are sometimes lent with _____ include money, shares, consumer goods through hire purchase, major assets such as aircraft, and even entire factories in finance lease arrangements.
a. ACNielsen
b. Interest
c. AMAX
d. ADTECH

36. In sociology, a _____ or angle of repose is the event of a previously rare phenomenon becoming rapidly and dramatically more common. The phrase was coined in its sociological use by Morton Grodzins, by analogy with the fact in physics that adding a small amount of weight to a balanced object can cause it to suddenly and completely topple.

Grodzins studied integrating American neighborhoods in the early 1960s.

a. Completely randomized designs
b. Manufacturers' representatives
c. Publicity
d. Tipping point

37. _____ is a sub-discipline and type of marketing. There are two main definitional characteristics which distinguish it from other types of marketing. The first is that it attempts to send its messages directly to consumers, without the use of intervening media.
a. Database marketing
b. Direct Marketing Associations
c. Power III
d. Direct marketing

38. _____ is a theory of how, why, and at what rate new ideas and technology spread through cultures. Everett Rogers introduced it in his 1962 book, _____s, writing that 'Diffusion is the process by which an innovation is communicated through certain channels over time among the members of a social system.' The adoption curve becomes an s-curve when cumulative adoption is used.

Rogers theorized that innovations would spread through a community in an S curve, as the early adopters select the innovation (which may be a technology) first, followed by the majority, until a technology or innovation has reached its saturation point in a community.

Chapter 8. CREATING THE PRODUCT

According to Rogers, diffusion research centers on the conditions which increase or decrease the likelihood that a new idea, product, or practice will be adopted by members of a given culture.

a. Power III
c. 6-3-5 Brainwriting
b. Diffusion of Innovation
d. 180SearchAssistant

39. Organizational culture is not the same as _____. It is wider and deeper concepts, something that an organization 'is' rather than what it 'has' (according to Buchanan and Huczynski.)

_____ is the total sum of the values, customs, traditions and meanings that make a company unique.

a. Corporate culture
c. Cross-functional team
b. 180SearchAssistant
d. Power III

40. In economics, business, retail, and accounting, a _____ is the value of money that has been used up to produce something, and hence is not available for use anymore. In economics, a _____ is an alternative that is given up as a result of a decision. In business, the _____ may be one of acquisition, in which case the amount of money expended to acquire it is counted as _____.

a. Variable cost
c. Fixed costs
b. Transaction cost
d. Cost

41. _____ is difficult to define. For example, in 1952, Alfred Kroeber and Clyde Kluckhohn compiled a list of 164 definitions of '_____' in _____: A Critical Review of Concepts and Definitions. However, the word '_____' is most commonly used in three basic senses:

- excellence of taste in the fine arts and humanities
- an integrated pattern of human knowledge, belief, and behavior that depends upon the capacity for symbolic thought and social learning
- the set of shared attitudes, values, goals, and practices that characterizes an institution, organization or group.

When the concept first emerged in eighteenth- and nineteenth-century Europe, it connoted a process of cultivation or improvement, as in agriculture or horticulture. In the nineteenth century, it came to refer first to the betterment or refinement of the individual, especially through education, and then to the fulfillment of national aspirations or ideals.

a. African Americans
c. Albert Einstein
b. AStore
d. Culture

Chapter 9. MANAGING THE PRODUCT

1. _____ is an organizational lifecycle function within a company dealing with the planning or marketing of a product or products at all stages of the product lifecycle.

   _____ and product marketing (outbound focused) are different yet complementary efforts with the objective of maximizing sales revenues, market share, and profit margins. The role of _____ spans many activities from strategic to tactical and varies based on the organizational structure of the company.

   a. Service product management
   c. Product information management
   b. Product management
   d. Requirement prioritization

2. _____ is the ongoing process of identifying and articulating market requirements that define a product's feature set.
   a. Market intelligence
   c. Brand parity
   b. Targeted advertising
   d. Product planning

3. _____ is defined by the American _____ Association as the activity, set of institutions, and processes for creating, communicating, delivering, and exchanging offerings that have value for customers, clients, partners, and society at large. The term developed from the original meaning which referred literally to going to market, as in shopping, or going to a market to sell goods or services.

   _____ practice tends to be seen as a creative industry, which includes advertising, distribution and selling.

   a. Marketing myopia
   c. Product naming
   b. Customer acquisition management
   d. Marketing

4. A _____ is a written document that details the necessary actions to achieve one or more marketing objectives. It can be for a product or service, a brand, or a product line. _____s cover between one and five years.
   a. Prosumer
   c. Marketing plan
   b. Disruptive technology
   d. Marketing strategy

5. _____ in organizations and public policy is both the organizational process of creating and maintaining a plan; and the psychological process of thinking about the activities required to create a desired goal on some scale. As such, it is a fundamental property of intelligent behavior. This thought process is essential to the creation and refinement of a plan, or integration of it with other plans, that is, it combines forecasting of developments with the preparation of scenarios of how to react to them.
   a. Power III
   c. Planning
   b. 6-3-5 Brainwriting
   d. 180SearchAssistant

6. A _____ is a plan of action designed to achieve a particular goal.

   _____ is different from tactics. In military terms, tactics is concerned with the conduct of an engagement while _____ is concerned with how different engagements are linked.

   a. 180SearchAssistant
   c. 6-3-5 Brainwriting
   b. Power III
   d. Strategy

Chapter 9. MANAGING THE PRODUCT

7. In economic models, the _____ time frame assumes no fixed factors of production. Firms can enter or leave the marketplace, and the cost (and availability) of land, labor, raw materials, and capital goods can be assumed to vary. In contrast, in the short-run time frame, certain factors are assumed to be fixed, because there is not sufficient time for them to change.
   a. 6-3-5 Brainwriting
   b. 180SearchAssistant
   c. Power III
   d. Long-run

8. There are many important decisions about product and service development and marketing. In the process of product development and marketing we should focus on strategic decisions about product attributes, product branding, product packaging, product labeling and product support services. But product strategy also calls for building a _____.
   a. Pinstorm
   b. Technology acceptance model
   c. Macromarketing
   d. Product line

9. In marketing and strategy, _____ refers to a reduction in the sales volume, sales revenue, or market share of one product as a result of the introduction of a new product by the same producer.

For example, if Coca Cola were to introduce a similar product (say, Diet Coke or Cherry Coke), this new product could take some of the sales away from the original Coke. _____ is a key consideration in product portfolio analysis.

   a. Marketing
   b. Cannibalization
   c. Business-to-consumer
   d. Co-marketing

10. _____ is a business management strategy aimed at embedding awareness of quality in all organizational processes. _____ has been widely used in manufacturing, education, call centers, government, and service industries, as well as NASA space and science programs.

When used together as a phrase, the three words in this expression have the following meanings:

- Total: Involving the entire organization, supply chain, and/or product life cycle
- Quality: With its usual definitions, with all its complexities
- Management: The system of managing with steps like Plan, Organize, Control, Lead, Staff, provisioning and organizing.

As defined by the International Organization for Standardization (ISO):

'_____ is a management approach for an organization, centered on quality, based on the participation of all its members and aiming at long-term success through customer satisfaction, and benefits to all members of the organization and to society.' ISO 8402:1994

One major aim is to reduce variation from every process so that greater consistency of effort is obtained. (Royse, D., Thyer, B., Padgett D., ' Logan T., 2006)

Chapter 9. MANAGING THE PRODUCT

In Japan, _____ comprises four process steps, namely:

1. Kaizen - Focuses on 'Continuous Process Improvement', to make processes visible, repeatable and measurable.
2. Atarimae Hinshitsu - The idea that 'things will work as they are supposed to'.
3. Kansei - Examining the way the user applies the product leads to improvement in the product itself.
4. Miryokuteki Hinshitsu - The idea that 'things should have an aesthetic quality' (for example, a pen will write in a way that is pleasing to the writer.)

_____ requires that the company maintain this quality standard in all aspects of its business. This requires ensuring that things are done right the first time and that defects and waste are eliminated from operations.

a. 180SearchAssistant
b. Total quality management
c. Power III
d. 6-3-5 Brainwriting

11. _____ is a broad label that refers to any individuals or households that use goods and services generated within the economy. The concept of a _____ is used in different contexts, so that the usage and significance of the term may vary.

A _____ is a person who uses any product or service.

a. 6-3-5 Brainwriting
b. Consumer
c. 180SearchAssistant
d. Power III

12. _____ is a technical term used in management science popularized by Joseph M. Juran

He defined an internal and external customers as anyone affected by the product or by the process used to produce the product, in the context of quality management. _____s may play the role as supplier, processer, and customer in the sequence of product development.

He claimed that the organization must understand and identify both internal and external customers and their needs.

a. Internal customer
b. AMAX
c. ADTECH
d. ACNielsen

13. _____ is a business management strategy, originally developed by Motorola, that today enjoys widespread application in many sectors of industry.

_____ seeks to identify and remove the causes of defects and errors in manufacturing and business processes. It uses a set of quality management methods, including statistical methods, and creates a special infrastructure of people within the organization ('Black Belts' etc.)

Chapter 9. MANAGING THE PRODUCT

a. Power III
b. 180SearchAssistant
c. 6-3-5 Brainwriting
d. Six Sigma

14. The _____ is generally accepted as the use and specification of the four p's describing the strategic position of a product in the marketplace. One version of the origins of the _____ starts in 1948 when James Culliton said that a marketing decision should be a result of something similar to a recipe. This version continued in 1953 when Neil Borden, in his American Marketing Association presidential address, took the recipe idea one step further and coined the term 'Marketing-Mix'.

a. 180SearchAssistant
b. Marketing mix
c. 6-3-5 Brainwriting
d. Power III

15. _____ in economics and business is the result of an exchange and from that trade we assign a numerical monetary value to a good, service or asset. If I trade 4 apples for an orange, the _____ of an orange is 4 - apples. Inversely, the _____ of an apple is 1/4 oranges.

a. Contribution margin-based pricing
b. Discounts and allowances
c. Pricing
d. Price

16. In operant conditioning, _____ occurs when an event following a response causes an increase in the probability of that response occurring in the future. Response strength can be assessed by measures such as the frequency with which the response is made (for example, a pigeon may peck a key more times in the session), or the speed with which it is made (for example, a rat may run a maze faster.) The environment change contingent upon the response is called a reinforcer.

a. Relationship Management Application
b. Completely randomized designs
c. Generic brands
d. Reinforcement

17. _____ is one of the four elements of marketing mix. An organization or set of organizations (go-betweens) involved in the process of making a product or service available for use or consumption by a consumer or business user.

The other three parts of the marketing mix are product, pricing, and promotion.

a. Japan Advertising Photographers' Association
b. Comparison-Shopping agent
c. Better Living Through Chemistry
d. Distribution

18. _____ Management is the succession of strategies used by management as a product goes through its _____. The conditions in which a product is sold changes over time and must be managed as it moves through its succession of stages.

The _____ goes through many phases, involves many professional disciplines, and requires many skills, tools and processes.

a. Supplier diversity
b. Customer satisfaction
c. Product life cycle
d. Chain stores

19. _____, also referred to as i-marketing, web marketing, online marketing is the marketing of products or services over the Internet.

The Internet has brought many unique benefits to marketing, one of which being lower costs for the distribution of information and media to a global audience. The interactive nature of _____, both in terms of providing instant response and eliciting responses, is a unique quality of the medium.

a. AMAX
b. Internet marketing
c. ACNielsen
d. ADTECH

20. A _____ is a collection of symbols, experiences and associations connected with a product, a service, a person or any other artifact or entity.

_____s have become increasingly important components of culture and the economy, now being described as 'cultural accessories and personal philosophies'.

Some people distinguish the psychological aspect of a _____ from the experiential aspect.

a. Brand equity
b. Store brand
c. Brandable software
d. Brand

21. A _____ is typically the attributes one associates with a brand, how the brand owner wants the consumer to perceive the brand - and by extension the branded company, organization, product or service. The brand owner will seek to bridge the gap between the _____ and the brand identity.
a. Brand equity
b. Brand loyalty
c. Status brand
d. Brand image

22. A _____ or trade mark, identified by the symbols â„¢ (not yet registered) and Â® (registered) business organization or other legal entity to identify that the products and/or services to consumers with which the _____ appears originate from a unique source of origin, and to distinguish its products or services from those of other entities. A _____ is a type of intellectual property, and typically a name, word, phrase, logo, symbol, design, image, or a combination of these elements. There is also a range of non-conventional _____s comprising marks which do not fall into these standard categories.
a. Power III
b. Risk management
c. 180SearchAssistant
d. Trademark

23. _____ refers to the marketing effects or outcomes that accrue to a product with its brand name compared with those that would accrue if the same product did not have the brand name . And, at the root of these marketing effects is consumers' knowledge. In other words, consumers' knowledge about a brand makes manufacturers/advertisers respond differently or adopt appropriately adapt measures for the marketing of the brand .
a. Brand aversion
b. Brand image
c. Product extension
d. Brand equity

24. _____ or self identity refers to the global understanding a sentient being has of him or herself. It presupposes but can be distinguished from self-consciousness, which is simply an awareness of one's self. It is also more general than self-esteem, which is the purely evaluative element of the _____.

Chapter 9. MANAGING THE PRODUCT

a. Self-concept
b. 180SearchAssistant
c. Need for cognition
d. Power III

25. _____, in marketing, consists of a consumer's commitment to repurchase the brand and can be demonstrated by repeated buying of a product or service or other positive behaviors such as word of mouth advocacy. True _____ implies that the consumer is willing, at least on occasion, to put aside their own desires in the interest of the brand. _____ has been proclaimed by some to be the ultimate goal of marketing.

a. Brand awareness
b. Trade Symbols
c. Brand implementation
d. Brand loyalty

26. Competitiveness is a comparative concept of the ability and performance of a firm, sub-sector or country to sell and supply goods and/or services in a given market. Although widely used in economics and business management, the usefulness of the concept, particularly in the context of national competitiveness, is vigorously disputed by economists, such as Paul Krugman .

The term may also be applied to markets, where it is used to refer to the extent to which the market structure may be regarded as perfectly _____.

a. Free trade zone
b. Customs union
c. Geographical pricing
d. Competitive

27. _____ is, in very basic words, a position a firm occupies against its competitors.

According to Michael Porter, the three methods for creating a sustainable _____ are through:

1. Cost leadership - Cost advantage occurs when a firm delivers the same services as its competitors but at a lower cost;

2.

a. 180SearchAssistant
b. Power III
c. 6-3-5 Brainwriting
d. Competitive advantage

28. _____ or brand stretching is a marketing strategy in which a firm marketing a product with a well-developed image uses the same brand name in a different product category. Organizations use this strategy to increase and leverage brand equity (definition: the net worth and long-term sustainability just from the renowned name.) An example of a _____ is Jello-gelatin creating Jello pudding pops.

a. Web 2.0
b. Brand orientation
c. Brand awareness
d. Brand extension

29. The brand name of a product that is distributed nationally under a brand name owned by the producer or distributor, as opposed to local brands (products distributed only in some areas of the country), and private label brands (products that carry the brand of the retailer rather than the producer.)

Chapter 9. MANAGING THE PRODUCT

_____s must compete with local and private brands. _____s are produced by, widely distuted by, and carry the name of the manufacturer.

- Local brands may appeal to those consumers who favor small, local producers over large national or global producers, and may be willing to pay a premium to 'buy local'

- The private label producer can offer lower prices because they avoid the cost of marketing and advertising to create and protect the brand. In North America, large retailers such as Loblaws, Walgreen and Wal-Mart all offer private label products.

a. Market intelligence
b. Specialty catalogs
c. National brand
d. Line extension

30. _____s (house brands in the United States, own brands in the UK, and home brands in Australia) are brands which are specific to a retail store or store chain. The retailer can manufacture goods under its own label, re-brand private label goods, or outsource manufacture of _____ items to multiple third parties - often the same manufacturers that produce brand label goods. _____ goods are generally cheaper than national brand goods because the retailer can optimize the production to suit consumer demand and reduce advertising costs.

a. Brand strength analysis
b. Brand loyalty
c. Brand ambassador
d. Store brand

31. An _____ is a brand that covers diverse kinds of products which are more or less related.

It applies also to any company that is identified only by its brand and history. Such a company now only acts as designer and distributor.

a. Electronic registration mark
b. ACNielsen
c. Umbrella brand
d. ADTECH

32. The verb _____ or grant _____ means to give permission. The noun _____ refers to that permission as well as to the document memorializing that permission. _____ may be granted by a party to another party as an element of an agreement between those parties.

a. Power III
b. 6-3-5 Brainwriting
c. 180SearchAssistant
d. License

33. A _____ is a list of the general tasks and responsibilities of a position. Typically, it also includes to whom the position reports, specifications such as the qualifications needed by the person in the job, salary range for the position, etc. A _____ is usually developed by conducting a job analysis, which includes examining the tasks and sequences of tasks necessary to perform the job.

a. 6-3-5 Brainwriting
b. Job description
c. 180SearchAssistant
d. Power III

34. The _____ is a US law that applies to labels on many consumer products. It requires the label to state:

- The identity of the product;
- The name and place of business of the manufacturer, packer, or distributor; and
- The net quantity of contents.

The contents statement must include both metric and U.S. customary units.

Passed under Lyndon B. Johnson in 1966, the law first took effect on July 1, 1967. The metric labeling requirement was added in 1992 and took effect on February 14, 1994.

a. 6-3-5 Brainwriting
c. Fair Packaging and Labeling Act
b. 180SearchAssistant
d. Power III

35. The _____ is an independent agency of the United States government, created, directed, and empowered by Congressional statute , and with the majority of its commissioners appointed by the current President.

a. 180SearchAssistant
c. 6-3-5 Brainwriting
b. Power III
d. Federal Communications Commission

36. The U.S. _____ is an agency of the United States Department of Health and Human Services and is responsible for regulating and supervising the safety of foods, dietary supplements, drugs, vaccines, biological medical products, blood products, medical devices, radiation-emitting devices, veterinary products, and cosmetics. The FDA also enforces section 361 of the Public Health Service Act and the associated regulations, including sanitation requirements on interstate travel as well as specific rules for control of disease on products ranging from pet turtles to semen donations for assisted reproductive medicine techniques.

The FDA is an agency within the United States Department of Health and Human Services responsible for protecting and promoting the nation's public health.

a. Power III
c. Food and Drug Administration
b. 6-3-5 Brainwriting
d. 180SearchAssistant

37. The _____ is a 1990 United States Federal law. It was signed into law on November 8, 1990 by the president.

The law gives the Food and Drug Administration (FDA) authority to require nutrition labeling of most foods regulated by the Agency; and to require that all nutrient content claims (for example, 'high fiber', 'low fat', etc.).

a. Nutrition Labeling and Education Act
c. Fair Debt Collection Practices Act
b. Trespass to land
d. Copyright infringement

38. Regulation refers to 'controlling human or societal behaviour by rules or restrictions.' Regulation can take many forms: legal restrictions promulgated by a government authority, self-regulation, social regulation (e.g. norms), co-regulation and market regulation. One can consider regulation as actions of conduct imposing sanctions (such as a fine.) This action of administrative law, or implementing _____ law, may be contrasted with statutory or case law.

a. Right to Financial Privacy Act
b. Regulatory
c. Robinson-Patman Act
d. Privacy law

39. _____ refers to 'controlling human or societal behaviour by rules or restrictions.' _____ can take many forms: legal restrictions promulgated by a government authority, self-_____, social _____, co-_____ and market _____. One can consider _____ as actions of conduct imposing sanctions (such as a fine.) This action of administrative law, or implementing regulatory law, may be contrasted with statutory or case law.
   a. Non-conventional trademark
   b. CAN-SPAM
   c. Rule of four
   d. Regulation

Chapter 10. SERVICES AND OTHER INTANGIBLES: Marketing the Product That Isn`t There

1. _____ is defined by the American _____ Association as the activity, set of institutions, and processes for creating, communicating, delivering, and exchanging offerings that have value for customers, clients, partners, and society at large. The term developed from the original meaning which referred literally to going to market, as in shopping, or going to a market to sell goods or services.

_____ practice tends to be seen as a creative industry, which includes advertising, distribution and selling.

a. Customer acquisition management
c. Marketing

b. Marketing myopia
d. Product naming

2. _____ is a broad label that refers to any individuals or households that use goods and services generated within the economy. The concept of a _____ is used in different contexts, so that the usage and significance of the term may vary.

A _____ is a person who uses any product or service.

a. 6-3-5 Brainwriting
c. Power III

b. 180SearchAssistant
d. Consumer

3. A _____ is a brief statement of the purpose of a company, organization. It is ideally used to guide the actions of the organization.

_____s often contain the following:

- Purpose of the organization
- The organization's primary stakeholders: clients, stockholders, etc.
- Responsibilities of the organization towards these stockholders
- Products and services offered

Generally shorter _____s are more effective than longer ones.

In developing a _____:

- Encourage input as feasible from employees, volunteers, and other stakeholders
- Publicize it broadly

The _____ can be used to resolve differences between business stakeholders. Stakeholders include: employees including managers and executives, stockholders, board of directors, customers, suppliers, distributors, creditors, governments (local, state, federal, etc.), unions, competitors, NGO's, and the general public.

a. 6-3-5 Brainwriting
c. Mission statement

b. 180SearchAssistant
d. Power III

Chapter 10. SERVICES AND OTHER INTANGIBLES: Marketing the Product That Isn't There

4. _____ is a strategic planning method used to evaluate the Strengths, Weaknesses, Opportunities, and Threats involved in a project or in a business venture. It involves specifying the objective of the business venture or project and identifying the internal and external factors that are favorable and unfavorable to achieving that objective. The technique is credited to Albert Humphrey, who led a research project at Stanford University in the 1960s and 1970s using data from Fortune 500 companies.

 a. Lead scoring
 b. SWOT analysis
 c. Market environment
 d. Product differentiation

5. _____ is a business term meaning the market segment to which a particular good or service is marketed. It is mainly defined by age, gender, geography, socio-economic grouping, technographic, or any other combination of demographics. It is generally studied and mapped by an organization through lists and reports containing demographic information that may have an effect on the marketing of key products or services.

 a. Market specialization
 b. Category Development Index
 c. Brando
 d. Distribution

6. _____ is a term commonly used to describe commerce transactions between businesses like the one between a manufacturer and a wholesaler or a wholesaler and a retailer i.e both the buyer and the seller are business entity. This is unlike business-to-consumers (B2C) which involve a business entity and end consumer, or business-to-government (B2G) which involve a business entity and government.

The volume of B2B transactions is much higher than the volume of B2C transactions. The primary reason for this is that in a typical supply chain there will be many B2B transactions involving subcomponent or raw materials, and only one B2C transaction, specifically sale of the finished product to the end customer.

 a. Disruptive technology
 b. Social marketing
 c. Business-to-business
 d. Customer relationship management

7. The _____ or gross domestic income (GDI) is one of the measures of national income and output for a given country's economy. It is the total value of all final goods and services produced in a particular economy; the dollar value of all goods and services produced within a country's borders in a given year. _____ can be defined in three ways, all of which are conceptually identical.

 a. Leading indicator
 b. Macroeconomics
 c. Microeconomics
 d. Gross domestic product

8. _____ is used in marketing to describe the inability to assess the value gained from engaging in an activity using any tangible evidence. It is often used to describe services where there isn't a tangible product that the customer can purchase, that can be seen, tasted or touched.

Other key characteristics of services include perishability, inseparability and variability.

 a. Individual branding
 b. Automated surveys
 c. Inseparability
 d. Intangibility

9. _____ is an advertisement in which a particular product specifically mentions a competitor by name for the express purpose of showing why the competitor is inferior to the product naming it.

Chapter 10. SERVICES AND OTHER INTANGIBLES: Marketing the Product That Isn`t There

This should not be confused with parody advertisements, where a fictional product is being advertised for the purpose of poking fun at the particular advertisement, nor should it be confused with the use of a coined brand name for the purpose of comparing the product without actually naming an actual competitor. ('Wikipedia tastes better and is less filling than the Encyclopedia Galactica.')

In the 1980s, during what has been referred to as the cola wars, soft-drink manufacturer Pepsi ran a series of advertisements where people, caught on hidden camera, in a blind taste test, chose Pepsi over rival Coca-Cola.

a. Comparative advertising
b. GL-70
c. Heavy-up
d. Cost per conversion

10. _____ is a marketing term, and involves evaluating the situation and trends in a particular company's market. _____ is often called the 'three c's', which refers to the three major elements that must be studied:

- Customers
- Costs
- Competition

The number of 'c's' is sometimes extended to four, five, or even six, with 'Collaboration', 'Company', and 'Competitive advantage'.

- Marketing mix
- SWOT analysis

a. 6-3-5 Brainwriting
b. Situation analysis
c. Power III
d. 180SearchAssistant

11. _____ is a process used to manage information technology (IT.) Its primary goal is to ensure that IT capacity meets current and future business requirements in a cost-effective manner. One common interpretation of _____ is described in the ITIL framework.

a. Pop-up ads
b. Project Portfolio Management
c. Power III
d. Capacity management

12. The _____ is generally accepted as the use and specification of the four p's describing the strategic position of a product in the marketplace. One version of the origins of the _____ starts in 1948 when James Culliton said that a marketing decision should be a result of something similar to a recipe. This version continued in 1953 when Neil Borden, in his American Marketing Association presidential address, took the recipe idea one step further and coined the term 'Marketing-Mix'.

a. 180SearchAssistant
b. Marketing mix
c. Power III
d. 6-3-5 Brainwriting

13. _____ is used in marketing to describe the way in which service capacity cannot be stored for sale in the future. It is a key concept of services marketing.

Chapter 10. SERVICES AND OTHER INTANGIBLES: Marketing the Product That Isn't There

Other key characteristics of services include intangibility, inseparability and variability.

a. Perishability
b. National brand
c. Specialty catalogs
d. Demonstrator model

14. In economics, _____ is the removal of intermediaries in a supply chain: 'cutting out the middleman'. Instead of going through traditional distribution channels, which had some type of intermediate (such as a distributor, wholesaler, broker, or agent), companies may now deal with every customer directly, for example via the Internet. One important factor is a drop in the cost of servicing customers directly.

a. Consumer-to-consumer
b. Spamvertising
c. Social shopping
d. Disintermediation

15. _____ is used in marketing to describe a key quality of services as distinct from goods. _____ is the characteristic that a service has which renders it impossible to divorce the supply or production of the service from its consumption.

Other key characteristics of services include perishability, intangibility and variability.

a. Online focus group
b. Individual branding
c. Inseparability
d. Engagement

16. _____ is a business management strategy aimed at embedding awareness of quality in all organizational processes. _____ has been widely used in manufacturing, education, call centers, government, and service industries, as well as NASA space and science programs.

When used together as a phrase, the three words in this expression have the following meanings:

- Total: Involving the entire organization, supply chain, and/or product life cycle
- Quality: With its usual definitions, with all its complexities
- Management: The system of managing with steps like Plan, Organize, Control, Lead, Staff, provisioning and organizing.

As defined by the International Organization for Standardization (ISO):

> '_____ is a management approach for an organization, centered on quality, based on the participation of all its members and aiming at long-term success through customer satisfaction, and benefits to all members of the organization and to society.' ISO 8402:1994

One major aim is to reduce variation from every process so that greater consistency of effort is obtained. (Royse, D., Thyer, B., Padgett D., ' Logan T., 2006)

Chapter 10. SERVICES AND OTHER INTANGIBLES: Marketing the Product That Isn`t There

In Japan, _____ comprises four process steps, namely:

1. Kaizen - Focuses on 'Continuous Process Improvement', to make processes visible, repeatable and measurable.
2. Atarimae Hinshitsu - The idea that 'things will work as they are supposed to' .
3. Kansei - Examining the way the user applies the product leads to improvement in the product itself.
4. Miryokuteki Hinshitsu - The idea that 'things should have an aesthetic quality' (for example, a pen will write in a way that is pleasing to the writer.)

_____ requires that the company maintain this quality standard in all aspects of its business. This requires ensuring that things are done right the first time and that defects and waste are eliminated from operations.

a. 6-3-5 Brainwriting
c. Power III
b. 180SearchAssistant
d. Total quality management

17. A _____ is the central part of a telecom network that provides various services to customers who are connected by the access network.

_____s typically providing the following functionality:

1. Aggregation: The highest level of aggregation in a service provider network. The next level in the hierarchy under the core nodes is the distribution networks and then the edge networks. Customer Premise Equipment (CPE) do not normally connect to the _____s of a large service provider.
2. Authentication: The function to decide whether the user requesting a service from the telecom network is authorized to do so within this network or not.
3. Call Control/Switching: Call control or switching functionality decides the future course of call based on the call signalling processing. E.g. switching functionality may decide based on the 'called number' that the call be routed towards a subscriber within this operator's network or with Number Portability more prevalent to another operator's network.
4. Charging: This functionality handles the collation and processing of charging data generated by various network nodes. Two common types of charging mechanisms found in present day networks are prepaid charging and postpaid charging. See Automatic Message Accounting
5. Service Invocation: _____ performs the task of service invocation for its subscribers. Service invocation may happen based on some explicit action (e.g. call transfer) by user or implicitly (call waiting.) Its important to note however that service 'execution' may or may not be a _____ functionality as third party network/nodes may take part in actual service execution.
6. Gateways: Gateways shall be present in the _____ to access other networks. Gateway functionality is dependent on the type of network it interfaces with.

Physically, one or more of these logical functionalities may simultaneously exist in a given _____ node.

Chapter 10. SERVICES AND OTHER INTANGIBLES: Marketing the Product That Isn't There

Besides above mentioned functionalities, following also form part of a _____:

- O'M: Operations ' Maintenance centre or Operations Support Systems to configure and provision the _____ nodes. Number of subscribers, peak hour call rate, nature of services, geographical preferences are some of the factors which impact the configuration. Network statistics collection, alarm monitoring and logging of various network nodes actions also happens in the O'M centre. These stats, alarms and traces form important tools for a network operator to monitor the network health and performance and improvise on the same.
- Subscriber Database: _____ also hosts the subscribers database (e.g. HLR in GSM systems.) Subscriber database is accessed by _____ nodes for functions like authentication, service invocation etc.

a. 180SearchAssistant
b. Power III
c. 6-3-5 Brainwriting
d. Core network

18. _____ is a contract between two parties, one being the employer and the other being the employee. An employee may be defined as: 'A person in the service of another under any contract of hire, express or implied, oral or written, where the employer has the power or right to control and direct the employee in the material details of how the work is to be performed.' Black's Law Dictionary page 471 (5th ed. 1979.)

a. ADTECH
b. ACNielsen
c. AMAX
d. Employment

19. In economic models, the _____ time frame assumes no fixed factors of production. Firms can enter or leave the marketplace, and the cost (and availability) of land, labor, raw materials, and capital goods can be assumed to vary. In contrast, in the short-run time frame, certain factors are assumed to be fixed, because there is not sufficient time for them to change.

a. Long-run
b. 6-3-5 Brainwriting
c. Power III
d. 180SearchAssistant

20. A _____ is a process that can allow an organization to concentrate its limited resources on the greatest opportunities to increase sales and achieve a sustainable competitive advantage. A _____ should be centered around the key concept that customer satisfaction is the main goal.

A _____ is most effective when it is an integral component of corporate strategy, defining how the organization will successfully engage customers, prospects, and competitors in the market arena.

a. Societal marketing
b. Marketing strategy
c. Cyberdoc
d. Psychographic

21. _____ is the practice of individuals including commercial businesses, governments and institutions, facilitating the sale of their products or services to other companies or organizations that in turn resell them, use them as components in products or services they offer _____ is also called business-to-_____ for short. (Note that while marketing to government entities shares some of the same dynamics of organizational marketing, B2G Marketing is meaningfully different.)

98   Chapter 10. SERVICES AND OTHER INTANGIBLES: Marketing the Product That Isn`t There

a. Disruptive technology
b. Mass marketing
c. Law of disruption
d. Business marketing

22. _____ is one of the four Ps of the marketing mix. The other three aspects are product, promotion, and place. It is also a key variable in microeconomic price allocation theory.
   a. Price
   b. Competitor indexing
   c. Pricing
   d. Relationship based pricing

23. Mystery shopping or Mystery Consumer is a tool used by market research companies to measure quality of retail service or gather specific information about products and services. _____ posing as normal customers perform specific tasks-- such as purchasing a product, asking questions, registering complaints or behaving in a certain way - and then provide detailed reports or feedback about their experiences.

Mystery shopping began in the 1940s as a way to measure employee integrity.

   a. Mystery shopping
   b. Questionnaire
   c. Market research
   d. Mystery shoppers

24. _____ is marketing based on relationship and value. It may be used to market a service or a product.

Marketing a service-base business is different from marketing a goods-base business.

   a. 180SearchAssistant
   b. Power III
   c. 6-3-5 Brainwriting
   d. Services marketing

25. _____ or _____ data refers to selected population characteristics as used in government, marketing or opinion research, or the _____ profiles used in such research. Note the distinction from the term 'demography' Commonly-used _____ include race, age, income, disabilities, mobility (in terms of travel time to work or number of vehicles available), educational attainment, home ownership, employment status, and even location.
   a. Demographic
   b. African Americans
   c. AStore
   d. Albert Einstein

26. _____ in its literal sense is the process of transformation of local or regional phenomena into global ones. It can be described as a process by which the people of the world are unified into a single society and function together.

This process is a combination of economic, technological, sociocultural and political forces.

   a. 180SearchAssistant
   b. Power III
   c. Globalization
   d. 6-3-5 Brainwriting

27. A _____ is a type of website, usually maintained by an individual with regular entries of commentary, descriptions of events, or other material such as graphics or video. Entries are commonly displayed in reverse-chronological order. '_____' can also be used as a verb, meaning to maintain or add content to a _____.
   a. Power III
   b. 180SearchAssistant
   c. 6-3-5 Brainwriting
   d. Blog

Chapter 10. SERVICES AND OTHER INTANGIBLES: Marketing the Product That Isn't There

28. In operant conditioning, _____ occurs when an event following a response causes an increase in the probability of that response occurring in the future. Response strength can be assessed by measures such as the frequency with which the response is made (for example, a pigeon may peck a key more times in the session), or the speed with which it is made (for example, a rat may run a maze faster.) The environment change contingent upon the response is called a reinforcer.
   a. Relationship Management Application
   b. Generic brands
   c. Completely randomized designs
   d. Reinforcement

29. _____ is one of the four elements of marketing mix. An organization or set of organizations (go-betweens) involved in the process of making a product or service available for use or consumption by a consumer or business user.

The other three parts of the marketing mix are product, pricing, and promotion.

   a. Better Living Through Chemistry
   b. Japan Advertising Photographers' Association
   c. Distribution
   d. Comparison-Shopping agent

30. A personal and cultural _____ is a relative ethic _____, an assumption upon which implementation can be extrapolated. A _____ system is a set of consistent _____s and measures that is soo not true. A principle _____ is a foundation upon which other _____s and measures of integrity are based.
   a. Perceptual maps
   b. Package-on-Package
   c. Value
   d. Supreme Court of the United States

31. _____ is a form of applied ethics that examines ethical principles and moral or ethical problems that arise in a business environment. It applies to all aspects of business conduct and is relevant to the conduct of individuals and business organizations as a whole. Applied ethics is a field of ethics that deals with ethical questions in many fields such as medical, technical, legal and _____.
   a. 6-3-5 Brainwriting
   b. Power III
   c. 180SearchAssistant
   d. Business ethics

32. _____ is a branch of philosophy which seeks to address questions about morality, such as how a moral outcome can be achieved in a specific situation (applied _____), how moral values should be determined (normative _____), what moral values people actually abide by (descriptive _____), what the fundamental semantic, ontological, and epistemic nature of _____ or morality is (meta-_____), and how moral capacity or moral agency develops and what its nature is (moral psychology.)

Socrates was one of the first Greek philosophers to encourage both scholars and the common citizen to turn their attention from the outside world to the condition of man. In this view, Knowledge having a bearing on human life was placed highest, all other knowledge being secondary.

   a. AMAX
   b. ADTECH
   c. ACNielsen
   d. Ethics

33. In the Mediterranean Basin and the Near East, a _____ is a small, separated garden pavilion open on some or all sides. _____s were common in Persia, India, Pakistan, and in the Ottoman Empire from the 13th century onward. Today, there are many _____s in and around the TopkapÄ± Palace in Istanbul, and they are still a relatively common sight in Greece.

Chapter 10. SERVICES AND OTHER INTANGIBLES: Marketing the Product That Isn`t There

a. 180SearchAssistant
b. 6-3-5 Brainwriting
c. Power III
d. Kiosk

34. Competitiveness is a comparative concept of the ability and performance of a firm, sub-sector or country to sell and supply goods and/or services in a given market. Although widely used in economics and business management, the usefulness of the concept, particularly in the context of national competitiveness, is vigorously disputed by economists, such as Paul Krugman .

The term may also be applied to markets, where it is used to refer to the extent to which the market structure may be regarded as perfectly _____.

a. Competitive
b. Geographical pricing
c. Customs union
d. Free trade zone

35. _____ is, in very basic words, a position a firm occupies against its competitors.

According to Michael Porter, the three methods for creating a sustainable _____ are through:

1. Cost leadership - Cost advantage occurs when a firm delivers the same services as its competitors but at a lower cost;

2.

a. 180SearchAssistant
b. 6-3-5 Brainwriting
c. Competitive advantage
d. Power III

36. A _____ or subscription radio is a digital radio signal that is broadcast by a communications satellite, which covers a much wider geographical range than terrestrial radio signals.

For now, _____ offers a meaningful alternative to ground-based radio services in some countries, notably the United States. Mobile services, such as Sirius, XM, and Worldspace, allow listeners to roam across an entire continent, listening to the same audio programming anywhere they go.

a. 6-3-5 Brainwriting
b. 180SearchAssistant
c. Satellite radio
d. Power III

Chapter 11. PRICING THE PRODUCT

1. _____ is one of the four Ps of the marketing mix. The other three aspects are product, promotion, and place. It is also a key variable in microeconomic price allocation theory.
   a. Competitor indexing
   b. Relationship based pricing
   c. Price
   d. Pricing

2. In economics, business, retail, and accounting, a _____ is the value of money that has been used up to produce something, and hence is not available for use anymore. In economics, a _____ is an alternative that is given up as a result of a decision. In business, the _____ may be one of acquisition, in which case the amount of money expended to acquire it is counted as _____.
   a. Fixed costs
   b. Variable cost
   c. Transaction cost
   d. Cost

3. _____ or economic opportunity loss is the value of the next best alternative forgone as the result of making a decision. _____ analysis is an important part of a company's decision-making processes but is not treated as an actual cost in any financial statement. The next best thing that a person can engage in is referred to as the _____ of doing the best thing and ignoring the next best thing to be done.
   a. AMAX
   b. Opportunity cost
   c. ACNielsen
   d. ADTECH

4. _____ in economics and business is the result of an exchange and from that trade we assign a numerical monetary value to a good, service or asset. If I trade 4 apples for an orange, the _____ of an orange is 4 - apples. Inversely, the _____ of an apple is 1/4 oranges.
   a. Pricing
   b. Contribution margin-based pricing
   c. Discounts and allowances
   d. Price

5. In operant conditioning, _____ occurs when an event following a response causes an increase in the probability of that response occurring in the future. Response strength can be assessed by measures such as the frequency with which the response is made (for example, a pigeon may peck a key more times in the session), or the speed with which it is made (for example, a rat may run a maze faster.) The environment change contingent upon the response is called a reinforcer.
   a. Reinforcement
   b. Completely randomized designs
   c. Generic brands
   d. Relationship Management Application

6. _____, in strategic management and marketing, is the percentage or proportion of the total available market or market segment that is being serviced by a company. It can be expressed as a company's sales revenue (from that market) divided by the total sales revenue available in that market. It can also be expressed as a company's unit sales volume (in a market) divided by the total volume of units sold in that market.
   a. Cyberdoc
   b. Demand generation
   c. Customer relationship management
   d. Market share

7. _____ is a term used in business to indicate a state of intense competitive rivalry accompanied by a multi-lateral series of price reduction. One competitor will lower its price, then others will lower their prices to match. If one of them reduces their price again, a new round of reductions starts.
   a. Price war
   b. Resale price maintenance
   c. Competitor indexing
   d. Pricing objectives

Chapter 11. PRICING THE PRODUCT

8. _____ or goals give direction to the whole pricing process. Determining what your objectives are is the first step in pricing. When deciding on _____ you must consider: 1) the overall financial, marketing, and strategic objectives of the company; 2) the objectives of your product or brand; 3) consumer price elasticity and price points; and 4) the resources you have available.
   a. Transfer pricing
   b. Discounts and allowances
   c. Competitor indexing
   d. Pricing objectives

9. _____ in organizations and public policy is both the organizational process of creating and maintaining a plan; and the psychological process of thinking about the activities required to create a desired goal on some scale. As such, it is a fundamental property of intelligent behavior. This thought process is essential to the creation and refinement of a plan, or integration of it with other plans, that is, it combines forecasting of developments with the preparation of scenarios of how to react to them.
   a. 6-3-5 Brainwriting
   b. 180SearchAssistant
   c. Power III
   d. Planning

10. Competitiveness is a comparative concept of the ability and performance of a firm, sub-sector or country to sell and supply goods and/or services in a given market. Although widely used in economics and business management, the usefulness of the concept, particularly in the context of national competitiveness, is vigorously disputed by economists, such as Paul Krugman .

   The term may also be applied to markets, where it is used to refer to the extent to which the market structure may be regarded as perfectly _____.

   a. Customs union
   b. Competitive
   c. Free trade zone
   d. Geographical pricing

11. A craze is a product, idea, cultural movement, or model that gains popularity among a small section of the populace then quickly migrates to the mainstream. Crazes are characterized by their lightning fast adoption and swift departure from public awareness. Crazes and _____s are also characterized by their unusually high interest and sales figures relative to the time they are active in the marketplace, as compared with other similar products, ideas, cultural movements or models.
   a. 180SearchAssistant
   b. 6-3-5 Brainwriting
   c. Power III
   d. Fad

12. _____, a business term, is a measure of how products and services supplied by a company meet or surpass customer expectation. It is seen as a key performance indicator within business and is part of the four perspectives of a Balanced Scorecard.

   In a competitive marketplace where businesses compete for customers, _____ is seen as a key differentiator and increasingly has become a key element of business strategy.

   a. Customer satisfaction
   b. Supplier diversity
   c. Customer base
   d. Psychological pricing

Chapter 11. PRICING THE PRODUCT

13. In economics, _____ is the desire to own something and the ability to pay for it. The term _____ signifies the ability or the willingness to buy a particular commodity at a given point of time .

a. Market dominance
c. Demand

b. Discretionary spending
d. Market system

14. In economics, the _____ can be defined as the graph depicting the relationship between the price of a certain commodity, and the amount of it that consumers are willing and able to purchase at that given price. It is a graphic representation of a demand schedule The _____ for all consumers together follows from the _____ of every individual consumer: the individual demands at each price are added together.

_____s are used to estimate behaviors in competitive markets, and are often combined with supply curves to estimate the equilibrium price (the price at which sellers together are willing to sell the same amount as buyers together are willing to buy, also known as market clearing price) and the equilibrium quantity (the amount of that good or service that will be produced and bought without surplus/excess supply or shortage/excess demand) of that market.

a. Power III
c. 6-3-5 Brainwriting

b. Demand curve
d. 180SearchAssistant

15. _____ is the process by which a new idea or new product is accepted by the market. The rate of _____ is the speed that the new idea spreads from one consumer to the next. Adoption is similar to _____ except that it deals with the psychological processes an individual goes through, rather than an aggregate market process.

a. Perceptual maps
c. Diffusion

b. Market development
d. Kano model

16. In economics, the _____ is an economic law that states that consumers buy more of a good when its price decreases and less when its price increases.

- Supply and Demand

as there is inverse relationship exists between price and demand so when price increases demand decreases but quantity demand is another factor due to other factors like taste fashion incme expectations related goods etc

a. Microeconomics
c. Market structure

b. Macroeconomics
d. Law of demand

17. In economics, _____ is the ratio of the percent change in one variable to the percent change in another variable. It is a tool for measuring the responsiveness of a function to changes in parameters in a relative way. Commonly analyzed are _____ of substitution, price and wealth.

a. Opinion leadership
c. ACNielsen

b. Elasticity
d. Intellectual property

Chapter 11. PRICING THE PRODUCT

18. Price _____ is defined as the measure of responsiveness in the quantity demanded for a commodity as a result of change in price of the same commodity. It is a measure of how consumers react to a change in price. In other words, it is percentage change in quantity demanded as per the percentage change in price of the same commodity.
    a. Elasticity of demand
    b. ADTECH
    c. ACNielsen
    d. AMAX

19. In economics, _____ describes demand that is not very sensitive to a change in price.
    a. AMAX
    b. ACNielsen
    c. ADTECH
    d. Inelastic

20. _____ is defined as the measure of responsiveness in the quantity demanded for a commodity as a result of change in price of the same commodity. It is a measure of how consumers react to a change in price. In other words, it is percentage change in quantity demanded as per the percentage change in price of the same commodity.
    a. Power III
    b. 180SearchAssistant
    c. 6-3-5 Brainwriting
    d. Price elasticity of demand

21. _____ is an advertisement in which a particular product specifically mentions a competitor by name for the express purpose of showing why the competitor is inferior to the product naming it.

    This should not be confused with parody advertisements, where a fictional product is being advertised for the purpose of poking fun at the particular advertisement, nor should it be confused with the use of a coined brand name for the purpose of comparing the product without actually naming an actual competitor. ('Wikipedia tastes better and is less filling than the Encyclopedia Galactica.')

    In the 1980s, during what has been referred to as the cola wars, soft-drink manufacturer Pepsi ran a series of advertisements where people, caught on hidden camera, in a blind taste test, chose Pepsi over rival Coca-Cola.

    a. Comparative advertising
    b. Heavy-up
    c. Cost per conversion
    d. GL-70

22. _____s are used in open sentences. For instance, in the formula x + 1 = 5, x is a _____ which represents an 'unknown' number. _____s are often represented by letters of the Roman alphabet, or those of other alphabets, such as Greek, and use other special symbols.
    a. Quantitative
    b. Book of business
    c. Variable
    d. Personalization

23. _____s are expenses that change in proportion to the activity of a business. In other words, _____ is the sum of marginal costs. It can also be considered normal costs.
    a. Fixed costs
    b. Transaction cost
    c. Marginal cost
    d. Variable cost

24. In mathematics, an _____, or central tendency of a data set refers to a measure of the 'middle' or 'expected' value of the data set. There are many different descriptive statistics that can be chosen as a measurement of the central tendency of the data items.

    An _____ is a single value that is meant to typify a list of values.

Chapter 11. PRICING THE PRODUCT

a. Average
b. AMAX
c. ADTECH
d. ACNielsen

25. _____ is an economics term used to describe the total fixed costs (TFC) divided by the quantity (Q) of units produced.

_____ is a per-unit measure of fixed costs. As the total number of goods produced increases, the _____ decreases because the same amount of fixed costs are being spread over a larger number of units.

a. ACNielsen
b. Average fixed cost
c. ADTECH
d. Average variable cost

26. In economics, _____ are business expenses that are not dependent on the activities of the business They tend to be time-related, such as salaries or rents being paid per month. This is in contrast to variable costs, which are volume-related (and are paid per quantity.)

In management accounting, _____ are defined as expenses that do not change in proportion to the activity of a business, within the relevant period or scale of production.

a. Fixed costs
b. Variable cost
c. Transaction cost
d. Marginal cost

27. In economics, and cost accounting, _____ describes the total economic cost of production and is made up of variable costs, which vary according to the quantity of a good produced and include inputs such as labor and raw materials, plus fixed costs, which are independent of the quantity of a good produced and include inputs (capital) that cannot be varied in the short term, such as buildings and machinery. _____ in economics includes the total opportunity cost of each factor of production in addition to fixed and variable costs.

The rate at which _____ changes as the amount produced changes is called marginal cost.

a. Household production function
b. Product proliferation
c. Hoarding
d. Total cost

28. The break-even point for a product is the point where total revenue received equals the total costs associated with the sale of the product (TR=TC.) A break-even point is typically calculated in order for businesses to determine if it would be profitable to sell a proposed product, as opposed to attempting to modify an existing product instead so it can be made lucrative. _____ can also be used to analyse the potential profitability of an expenditure in a sales-based business.

In _____, margin of safety is how much output or sales level can fall before a business reaches its break-even point (BEP).

a. Pay Per Sale
b. Contribution margin-based pricing
c. Price skimming
d. Break even analysis

29. In economics ' business, specifically cost accounting, the _____ is the point at which cost or expenses and revenue are equal: there is no net loss or gain, and one has 'broken even'. A profit or a loss has not been made, although opportunity costs have been paid, and capital has received the risk-adjusted, expected return.

For example, if the business sells less than 200 tables each month, it will make a loss, if it sells more, it will be a profit.

a. Total revenue
b. Power III
c. 180SearchAssistant
d. Break-even point

30. _____ is the use of marginal concepts within economics. (Marginal concepts are associated with a specific change in the quantity used of a good or of a service, as opposed to some notion of the over-all significance of that class of good or service, or of some total quantity thereof.) The central concept of _____ proper is that of marginal utility, but marginalists following the lead of Alfred Marshall were further heavily dependent upon the concept of marginal physical productivity in their explanation of cost; and the neoclassical tradition that emerged from British _____ generally abandoned the concept of utility and gave marginal rates of substitution a more fundamental rôle in analysis.

a. Marginalism
b. 180SearchAssistant
c. 6-3-5 Brainwriting
d. Power III

31. _____ is, in very basic words, a position a firm occupies against its competitors.

According to Michael Porter, the three methods for creating a sustainable _____ are through:

1. Cost leadership - Cost advantage occurs when a firm delivers the same services as its competitors but at a lower cost;

2.

a. 6-3-5 Brainwriting
b. 180SearchAssistant
c. Power III
d. Competitive advantage

32. In economics and finance, _____ is the change in total cost that arises when the quantity produced changes by one unit. It is the cost of producing one more unit of a good. Mathematically, the _____ function is expressed as the first derivative of the total cost (TC) function with respect to quantity (Q.)

a. Transaction cost
b. Variable cost
c. Marginal cost
d. Fixed costs

33. In microeconomics, _____ is the extra revenue that an additional unit of product will bring. It is the additional income from selling one more unit of a good; sometimes equal to price. It can also be described as the change in total revenue/change in number of units sold.

a. Marginal revenue
b. Product proliferation
c. Total cost
d. Hoarding

Chapter 11. PRICING THE PRODUCT

34. _____ is a rivalry between individuals, groups, nations for territory, a niche, or allocation of resources. It arises whenever two or more parties strive for a goal which cannot be shared. _____ occurs naturally between living organisms which co-exist in the same environment.
   a. Price competition
   b. Competition
   c. Non-price competition
   d. Price fixing

35. In economics, _____ is a rise in the general level of prices of goods and services in an economy over a period of time. The term '_____' once referred to increases in the money supply (monetary _____); however, economic debates about the relationship between money supply and price levels have led to its primary use today in describing price _____. Inflation can also be described as a decline in the real value of money--a loss of purchasing power in the medium of exchange which is also the monetary unit of account.
   a. ADTECH
   b. Inflation
   c. ACNielsen
   d. Industrial organization

36. _____ is a common market form. Many markets can be considered monopolistically competitive, often including the markets for restaurants, cereal, clothing, shoes and service industries in large cities. Short-run equilibrium of the firm under _____

Monopolistically competitive markets have the following characteristics:

- There are many producers and many consumers in a given market, and no business has total control over the market price.
- Consumers perceive that there are non-price differences among the competitors' products.
- There are few barriers to entry and exit.
- Producers have a degree of control over price.

Long-run equilibrium of the firm under _____

The characteristics of a monopolistically competitive market are almost the same as in perfect competition, with the exception of heterogeneous products, and that _____ involves a great deal of non-price competition (based on subtle product differentiation.) A firm making profits in the short run will break even in the long run because demand will decrease and average total cost will increase.

   a. Macroeconomics
   b. Monopolistic competition
   c. Recession
   d. Gross domestic product

37. An _____ is a market form in which a market or industry is dominated by a small number of sellers (oligopolists.) Because there are few participants in this type of market, each oligopolist is aware of the actions of the others. The decisions of one firm influence, and are influenced by, the decisions of other firms.
   a. ADTECH
   b. AMAX
   c. Oligopoly
   d. ACNielsen

38. In economics, the term _____ describes the reduction of a country's gross domestic product (GDP) for at least two quarters. The usual dictionary definition is 'a period of reduced economic activity', a business cycle contraction.

Chapter 11. PRICING THE PRODUCT

The United States-based National Bureau of Economic Research (NBER) defines economic _____ as: 'a significant decline in [the] economic activity spread across the country, lasting more than a few months, normally visible in real GDP growth, real personal income, employment (non-farm payrolls), industrial production, and wholesale-retail sales.' The NBER's Business Cycle Dating Committee is generally seen as the authority for dating US _____s.

 a. Law of demand   b. Leading indicator
 c. Macroeconomics   d. Recession

39. _____ is a broad label that refers to any individuals or households that use goods and services generated within the economy. The concept of a _____ is used in different contexts, so that the usage and significance of the term may vary.

A _____ is a person who uses any product or service.

 a. Power III   b. Consumer
 c. 6-3-5 Brainwriting   d. 180SearchAssistant

40. _____ is the examining of goods or services from retailers with the intent to purchase at that time. _____ is an activity of selection and/or purchase. In some contexts it is considered a leisure activity as well as an economic one.

 a. Shopping   b. Khodebshchik
 c. Discount store   d. Hawkers

41. A _____ is a plan of action designed to achieve a particular goal.

_____ is different from tactics. In military terms, tactics is concerned with the conduct of an engagement while _____ is concerned with how different engagements are linked.

 a. Power III   b. 180SearchAssistant
 c. 6-3-5 Brainwriting   d. Strategy

42. _____ is defined by the American _____ Association as the activity, set of institutions, and processes for creating, communicating, delivering, and exchanging offerings that have value for customers, clients, partners, and society at large. The term developed from the original meaning which referred literally to going to market, as in shopping, or going to a market to sell goods or services.

_____ practice tends to be seen as a creative industry, which includes advertising, distribution and selling.

 a. Customer acquisition management   b. Marketing myopia
 c. Product naming   d. Marketing

43. _____ is a pricing method used by companies. It is used primarily because it is easy to calculate and requires little information. There are several varieties, but the common thread in all of them is that one first calculates the cost of the product, then includes an additional amount to represent profit.

Chapter 11. PRICING THE PRODUCT

a. Relationship based pricing
c. Break even analysis
b. Loss leader
d. Cost-plus pricing

44. _____ is a process used to manage information technology (IT.) Its primary goal is to ensure that IT capacity meets current and future business requirements in a cost-effective manner. One common interpretation of _____ is described in the ITIL framework.
a. Project Portfolio Management
c. Power III
b. Pop-up ads
d. Capacity management

45. _____ is a pricing method used by firms. It is defined as 'a cost management tool for reducing the overall cost of a product over its entire life-cycle with the help of production, engineering, research and design'. _____ finds the maximum amount of cost that can be incurred on a product and with it the firm can still earn the required profit margin from that product at a particular selling price.
a. Target costing
c. Premium pricing
b. Competitor indexing
d. Fee

46. _____ is the process of understanding, anticipating and influencing consumer behavior in order to maximize revenue or profits from a fixed, perishable resource This process was first discovered by Dr. Matt H. Keller. The challenge is to sell the right resources to the right customer at the right time for the right price. This process can result in price discrimination, where a firm charges customers consuming otherwise identical goods or services a different price for doing so.
a. Service provider
c. Cross-selling
b. Multi-level marketing
d. Yield management

47. In economic models, the _____ time frame assumes no fixed factors of production. Firms can enter or leave the marketplace, and the cost (and availability) of land, labor, raw materials, and capital goods can be assumed to vary. In contrast, in the short-run time frame, certain factors are assumed to be fixed, because there is not sufficient time for them to change.
a. 180SearchAssistant
c. Power III
b. 6-3-5 Brainwriting
d. Long-run

48. A personal and cultural _____ is a relative ethic _____, an assumption upon which implementation can be extrapolated. A _____ system is a set of consistent _____s and measures that is soo not true. A principle _____ is a foundation upon which other _____s and measures of integrity are based.
a. Supreme Court of the United States
c. Perceptual maps
b. Package-on-Package
d. Value

49. _____ is the ongoing process of identifying and articulating market requirements that define a product's feature set.
a. Brand parity
c. Product planning
b. Targeted advertising
d. Market intelligence

50. _____ is the pricing technique of setting a relatively low initial entry price, often lower than the eventual market price, to attract new customers. The strategy works on the expectation that customers will switch to the new brand because of the lower price. _____ is most commonly associated with a marketing objective of increasing market share or sales volume, rather than to make profit in the short term.

a. Competitor indexing
b. Penetration pricing
c. Price war
d. Fee

51. _____ is one of the four elements of marketing mix. An organization or set of organizations (go-betweens) involved in the process of making a product or service available for use or consumption by a consumer or business user.

The other three parts of the marketing mix are product, pricing, and promotion.

a. Comparison-Shopping agent
b. Japan Advertising Photographers' Association
c. Better Living Through Chemistry
d. Distribution

52. The (manufacturer's) suggested retail price (MSRP or SRP), _____ or recommended retail price (RRP) of a product is the price the manufacturer recommends that the retailer sell it for. The intention was to help to standardize prices among locations. While some stores always sell at, or below, the suggested retail price, others do so only when items are on sale or closeout.

a. Predatory pricing
b. Power III
c. 180SearchAssistant
d. List price

53. _____ is a term commonly used to describe commerce transactions between businesses like the one between a manufacturer and a wholesaler or a wholesaler and a retailer i.e both the buyer and the seller are business entity. This is unlike business-to-consumers (B2C) which involve a business entity and end consumer, or business-to-government (B2G) which involve a business entity and government.

The volume of B2B transactions is much higher than the volume of B2C transactions. The primary reason for this is that in a typical supply chain there will be many B2B transactions involving subcomponent or raw materials, and only one B2C transaction, specifically sale of the finished product to the end customer.

a. Customer relationship management
b. Social marketing
c. Disruptive technology
d. Business-to-business

54. A _____ is an amount paid by way of reduction, return, or refund on what has already been paid or contributed. It is a type of sales promotion marketers use primarily as incentives or supplements to product sales. The mail-in _____ is the most common.

a. Personalization
b. Strand
c. Lifestyle city
d. Rebate

55. _____ (or citizen-to-citizen) electronic commerce involves the electronically-facilitated transactions between consumers through some third party. A common example is the online auction, in which a consumer posts an item for sale and other consumers bid to purchase it; the third party generally charges a flat fee or commission. The sites are only intermediaries, just there to match consumers.

a. Business-to-government
b. Locator software
c. Web banner
d. Consumer-to-consumer

Chapter 11. PRICING THE PRODUCT

56. Electronic commerce, commonly known as _____ or eCommerce, consists of the buying and selling of products or services over electronic systems such as the Internet and other computer networks. The amount of trade conducted electronically has grown extraordinarily with wide-spread Internet usage. A wide variety of commerce is conducted in this way, spurring and drawing on innovations in electronic funds transfer, supply chain management, Internet marketing, online transaction processing, electronic data interchange (EDI), inventory management systems, and automated data collection systems.
   a. ACNielsen
   b. E-commerce
   c. AMAX
   d. ADTECH

57. _____, commonly known as e-commerce or eCommerce, consists of the buying and selling of products or services over electronic systems such as the Internet and other computer networks. The amount of trade conducted electronically has grown extraordinarily with wide-spread Internet usage. A wide variety of commerce is conducted in this way, spurring and drawing on innovations in electronic funds transfer, supply chain management, Internet marketing, online transaction processing, electronic data interchange (EDI), inventory management systems, and automated data collection systems.
   a. Electronic commerce
   b. AMAX
   c. ACNielsen
   d. ADTECH

58. Why do retail stores need _____? With respect to the key objectives of growth and profit for any retail entity, _____ should significantly improve sales margins and increase sales by enabling the vendor to price variably and hence suitably and to control its product range based on profit margins. The retail stores will be able to compete more effectively with rivals in the form of mixed multiples, mail order and online retailers, who are often able to undercut but who do not generally have the same understanding of the retail market. In particular _____ is recognised as encouraging impulse buys, cross-selling of products and repeat sales.
   a. 6-3-5 Brainwriting
   b. 180SearchAssistant
   c. Dynamic pricing
   d. Power III

59. The _____ business model is one in which participants bid for products and services over the Internet. The functionality of buying and selling in an auction format is made possible through auction software which regulates the various processes involved.

   Several types of _____s are possible.

   a. Online auction
   b. ACNielsen
   c. AMAX
   d. ADTECH

60. A _____ is a tool used in industrial business-to-business procurement. It is a type of auction in which the role of the buyer and seller are reversed, with the primary objective to drive purchase prices downward. In an ordinary auction, buyers compete to obtain a good or service.
   a. Vendor Managed Inventory
   b. Fulfillment house
   c. Materials management
   d. Reverse auction

61. _____s are Web-based intelligent software applications that can help online shoppers find lower price for commodities or services. Price comparison services was the earliest service a _____ provides. To search the price of a particular item, a _____ would search multiple online stores based on the keyword the online shopper provides.

a. Net Promoter^R score
b. Book of business
c. Comparison-Shopping agent
d. Distribution

62. _____ is a branch of philosophy which seeks to address questions about morality, such as how a moral outcome can be achieved in a specific situation (applied _____), how moral values should be determined (normative _____), what moral values people actually abide by (descriptive _____), what the fundamental semantic, ontological, and epistemic nature of _____ or morality is (meta-_____), and how moral capacity or moral agency develops and what its nature is (moral psychology.)

Socrates was one of the first Greek philosophers to encourage both scholars and the common citizen to turn their attention from the outside world to the condition of man. In this view, Knowledge having a bearing on human life was placed highest, all other knowledge being secondary.

a. ACNielsen
b. ADTECH
c. AMAX
d. Ethics

63. In psychology, philosophy, and the cognitive sciences, _____ is the process of attaining awareness or understanding of sensory information. It is a task far more complex than was imagined in the 1950s and 1960s, when it was predicted that building perceiving machines would take about a decade, a goal which is still very far from fruition. The word _____ comes from the Latin words _____, percepio, meaning 'receiving, collecting, action of taking possession, apprehension with the mind or senses.'

_____ is one of the oldest fields in psychology.

a. 180SearchAssistant
b. Groupthink
c. Power III
d. Perception

64. _____ are prices at which demand is relatively high. In introductory microeconomics, a demand curve is downward sloping to the right and either linear or gently convex to the origin. The first is usually true, but the second is only piecewise true, as price surveys indicate that demand for a product is not a linear function of its price and not even a smooth function.

a. Relationship based pricing
b. Fee
c. Price markdown
d. Price points

65. _____ or price ending is a marketing practice based on the theory that certain prices have a psychological impact. The retail prices are often expressed as 'odd prices': a little less than a round number, e.g. $19.99 or £6.95 (but not necessarily mathematically odd, it could also be 2.98.) The theory is this drives demand greater than would be expected if consumers were perfectly rational.

a. Supplier diversity
b. Chain stores
c. First-mover advantage
d. Psychological pricing

Chapter 11. PRICING THE PRODUCT

66. _____ is a form of communication that typically attempts to persuade potential customers to purchase or to consume more of a particular brand of product or service. 'While now central to the contemporary global economy and the reproduction of global production networks, it is only quite recently that _____ has been more than a marginal influence on patterns of sales and production. The formation of modern _____ was intimately bound up with the emergence of new forms of monopoly capitalism around the end of the 19th and beginning of the 20th century as one element in corporate strategies to create, organize and where possible control markets, especially for mass produced consumer goods.
   a. ADTECH
   b. AMAX
   c. ACNielsen
   d. Advertising

67. The _____ is an economic and political union of 27 member states, located primarily in Europe. It was established by the Treaty of Maastricht on 1 November 1993 upon the foundations of the pre-existing European Economic Community. With almost 500 million citizens, the _____ combined generates an estimated 30% share (US$16.8 trillion in 2007) of the nominal gross world product.
   a. European Union
   b. ADTECH
   c. ACNielsen
   d. Eurozone

68. The _____ is an independent agency of the United States government, established in 1914 by the _____ Act. Its principal mission is the promotion of 'consumer protection' and the elimination and prevention of what regulators perceive to be harmfully 'anti-competitive' business practices, such as coercive monopoly.

The _____ Act was one of President Wilson's major acts against trusts.

   a. Federal Trade Commission
   b. Power III
   c. 6-3-5 Brainwriting
   d. 180SearchAssistant

69. The _____ of 1914 (15 U.S.C §§ 41-58, as amended) established the Federal Trade Commission (FTC), a bipartisan body of five members appointed by the President of the United States for seven year terms. This Commission was authorized to issue Cease and Desist orders to large corporations to curb unfair trade practices. This Act also gave more flexibility to the US congress for judicial matters.
   a. Gripe site
   b. Federal Trade Commission Act
   c. Comparative negligence
   d. Product liability

70. A _____ or leader is a product sold at a low price (at cost or below cost) to stimulate other, profitable sales. It is a kind of sales promotion, in other words marketing concentrating on a pricing strategy. The price can even be so low that the product is sold at a loss.
   a. Price shading
   b. Loss leader
   c. Resale price maintenance
   d. Penetration pricing

71. Merchandising refers to the methods, practices and operations conducted to promote and sustain certain categories of commercial activity. The term is understood to have different specific meanings depending on the context. _____ is a sale goods at a store

In marketing, one of the definitions of merchandising is the practice in which the brand or image from one product or service is used to sell another.

a. New Media Strategies
b. Merchandise
c. Merchandising
d. Sales promotion

72. _____ are final goods specifically intended for the mass market. For instance, _____ do not include investment assets, like precious antiques, even though these antiques are final goods.

Manufactured goods are goods that have been processed by way of machinery.

a. Power III
b. Consumer Goods
c. Free good
d. Durable good

73. _____ is the practice of selling a product or service at a very low price, intending to drive competitors out of the market, or create barriers to entry for potential new competitors. If competitors or potential competitors cannot sustain equal or lower prices without losing money, they go out of business or choose not to enter the business. The predatory merchant then has fewer competitors or is even a de facto monopoly, and can then raise prices above what the market would otherwise bear.

a. List price
b. Power III
c. 180SearchAssistant
d. Predatory pricing

74. _____ exists when sales of identical goods or services are transacted at different prices from the same provider. In a theoretical market with perfect information, no transaction costs or prohibition on secondary exchange (or re-selling) to prevent arbitrage, _____ can only be a feature of monopoly and oligopoly markets, where market power can be exercised. Otherwise, the moment the seller tries to sell the same good at different prices, the buyer at the lower price can arbitrage by selling to the consumer buying at the higher price but with a tiny discount.

a. Penetration pricing
b. Price
c. Resale price maintenance
d. Price discrimination

75. _____ is an agreement between business competitors to sell the same product or service at the same price. In general, it is an agreement intended to ultimately push the price of a product as high as possible, leading to profits for all the sellers. _____ can also involve any agreement to fix, peg, discount or stabilize prices.

a. Direct competition
b. Non-price competition
c. Price competition
d. Price fixing

76. The _____ of 1936 (or Anti-Price Discrimination Act, 15 U.S.C. § 13) is a United States federal law that prohibits what were considered, at the time of passage, to be anticompetitive practices by producers, specifically price discrimination. It grew out of practices in which chain stores were allowed to purchase goods at lower prices than other retailers.

a. Trademark infringement
b. Robinson-Patman Act
c. Fair Debt Collection Practices Act
d. Registered trademark symbol

77. The _____ requires the Federal government to investigate and pursue trusts, companies and organizations suspected of violating the Act. It was the first United States Federal statute to limit cartels and monopolies, and today still forms the basis for most antitrust litigation by the federal government.

a. Sherman Antitrust Act
b. 180SearchAssistant
c. Power III
d. 6-3-5 Brainwriting

Chapter 12. CATCHING THE BUZZ

1. _____ is a sub-discipline and type of marketing. There are two main definitional characteristics which distinguish it from other types of marketing. The first is that it attempts to send its messages directly to consumers, without the use of intervening media.
   a. Direct Marketing Associations
   b. Database marketing
   c. Direct marketing
   d. Power III

2. _____ involves disseminating information about a product, product line, brand, or company. It is one of the four key aspects of the marketing mix. (The other three elements are product marketing, pricing, and distribution). P>_____ is generally sub-divided into two parts:

   - Above the line _____: Promotion in the media (e.g. TV, radio, newspapers, Internet and Mobile Phones) in which the advertiser pays an advertising agency to place the ad
   - Below the line _____: All other _____. Much of this is intended to be subtle enough for the consumer to be unaware that _____ is taking place. E.g. sponsorship, product placement, endorsements, sales _____, merchandising, direct mail, personal selling, public relations, trade shows

   a. Bottling lines
   b. Davie Brown Index
   c. Cashmere Agency
   d. Promotion

3. Importance of _____ is critical for any commercial organization. Expanding business is not possible without increasing sales volumes, and effective _____ goal is to organize sales team work in such a manner that ensures a growing flow of regular customers and increasing amount of sales.

The four phase-model of Management Process

   1. Conception
   2. Planning
   3. Execution
   4. Control

This model is cyclical, so it is a constant/continuous process.

===_____ is attainment of sales force goals in a effective ' efficient manner through planning, staffing, training, leading ' controlling organizational resources.

   a. Hit rate
   b. Request for proposal
   c. Sales process
   d. Sales management

4. _____ generally refers to a list of all planned expenses and revenues. It is a plan for saving and spending. A _____ is an important concept in microeconomics, which uses a _____ line to illustrate the trade-offs between two or more goods.
   a. Power III
   b. 180SearchAssistant
   c. 6-3-5 Brainwriting
   d. Budget

Chapter 12. CATCHING THE BUZZ

5. In economic models, the _____ time frame assumes no fixed factors of production. Firms can enter or leave the marketplace, and the cost (and availability) of land, labor, raw materials, and capital goods can be assumed to vary. In contrast, in the short-run time frame, certain factors are assumed to be fixed, because there is not sufficient time for them to change.
   a. 6-3-5 Brainwriting
   b. 180SearchAssistant
   c. Power III
   d. Long-run

6. _____ is defined by the American _____ Association as the activity, set of institutions, and processes for creating, communicating, delivering, and exchanging offerings that have value for customers, clients, partners, and society at large. The term developed from the original meaning which referred literally to going to market, as in shopping, or going to a market to sell goods or services.

   _____ practice tends to be seen as a creative industry, which includes advertising, distribution and selling.

   a. Marketing myopia
   b. Product naming
   c. Customer acquisition management
   d. Marketing

7. _____ refers to messages and related media used to communicate with a market. Those who practice advertising, branding, direct marketing, graphic design, marketing, packaging, promotion, publicity, sponsorship, public relations, sales, sales promotion and online marketing are termed marketing communicators, _____ managers, or more briefly as marcom managers.
   a. Marketing communication
   b. Merchandising
   c. Merchandise
   d. Sales promotion

8. _____ is a form of communication that typically attempts to persuade potential customers to purchase or to consume more of a particular brand of product or service. 'While now central to the contemporary global economy and the reproduction of global production networks, it is only quite recently that _____ has been more than a marginal influence on patterns of sales and production. The formation of modern _____ was intimately bound up with the emergence of new forms of monopoly capitalism around the end of the 19th and beginning of the 20th century as one element in corporate strategies to create, organize and where possible control markets, especially for mass produced consumer goods.
   a. AMAX
   b. ADTECH
   c. Advertising
   d. ACNielsen

9. _____ is an unconventional system of promotions that relies on time, energy and imagination rather than a big marketing budget. Typically, _____ tactics are unexpected and unconventional; consumers are targeted in unexpected places, which can make the idea that's being marketed memorable, generate buzz, and even spread virally. The term was coined and defined by Jay Conrad Levinson in his 1984 book _____.
   a. Diversity marketing
   b. Cause-related Marketing
   c. Digital marketing
   d. Guerrilla marketing

10. _____ , according to The American Marketing Association, is 'a planning process designed to assure that all brand contacts received by a customer or prospect for a product, service, or organization are relevant to that person and consistent over time.' (Marketing Power Dictionary)

    _____ is a term used to describe a holistic approach to marketing. It aims to ensure consistency of message and the complementary use of media. The concept includes online and offline marketing channels.

Chapter 12. CATCHING THE BUZZ

a. ACNielsen
c. AMAX
b. Integrated marketing communications
d. ADTECH

11. _____ is the practice of managing the flow of information between an organization and its publics. _____ - often referred to as _____ - gains an organization or individual exposure to their audiences using topics of public interest and news items that do not require direct payment. Because _____ places exposure in credible third-party outlets, it offers a third-party legitimacy that advertising does not have.
   a. Graphic communication
   c. Power III
   b. Symbolic analysis
   d. Public relations

12. _____ is one of the four aspects of promotional mix. (The other three parts of the promotional mix are advertising, personal selling, and publicity/public relations.) Media and non-media marketing communication are employed for a pre-determined, limited time to increase consumer demand, stimulate market demand or improve product availability.
   a. Marketing communication
   c. Sales promotion
   b. Merchandise
   d. New Media Strategies

13. _____ and viral advertising refer to marketing techniques that use pre-existing social networks to produce increases in brand awareness or to achieve other marketing objectives (such as product sales) through self-replicating viral processes, analogous to the spread of pathological and computer viruses. It can be word-of-mouth delivered or enhanced by the network effects of the Internet. Viral promotions may take the form of video clips, interactive Flash games, advergames, ebooks, brandable software, images, or even text messages.
   a. New Media Marketing
   c. 180SearchAssistant
   b. Power III
   d. Viral marketing

14. _____ is a term commonly used to describe commerce transactions between businesses like the one between a manufacturer and a wholesaler or a wholesaler and a retailer i.e both the buyer and the seller are business entity.This is unlike business-to-consumers (B2C) which involve a business entity and end consumer, or business-to-government (B2G) which involve a business entity and government.

The volume of B2B transactions is much higher than the volume of B2C transactions. The primary reason for this is that in a typical supply chain there will be many B2B transactions involving subcomponent or raw materials, and only one B2C transaction, specifically sale of the finished product to the end customer.

   a. Business-to-business
   c. Customer relationship management
   b. Disruptive technology
   d. Social marketing

15. _____ is the process of transforming information from one format into another. The opposite operation is called decoding.

There are a number of more specific meanings that apply in certain contexts:

- _____ is a basic perceptual process of interpreting incoming stimuli; technically speaking, it is a complex, multi-stage process of converting relatively objective sensory input (e.g., light, sound) into subjectively meaningful experience.
- A content format is a specific _____ format for converting a specific type of data to information.
- Character _____ is a code that pairs a set of natural language characters (such as an alphabet or syllabary) with a set of something else, such as numbers or electrical pulses.
- Text _____ uses a markup language to tag the structure and other features of a text to facilitate processing by computers.
- Semantics _____ of formal language A in formal language B is a method of representing all terms (e.g. programs or descriptions) of language A using language B.
- Electronic _____ transforms a signal into a code optimized for transmission or storage, generally done with a codec.
- Neural _____ is the way in which information is represented in neurons.
- Memory _____ is the process of converting sensations into memories.
- Encryption transforms information for secrecy.

a. ACNielsen
b. Encoding
c. AMAX
d. ADTECH

16. _____ is the reverse of encoding, which is the process of transforming information from one format into another. Information about _____ can be found in the following:

- Digital-to-analog converter, the use of analog circuit for _____ operations
- Code, a rule for converting a piece of information into another form or representation
- Code (cryptography), a method used to transform a message into an obscured form
- _____
- _____ methods, methods in communication theory for _____ codewords sent over a noisy channel
- Digital signal processing, the study of signals in a digital representation and the processing methods of these signals
- Word _____, the use of phonics to decipher print patterns and translate them into the sounds of language
- deCODE genetics

a. 180SearchAssistant
b. Power III
c. 6-3-5 Brainwriting
d. Decoding

17. _____ describes the situation when output from (or information about the result of) an event or phenomenon in the past will influence the same event/phenomenon in the present or future. When an event is part of a chain of cause-and-effect that forms a circuit or loop, then the event is said to 'feed back' into itself.

Chapter 12. CATCHING THE BUZZ

_____ is also a synonym for:

- _____ Signal; the information about the initial event that is the basis for subsequent modification of the event.
- _____ Loop; the causal path that leads from the initial generation of the _____ signal to the subsequent modification of the event.

_____ is a mechanism, process or signal that is looped back to control a system within itself. Such a loop is called a _____ loop.

a. 180SearchAssistant
b. Power III
c. 6-3-5 Brainwriting
d. Feedback

18. The _____ is generally accepted as the use and specification of the four p's describing the strategic position of a product in the marketplace. One version of the origins of the _____ starts in 1948 when James Culliton said that a marketing decision should be a result of something similar to a recipe. This version continued in 1953 when Neil Borden, in his American Marketing Association presidential address, took the recipe idea one step further and coined the term 'Marketing-Mix'.

a. Marketing mix
b. 180SearchAssistant
c. 6-3-5 Brainwriting
d. Power III

19. _____ is a market coverage strategy in which a firm decides to ignore market segment differences and go after the whole market with one offer.it is type of marketing (or attempting to sell through persuasion) of a product to a wide audience. The idea is to broadcast a message that will reach the largest number of people possible. Traditionally _____ has focused on radio, television and newspapers as the medium used to reach this broad audience.

a. Cyberdoc
b. Mass marketing
c. Marketspace
d. Business-to-consumer

20. _____ is a reference to the passing of information from person to person. Originally the term referred specifically to oral communication (literally words from the mouth), but now includes any type of human communication, such as face to face, telephone, email, and text messaging.

Word-of-mouth marketing, which encompasses a variety of subcategories, including buzz, blog, viral, grassroots, cause influencers and social media marketing, as well as ambassador programs, work with consumer-generated media and more, can be highly valued by product marketers.

a. Word of mouth
b. Merchandise
c. Marketing communication
d. New Media Strategies

21. A _____ is a plan of action designed to achieve a particular goal.

_____ is different from tactics. In military terms, tactics is concerned with the conduct of an engagement while _____ is concerned with how different engagements are linked.

a. 180SearchAssistant
c. Power III
b. 6-3-5 Brainwriting
d. Strategy

22. A _____ is a type of website, usually maintained by an individual with regular entries of commentary, descriptions of events, or other material such as graphics or video. Entries are commonly displayed in reverse-chronological order. '_____' can also be used as a verb, meaning to maintain or add content to a _____.

a. 6-3-5 Brainwriting
c. Power III
b. 180SearchAssistant
d. Blog

23. _____ or simply buzz is a term used in word-of-mouth marketing. The interaction of consumers and users of a product or service serve to amplify the original marketing message.

Some describe buzz as a form of hype among consumers, a vague but positive association, excitement, or anticipation about a product or service.

a. Consumption smoothing
c. Consumer confidence
b. Multidimensional scaling
d. Marketing buzz

24. _____ is one of the four elements of marketing mix. An organization or set of organizations (go-betweens) involved in the process of making a product or service available for use or consumption by a consumer or business user.

The other three parts of the marketing mix are product, pricing, and promotion.

a. Better Living Through Chemistry
c. Japan Advertising Photographers' Association
b. Distribution
d. Comparison-Shopping agent

25. _____ is a form of advertisement, where branded goods or services are placed in a context usually devoid of ads, such as movies, the story line of television shows Broadcasting ' Cable reported, 'Two thirds of advertisers employ 'branded entertainment'--_____--with the vast majority of that (80%) in commercial TV programming.' The story, based on a survey by the Association of National Advertisers, added, 'Reasons for using in-show plugs varied from 'stronger emotional connection' to better dovetailing with relevant content, to targetting a specific group.'

_____ became common in the 1980s, but can be traced back to the nineteenth century in publishing.

a. Power III
c. Product placement
b. 6-3-5 Brainwriting
d. 180SearchAssistant

26. _____ refer to a collection of facts usually collected as the result of experience, observation or experiment or a set of premises. This may consist of numbers, words particularly as measurements or observations of a set of variables. _____ are often viewed as a lowest level of abstraction from which information and knowledge are derived.

a. Pearson product-moment correlation coefficient
c. Sample size
b. Mean
d. Data

Chapter 12. CATCHING THE BUZZ

27. _____ is the process of extracting hidden patterns from data. As more data is gathered, with the amount of data doubling every three years, _____ is becoming an increasingly important tool to transform this data into information. It is commonly used in a wide range of profiling practices, such as marketing, surveillance, fraud detection and scientific discovery.
    a. Data mining
    b. 180SearchAssistant
    c. Structure mining
    d. Power III

28. A _____ is a structured collection of records or data that is stored in a computer system. The structure is achieved by organizing the data according to a _____ model. The model in most common use today is the relational model.
    a. 6-3-5 Brainwriting
    b. Power III
    c. 180SearchAssistant
    d. Database

29. _____ is a form of direct marketing using databases of customers or potential customers to generate personalized communications in order to promote a product or service for marketing purposes. The method of communication can be any addressable medium, as in direct marketing.

    The distinction between direct and _____ stems primarily from the attention paid to the analysis of data.

    a. Direct marketing
    b. Database marketing
    c. Power III
    d. Direct Marketing Associations

30. _____ refers to the evolving trend in marketing whereby marketing has moved from a transaction-based effort to a conversation. The definition of _____ comes from John Deighton at Harvard, who says _____ is the ability to address the customer, remember what the customer says and address the customer again in a way that illustrates that we remember what the customer has told us (Deighton 1996.) _____ is not synonymous with online marketing, although _____ processes are facilitated by internet technology.
    a. Outsourcing relationship management
    b. Interactive marketing
    c. InfoNU
    d. European Information Technology Observatory

31. _____ consists of the processes a company uses to track and organize its contacts with its current and prospective customers. _____ software is used to support these processes; information about customers and customer interactions can be entered, stored and accessed by employees in different company departments. Typical _____ goals are to improve services provided to customers, and to use customer contact information for targeted marketing.
    a. Commercialization
    b. Demand generation
    c. Product bundling
    d. Customer relationship management

32. Customer _____ consists of the processes a company uses to track and organize its contacts with its current and prospective customers. CRelationship management software is used to support these processes; information about customers and customer interactions can be entered, stored and accessed by employees in different company departments. Typical CRelationship management goals are to improve services provided to customers, and to use customer contact information for targeted marketing.
    a. Green marketing
    b. Product bundling
    c. Marketing
    d. Relationship management

Chapter 12. CATCHING THE BUZZ

33. _____ is a broad label that refers to any individuals or households that use goods and services generated within the economy. The concept of a _____ is used in different contexts, so that the usage and significance of the term may vary.

A _____ is a person who uses any product or service.

- a. Power III
- c. 180SearchAssistant
- b. 6-3-5 Brainwriting
- d. Consumer

34. _____ is defined by the Oxford English Dictionary as 'the action or practice of selling among or between established clients, markets, traders, etc.' or 'that of selling an additional product or service to an existing customer'. In practice businesses define _____ in many different ways. Elements that might influence the definition might include: the size of the business, the industry sector it operates within and the financial motivations of those required to define the term.

- a. Freebie marketing
- c. Service provider
- b. Cross-selling
- d. Yield management

35. In marketing and advertising, a _____ usually an advertising campaign, is aimed at appealing to. A _____ can be people of a certain age group, gender, marital status, etc. (ex: teenagers, females, single people, etc.)

- a. Brand Development Index
- c. National brand
- b. Target audience
- d. Targeted advertising

36. _____ is a business term meaning the market segment to which a particular good or service is marketed. It is mainly defined by age, gender, geography, socio-economic grouping, technographic, or any other combination of demographics. It is generally studied and mapped by an organization through lists and reports containing demographic information that may have an effect on the marketing of key products or services.

- a. Brando
- c. Category Development Index
- b. Market specialization
- d. Distribution

37. An _____ is a series of advertisement messages that share a single idea and theme which make up an integrated marketing communication (IMC.) _____s appear in different media across a specific time frame.

The critical part of making an _____ is determining a campaign theme, as it sets the tone for the individual advertisements and other forms of marketing communications that will be used.

- a. ACNielsen
- c. Advertising campaign
- b. AMAX
- d. ADTECH

38. In operant conditioning, _____ occurs when an event following a response causes an increase in the probability of that response occurring in the future. Response strength can be assessed by measures such as the frequency with which the response is made (for example, a pigeon may peck a key more times in the session), or the speed with which it is made (for example, a rat may run a maze faster.) The environment change contingent upon the response is called a reinforcer.

- a. Reinforcement
- c. Generic brands
- b. Completely randomized designs
- d. Relationship Management Application

Chapter 12. CATCHING THE BUZZ

39. A _____ is a collection of symbols, experiences and associations connected with a product, a service, a person or any other artifact or entity.

_____s have become increasingly important components of culture and the economy, now being described as 'cultural accessories and personal philosophies'.

Some people distinguish the psychological aspect of a _____ from the experiential aspect.

a. Brandable software
c. Store brand
b. Brand equity
d. Brand

40. _____ Management is the succession of strategies used by management as a product goes through its _____. The conditions in which a product is sold changes over time and must be managed as it moves through its succession of stages.

The _____ goes through many phases, involves many professional disciplines, and requires many skills, tools and processes.

a. Supplier diversity
c. Chain stores
b. Product life cycle
d. Customer satisfaction

41. The business terms _____ and pull originated in the logistic and supply chain management, but are also widely used in marketing.

A _____-pull-system in business describes the move of a product or information between two subjects. On markets the consumers usually 'pulls' the goods or information they demand for their needs, while the offerers or suppliers '_____es' them toward the consumers.

a. Gold Key Matching Service
c. Push
b. Manufacturers' representatives
d. Completely randomized designs

42. _____ is a term used to denote a section of the media specifically designed to reach a very large audience such as the population of a nation state. It was coined in the 1920s with the advent of nationwide radio networks, mass-circulation newspapers and magazines, although _____ were present centuries before the term became common. The term public media has a similar meaning: it is the sum of the public mass distributors of news and entertainment across media such as newspapers, television, radio, broadcasting, which may require union membership in some large markets such as Newspaper Guild, AFTRA, ' text publishers.
a. 6-3-5 Brainwriting
c. 180SearchAssistant
b. Power III
d. Mass media

43. _____ is either an activity of a living being (such as a human), consisting of receiving knowledge of the outside world through the senses, or the recording of data using scientific instruments. The term may also refer to any datum collected during this activity.

The scientific method requires _____s of nature to formulate and test hypotheses.

a. ADTECH
b. ACNielsen
c. Observation
d. AMAX

Chapter 13. ADVERTISING, SALES PROMOTION, AND PUBLIC RELATIONS

1. _____ is a form of communication that typically attempts to persuade potential customers to purchase or to consume more of a particular brand of product or service. 'While now central to the contemporary global economy and the reproduction of global production networks, it is only quite recently that _____ has been more than a marginal influence on patterns of sales and production. The formation of modern _____ was intimately bound up with the emergence of new forms of monopoly capitalism around the end of the 19th and beginning of the 20th century as one element in corporate strategies to create, organize and where possible control markets, especially for mass produced consumer goods.
   a. AMAX
   b. ADTECH
   c. ACNielsen
   d. Advertising

2. _____ is the pursuit of influencing outcomes -- including public-policy and resource allocation decisions within political, economic, and social systems and institutions -- that directly affect people's current lives. (Cohen, 2001)

   Therefore, _____ can be seen as a deliberate process of speaking out on issues of concern in order to exert some influence on behalf of ideas or persons. Based on this definition, Cohen (2001) states that 'ideologues of all persuasions advocate' to bring a change in people's lives.

   a. Advocacy
   b. ACNielsen
   c. ADTECH
   d. AMAX

3. A _____ is a type of website, usually maintained by an individual with regular entries of commentary, descriptions of events, or other material such as graphics or video. Entries are commonly displayed in reverse-chronological order. '_____' can also be used as a verb, meaning to maintain or add content to a _____.
   a. Blog
   b. 6-3-5 Brainwriting
   c. Power III
   d. 180SearchAssistant

4. _____ is a branch of philosophy which seeks to address questions about morality, such as how a moral outcome can be achieved in a specific situation (applied _____), how moral values should be determined (normative _____), what moral values people actually abide by (descriptive _____), what the fundamental semantic, ontological, and epistemic nature of _____ or morality is (meta-_____), and how moral capacity or moral agency develops and what its nature is (moral psychology.)

   Socrates was one of the first Greek philosophers to encourage both scholars and the common citizen to turn their attention from the outside world to the condition of man. In this view, Knowledge having a bearing on human life was placed highest, all other knowledge being secondary.

   a. ACNielsen
   b. AMAX
   c. ADTECH
   d. Ethics

5. _____ refers to optimizing delivering ads according to the position of the recipient (client, user.) It is used in Geo (marketing.) Local search (Internet) often fuels uses optimization for targeting the advertising.
   a. Bumvertising
   b. Puffery
   c. Jingle
   d. Local advertising

6. _____ is the practice of managing the flow of information between an organization and its publics. _____ - often referred to as _____ - gains an organization or individual exposure to their audiences using topics of public interest and news items that do not require direct payment. Because _____ places exposure in credible third-party outlets, it offers a third-party legitimacy that advertising does not have.

a. Symbolic analysis
b. Public relations
c. Power III
d. Graphic communication

7. _____ is an advertisement in which a particular product specifically mentions a competitor by name for the express purpose of showing why the competitor is inferior to the product naming it.

This should not be confused with parody advertisements, where a fictional product is being advertised for the purpose of poking fun at the particular advertisement, nor should it be confused with the use of a coined brand name for the purpose of comparing the product without actually naming an actual competitor. ('Wikipedia tastes better and is less filling than the Encyclopedia Galactica.')

In the 1980s, during what has been referred to as the cola wars, soft-drink manufacturer Pepsi ran a series of advertisements where people, caught on hidden camera, in a blind taste test, chose Pepsi over rival Coca-Cola.

a. Comparative advertising
b. Cost per conversion
c. GL-70
d. Heavy-up

8. An _____ is a series of advertisement messages that share a single idea and theme which make up an integrated marketing communication (IMC.) _____s appear in different media across a specific time frame.

The critical part of making an _____ is determining a campaign theme, as it sets the tone for the individual advertisements and other forms of marketing communications that will be used.

a. ACNielsen
b. AMAX
c. ADTECH
d. Advertising campaign

9. A _____ is a relatively new executive level position at a corporation, company, organization typically reporting directly to the CEO or board of directors. The _____ is responsible for a brand's image, experience, and promise, and propagating it throughout all aspects of the company. The brand officer oversees marketing, advertising, design, public relations and customer service departments.
a. Power III
b. Chief executive officer
c. Financial analyst
d. Chief brand officer

10. _____ is a sub-discipline and type of marketing. There are two main definitional characteristics which distinguish it from other types of marketing. The first is that it attempts to send its messages directly to consumers, without the use of intervening media.
a. Direct marketing
b. Power III
c. Direct Marketing Associations
d. Database marketing

11. _____ , according to The American Marketing Association, is 'a planning process designed to assure that all brand contacts received by a customer or prospect for a product, service, or organization are relevant to that person and consistent over time.' (Marketing Power Dictionary)

_____ is a term used to describe a holistic approach to marketing. It aims to ensure consistency of message and the complementary use of media. The concept includes online and offline marketing channels.

Chapter 13. ADVERTISING, SALES PROMOTION, AND PUBLIC RELATIONS

a. Integrated marketing communications
b. ACNielsen
c. AMAX
d. ADTECH

12. _____ is defined by the American _____ Association as the activity, set of institutions, and processes for creating, communicating, delivering, and exchanging offerings that have value for customers, clients, partners, and society at large. The term developed from the original meaning which referred literally to going to market, as in shopping, or going to a market to sell goods or services.

_____ practice tends to be seen as a creative industry, which includes advertising, distribution and selling.

a. Product naming
b. Marketing
c. Marketing myopia
d. Customer acquisition management

13. _____ in economics and business is the result of an exchange and from that trade we assign a numerical monetary value to a good, service or asset. If I trade 4 apples for an orange, the _____ of an orange is 4 - apples. Inversely, the _____ of an apple is 1/4 oranges.

a. Pricing
b. Contribution margin-based pricing
c. Discounts and allowances
d. Price

14. Importance of _____ is critical for any commercial organization. Expanding business is not possible without increasing sales volumes, and effective _____ goal is to organize sales team work in such a manner that ensures a growing flow of regular customers and increasing amount of sales.

The four phase-model of Management Process

1. Conception
2. Planning
3. Execution
4. Control

This model is cyclical, so it is a constant/continuous process.

===_____ is attainment of sales force goals in a effective ' efficient manner through planning, staffing, training, leading ' controlling organizational resources.

a. Hit rate
b. Sales process
c. Request for proposal
d. Sales management

15. _____ is an organization's process of defining its strategy and making decisions on allocating its resources to pursue this strategy, including its capital and people. Various business analysis techniques can be used in _____, including SWOT analysis (Strengths, Weaknesses, Opportunities, and Threats) and PEST analysis (Political, Economic, Social, and Technological analysis) or STEER analysis involving Socio-cultural, Technological, Economic, Ecological, and Regulatory factors and EPISTEL (Environment, Political, Informatic, Social, Technological, Economic and Legal)

Chapter 13. ADVERTISING, SALES PROMOTION, AND PUBLIC RELATIONS

_____ is the formal consideration of an organization's future course. All _____ deals with at least one of three key questions:

1. 'What do we do?'
2. 'For whom do we do it?'
3. 'How do we excel?'

In business _____, the third question is better phrased 'How can we beat or avoid competition?'. (Bradford and Duncan, page 1.)

a. 6-3-5 Brainwriting
b. Power III
c. 180SearchAssistant
d. Strategic planning

16. In marketing and advertising, a _____ usually an advertising campaign, is aimed at appealing to. A _____ can be people of a certain age group, gender, marital status, etc. (ex: teenagers, females, single people, etc.)

a. Target audience
b. Targeted advertising
c. Brand Development Index
d. National brand

17. _____ generally refers to a list of all planned expenses and revenues. It is a plan for saving and spending. A _____ is an important concept in microeconomics, which uses a _____ line to illustrate the trade-offs between two or more goods.

a. Budget
b. 6-3-5 Brainwriting
c. Power III
d. 180SearchAssistant

18. _____ refers to messages and related media used to communicate with a market. Those who practice advertising, branding, direct marketing, graphic design, marketing, packaging, promotion, publicity, sponsorship, public relations, sales, sales promotion and online marketing are termed marketing communicators, _____ managers, or more briefly as marcom managers.

a. Sales promotion
b. Marketing communication
c. Merchandise
d. Merchandising

19. _____ in organizations and public policy is both the organizational process of creating and maintaining a plan; and the psychological process of thinking about the activities required to create a desired goal on some scale. As such, it is a fundamental property of intelligent behavior. This thought process is essential to the creation and refinement of a plan, or integration of it with other plans, that is, it combines forecasting of developments with the preparation of scenarios of how to react to them.

a. 180SearchAssistant
b. Power III
c. 6-3-5 Brainwriting
d. Planning

20. _____ measures the extent to which a consumer has a meaningful brand experience when exposed to commercial advertising, sponsorship, television contact, or other experience.

In March 2006 the Advertising Research Foundation defined _____ as 'turning on a prospect to a brand idea enhanced by the surrounding context'. The ARF has also defined the function whereby _____ impacts a brand:

Chapter 13. ADVERTISING, SALES PROMOTION, AND PUBLIC RELATIONS

_____ is complex because a variety of exposure and relationship factors affect _____, making simplified rankings misleading.

a. Inseparability
b. Individual branding
c. Automated surveys
d. Engagement

21. A _____ is a plan of action designed to achieve a particular goal.

_____ is different from tactics. In military terms, tactics is concerned with the conduct of an engagement while _____ is concerned with how different engagements are linked.

a. 6-3-5 Brainwriting
b. 180SearchAssistant
c. Power III
d. Strategy

22. In grammar, the _____ is the form of an adjective or adverb which denotes the degree or grade by which a person, thing and is used in this context with a subordinating conjunction, such as than, as...as, etc.

The structure of a _____ in English consists normally of the positive form of the adjective or adverb, plus the suffix -er e.g. 'he is taller than his father is', or 'the village is less picturesque than the town nearby'.

a. 180SearchAssistant
b. Power III
c. Comparative
d. 6-3-5 Brainwriting

23. The _____ is a marketing concept that was first proposed as a theory to explain a pattern among successful advertising campaigns of the early 1940s. It states that such campaigns made unique propositions to the customer and that this convinced them to switch brands. The term was invented by Rosser Reeves of Ted Bates ' Company.

a. Unique selling proposition
b. ADTECH
c. ACNielsen
d. AMAX

24. _____ are uniquely different from the rhetorical appeal to fear. There has been nearly 50 years of research on _____ in various disciplines and these studies have collectively garnered mixed results However, _____ are commonly used in persuasive health campaigns designed to modify behavior.

a. 180SearchAssistant
b. Power III
c. 6-3-5 Brainwriting
d. Fear appeals

25. _____ was originally coined by Austrian psychologist Alfred Adler in 1929. The current broader sense of the word dates from 1961.

In sociology, a _____ is the way a person lives.

a. Power III
b. 6-3-5 Brainwriting
c. 180SearchAssistant
d. Lifestyle

Chapter 13. ADVERTISING, SALES PROMOTION, AND PUBLIC RELATIONS

26. _____ is the use of sexual or erotic imagery in advertising to draw interest to a particular product, for purpose of sale. A feature of _____ is that the imagery used, such as that of a pretty woman, typically has no connection to the product being advertised. The purpose of the imagery is to attract attention of the potential customer or user.

a. 6-3-5 Brainwriting
b. 180SearchAssistant
c. Power III
d. Sex in advertising

27. In promotion and of advertising, a _____ or endorsement consists of a written or spoken statement, sometimes from a person figure, sometimes from a private citizen, extolling the virtue of some product. The term '_____' most commonly applies to the sales-pitches attributed to ordinary citizens, whereas 'endorsement' usually applies to pitches by celebrities. See also Testify, Testimony, for historical context and etymology.

a. Roll-in
b. Promotional products
c. Transpromotional
d. Testimonial

28. _____ is a broad label that refers to any individuals or households that use goods and services generated within the economy. The concept of a _____ is used in different contexts, so that the usage and significance of the term may vary.

A _____ is a person who uses any product or service.

a. 180SearchAssistant
b. Power III
c. Consumer
d. 6-3-5 Brainwriting

29. _____ is a specialized field of marketing research, it is the study of television commercials prior to airing them. It is defined as research to determine an ad's effectiveness based on consumers' responses to the ad and covers all media including print, TV, radio, Internet etcAlthough also known as _____, pre-testing is considered the more accurate, modern name (Young, p.4) for the prediction of how effectively an ad will perform, based on the analysis of feedback gathered from the target audience. Each test will either qualify the ad as strong enough to meet company action standards for airing or identify opportunities to improve the performance of the ad through editing.

a. Custom media
b. Johnson Box
c. Heinz pickle pin
d. Copy testing

30. A _____ is a memorable slogan, set to an engaging melody, mainly broadcast on radio and sometimes on television commercials.

The _____ had no definitive debut: its infiltration of the radio was more of an evolutionary process than a sudden innovation. Product advertisements with a musical tilt can be traced back to 1923, around the same time commercial radio came to the public.

a. Custom media
b. Jingle
c. Link flooding
d. Non-commercial advertising

31. _____ is a business term meaning the market segment to which a particular good or service is marketed. It is mainly defined by age, gender, geography, socio-economic grouping, technographic, or any other combination of demographics. It is generally studied and mapped by an organization through lists and reports containing demographic information that may have an effect on the marketing of key products or services.

Chapter 13. ADVERTISING, SALES PROMOTION, AND PUBLIC RELATIONS

a. Category Development Index
c. Brando
b. Distribution
d. Market specialization

32. _____ is a term commonly used to describe commerce transactions between businesses like the one between a manufacturer and a wholesaler or a wholesaler and a retailer i.e both the buyer and the seller are business entity.This is unlike business-to-consumers (B2C) which involve a business entity and end consumer, or business-to-government (B2G) which involve a business entity and government.

The volume of B2B transactions is much higher than the volume of B2C transactions. The primary reason for this is that in a typical supply chain there will be many B2B transactions involving subcomponent or raw materials, and only one B2C transaction, specifically sale of the finished product to the end customer.

a. Social marketing
c. Customer relationship management
b. Disruptive technology
d. Business-to-business

33. _____ is either an activity of a living being (such as a human), consisting of receiving knowledge of the outside world through the senses, or the recording of data using scientific instruments. The term may also refer to any datum collected during this activity.

The scientific method requires _____s of nature to formulate and test hypotheses.

a. AMAX
c. ACNielsen
b. ADTECH
d. Observation

34. A _____ is a large outdoor advertising structure (a billing board), typically found in high traffic areas such as alongside busy roads. _____s present large advertisements to passing pedestrians and drivers. Typically showing large, ostensibly witty slogans, and distinctive visuals, _____s are highly visible in the top designated market areas.

a. Billboard
c. 180SearchAssistant
b. 6-3-5 Brainwriting
d. Power III

35. Radio-frequency identification (_____) is the use of an object (typically referred to as an _____ tag) applied to or incorporated into a product, animal, or person for the purpose of identification and tracking using radio waves. Some tags can be read from several meters away and beyond the line of sight of the reader.

Most _____ tags contain at least two parts.

a. Power III
c. 6-3-5 Brainwriting
b. 180SearchAssistant
d. RFID

36. _____ is the use of an object (typically referred to as an RFID tag) applied to or incorporated into a product, animal, or person for the purpose of identification and tracking using radio waves. Some tags can be read from several meters away and beyond the line of sight of the reader.

Most RFID tags contain at least two parts.

a. 180SearchAssistant
c. 6-3-5 Brainwriting
b. Power III
d. Radio-frequency identification

37. _____, commonly known as e-commerce or eCommerce, consists of the buying and selling of products or services over electronic systems such as the Internet and other computer networks. The amount of trade conducted electronically has grown extraordinarily with wide-spread Internet usage. A wide variety of commerce is conducted in this way, spurring and drawing on innovations in electronic funds transfer, supply chain management, Internet marketing, online transaction processing, electronic data interchange (EDI), inventory management systems, and automated data collection systems.

a. Electronic commerce
c. ADTECH
b. ACNielsen
d. AMAX

38. _____ is a term used in marketing in general and e-marketing specifically. Marketers will ask permission before advancing to the next step in the purchasing process. For example, they ask permission to send advertisements to prospective customers.

a. Personalized marketing
c. Live banner
b. Spam Lit
d. Permission marketing

39. _____ are a form of online advertising on the World Wide Web intended to attract web traffic or capture email addresses. It works when certain web sites open a new web browser window to display advertisements. The pop-up window containing an advertisement is usually generated by JavaScript, but can be generated by other means as well.

a. Customer intelligence
c. Project Portfolio Management
b. Power III
d. Pop-up ads

40. In economics, business, retail, and accounting, a _____ is the value of money that has been used up to produce something, and hence is not available for use anymore. In economics, a _____ is an alternative that is given up as a result of a decision. In business, the _____ may be one of acquisition, in which case the amount of money expended to acquire it is counted as _____.

a. Fixed costs
c. Variable cost
b. Transaction cost
d. Cost

41. _____ is an advertising term for a timing pattern in which commercials are scheduled to run during intervals that are separated by periods in which no advertising messages appear for the advertised item. Any period of time during which the messages are appearing is called a flight, and a period of message inactivity is usually called a hiatus.

The advantage of the _____ technique is that it allows an advertiser who does not have funds for running spots continuously to conserve money and maximize the impact of the commercials by airing them at key strategic times.

a. Flighting
c. Strict liability
b. Concession
d. Consumocracy

42. _____ is one of the four aspects of promotional mix. (The other three parts of the promotional mix are advertising, personal selling, and publicity/public relations.) Media and non-media marketing communication are employed for a pre-determined, limited time to increase consumer demand, stimulate market demand or improve product availability.

Chapter 13. ADVERTISING, SALES PROMOTION, AND PUBLIC RELATIONS 133

a. Marketing communication
c. New Media Strategies

b. Sales promotion
d. Merchandise

43. _____ is systematic determination of merit, worth, and significance of something or someone using criteria against a set of standards. _____ often is used to characterize and appraise subjects of interest in a wide range of human enterprises, including the arts, criminal justice, foundations and non-profit organizations, government, health care, and other human services.

Depending on the topic of interest, there are professional groups which look to the quality and rigor of the _____ process.

a. ADTECH
c. ACNielsen

b. AMAX
d. Evaluation

44. _____ involves disseminating information about a product, product line, brand, or company. It is one of the four key aspects of the marketing mix. (The other three elements are product marketing, pricing, and distribution). P>_____ is generally sub-divided into two parts:

- Above the line _____: Promotion in the media (e.g. TV, radio, newspapers, Internet and Mobile Phones) in which the advertiser pays an advertising agency to place the ad
- Below the line _____: All other _____. Much of this is intended to be subtle enough for the consumer to be unaware that _____ is taking place. E.g. sponsorship, product placement, endorsements, sales _____, merchandising, direct mail, personal selling, public relations, trade shows

a. Cashmere Agency
c. Promotion

b. Davie Brown Index
d. Bottling lines

45. _____ refers to the methods, practices and operations conducted to promote and sustain certain categories of commercial activity. The term is understood to have different specific meanings depending on the context. Merchandise is a sale goods at a store

In marketing, one of the definitions of _____ is the practice in which the brand or image from one product or service is used to sell another.

a. Word of mouth
c. Merchandising

b. New Media Strategies
d. Marketing communication

46. In operant conditioning, _____ occurs when an event following a response causes an increase in the probability of that response occurring in the future. Response strength can be assessed by measures such as the frequency with which the response is made (for example, a pigeon may peck a key more times in the session), or the speed with which it is made (for example, a rat may run a maze faster.) The environment change contingent upon the response is called a reinforcer.

a. Reinforcement
c. Completely randomized designs

b. Relationship Management Application
d. Generic brands

Chapter 13. ADVERTISING, SALES PROMOTION, AND PUBLIC RELATIONS

47. In economics and sociology, an _____ is any factor (financial or non-financial) that enables or motivates a particular course of action, or counts as a reason for preferring one choice to the alternatives. It is an expectation that encourages people to behave in a certain way. Since human beings are purposeful creatures, the study of _____ structures is central to the study of all economic activity (both in terms of individual decision-making and in terms of co-operation and competition within a larger institutional structure.)
   a. ADTECH
   b. ACNielsen
   c. AMAX
   d. Incentive

48. An _____ is a formal scheme used to promote or encourage specific actions or behavior by a specific group of people during a defined period of time. _____s are particularly used in business management to motivate employees, and in sales in order to attract and retain customers.

If programs are to be effective, all the factors that affect behavior must be recognized, including: motivation, skills, recognition, an understanding of the goals, and the ability to measure progress.

   a. Electronic retailing self-regulation program
   b. Advertiser funded programming
   c. Incentive program
   d. All commodity volume

49. _____ refers to articles of merchandise that are used in marketing and communication programs. These items are usually imprinted with a company's name, logo or slogan, and given away at trade shows, conferences, and as part of guerrilla marketing campaigns.

Almost anything can be branded with a company's name or logo and used for promotion.

   a. Testimonial
   b. Transpromotional
   c. Roll-in
   d. Promotional products

50. The business terms _____ and pull originated in the logistic and supply chain management, but are also widely used in marketing.

A _____-pull-system in business describes the move of a product or information between two subjects. On markets the consumers usually 'pulls' the goods or information they demand for their needs, while the offerers or suppliers '_____es' them toward the consumers.

   a. Completely randomized designs
   b. Gold Key Matching Service
   c. Manufacturers' representatives
   d. Push

51. A trade fair (trade show or expo) is an exhibition organized so that companies in a specific industry can showcase and demonstrate their latest products, service, study activities of rivals and examine recent trends and opportunities. Some trade fairs are open to the public, while others can only be attended by company representatives (members of the trade) and members of the press, therefore _____ are classified as either 'Public' or 'Trade Only'. They are held on a continuing basis in virtually all markets and normally attract companies from around the globe.
   a. 180SearchAssistant
   b. 6-3-5 Brainwriting
   c. Power III
   d. Trade shows

Chapter 13. ADVERTISING, SALES PROMOTION, AND PUBLIC RELATIONS 135

52. In calculus, a function f defined on a subset of the real numbers with real values is called _____, if for all x and y such that x ≤ y one has f(x) ≤ f(y), so f preserves the order. In layman's terms, the sign of the slope is always positive (the curve tending upwards) or zero (i.e., non-decreasing, or asymptotic, or depicted as a horizontal, flat line) Likewise, a function is called monotonically decreasing (non-increasing) if, whenever x ≤ y, then f(x) ≥ f(y), so it reverses the order.
   a. Power III
   b. 180SearchAssistant
   c. 6-3-5 Brainwriting
   d. Monotonic

53. An _____ is the manufacturing of a good or service within a category. Although _____ is a broad term for any kind of economic production, in economics and urban planning _____ is a synonym for the secondary sector, which is a type of economic activity involved in the manufacturing of raw materials into goods and products.

There are four key industrial economic sectors: the primary sector, largely raw material extraction industries such as mining and farming; the secondary sector, involving refining, construction, and manufacturing; the tertiary sector, which deals with services (such as law and medicine) and distribution of manufactured goods; and the quaternary sector, a relatively new type of knowledge _____ focusing on technological research, design and development such as computer programming, and biochemistry.

   a. ADTECH
   b. Industry
   c. AMAX
   d. ACNielsen

54. _____ is anything that is generally accepted as payment for goods and services and repayment of debts. The main uses of _____ are as a medium of exchange, a unit of account, and a store of value. Some authors explicitly require _____ to be a standard of deferred payment.
   a. Microeconomics
   b. Law of supply
   c. Leading indicator
   d. Money

55. In marketing a _____ is a ticket or document that can be exchanged for a financial discount or rebate when purchasing a product. Customarily, _____s are issued by manufacturers of consumer packaged goods or by retailers, to be used in retail stores as a part of sales promotions. They are often widely distributed through mail, magazines, newspapers, the Internet, and mobile devices such as cell phones.
   a. Merchandising
   b. Merchandise
   c. Coupon
   d. Marketing communication

56. _____s are structured marketing efforts that reward, and therefore encourage, loyal buying behaviour -- behaviour which is potentially of benefit to the firm.

In marketing generally and in retailing more specifically, a loyalty card, rewards card, points card, advantage card, or club card is a plastic or paper card, visually similar to a credit card or debit card, that identifies the card holder as a member in a _____. Loyalty cards are a system of the loyalty business model.

   a. 6-3-5 Brainwriting
   b. Loyalty program
   c. Power III
   d. 180SearchAssistant

57. A _____ is an amount paid by way of reduction, return, or refund on what has already been paid or contributed. It is a type of sales promotion marketers use primarily as incentives or supplements to product sales. The mail-in _____ is the most common.

Chapter 13. ADVERTISING, SALES PROMOTION, AND PUBLIC RELATIONS

    a. Personalization
    c. Strand

    b. Lifestyle city
    d. Rebate

58. In the United States consumer sales promotions known as _____ or simply sweeps (both single and plural) have become associated with marketing promotions targeted toward both generating enthusiasm and providing incentive reactions among customers by enticing consumers to submit free entries into drawings of chance (and not skill) that are tied to product or service awareness wherein the featured prizes are given away by sponsoring companies. Prizes can vary in value from less than one dollar to more than one million U.S. dollars and can be in the form of cash, cars, homes, electronics, etc.

_____ frequently have eligibility limited by international, national, state, local, or other geographical factors.

    a. Claritas Prizm
    c. Commercial planning

    b. Market segment
    d. Sweepstakes

59. _____ is the practice of using video games to advertise a product, organization or viewpoint. The term 'advergames' was coined in January 2000 by Anthony Giallourakis, and later mentioned by Wired's 'Jargon Watch' column in 2001. It has been applied to various free online games commissioned by major companies.
    a. ADTECH
    c. ACNielsen

    b. AMAX
    d. Advergaming

60. A _____ is a collection of symbols, experiences and associations connected with a product, a service, a person or any other artifact or entity.

_____s have become increasingly important components of culture and the economy, now being described as 'cultural accessories and personal philosophies'.

Some people distinguish the psychological aspect of a _____ from the experiential aspect.

    a. Brandable software
    c. Brand

    b. Brand equity
    d. Store brand

61. _____ is that part of statistical practice concerned with the selection of individual observations intended to yield some knowledge about a population of concern, especially for the purposes of statistical inference. Each observation measures one or more properties (weight, location, etc.) of an observable entity enumerated to distinguish objects or individuals.
    a. Richard Buckminster 'Bucky' Fuller
    c. AStore

    b. Sampling
    d. Sports Marketing Group

62. A _____ is defined by the International Co-operative Alliance's Statement on the Co-operative Identity as an autonomous association of persons united voluntarily to meet their common economic, social, and cultural needs and aspirations through a jointly-owned and democratically-controlled enterprise. It is a business organization owned and operated by a group of individuals for their mutual benefit. A _____ may also be defined as a business owned and controlled equally by the people who use its services or who work at it.

Chapter 13. ADVERTISING, SALES PROMOTION, AND PUBLIC RELATIONS

a. 6-3-5 Brainwriting
b. 180SearchAssistant
c. Cooperative
d. Power III

63. _____ is the deliberate attempt to manage the public's perception of a subject. The subjects of _____ include people (for example, politicians and performing artists), goods and services, organizations of all kinds, and works of art or entertainment.

From a marketing perspective, _____ is one component of promotion.

a. Pearson's chi-square
b. Little value placed on potential benefits
c. Publicity
d. Brando

64. A _____ is a type of wholesale merchant business that buys goods and bulk products from importers, other wholesalers and then sells to retailers. _____s can deal in any commodity destined for the retail market. Typical categories are food, lumber, hardware, fuel, and textiles.

a. Refusal to deal
b. Chief privacy officer
c. Tacit collusion
d. Jobbing house

65. _____ is the ongoing process of identifying and articulating market requirements that define a product's feature set.

a. Brand parity
b. Targeted advertising
c. Market intelligence
d. Product planning

66. _____ is a strategic management responsibility that integrates finance, communication, marketing and securities law compliance to enable the most effective two-way communication between a company, the financial community, and other constituencies, which ultimately contributes to a company's securities achieving fair valuation. (Adopted by the Ninvestor relationsl Board of Directors, March 2003.) The term describes the department of a company devoted to handling inquiries from shareholders and investors, as well as others who might be interested in a company's stock or financial stability.

a. ACNielsen
b. AMAX
c. ADTECH
d. Investor relations

67. A _____ is a video segment created by a PR firm, advertising agency, marketing firm, corporation or government agency and provided to television news stations for the purpose of informing, shaping public opinion commercial products and services.

News reports may incorporate a _____ in whole or part if the news producer feels it contains information appropriate to the story or of interest to viewers.

a. 180SearchAssistant
b. 6-3-5 Brainwriting
c. Power III
d. Video news release

68. In marketing, a _____ is the 'persona' of a corporation which is designed to accord with and facilitate the attainment of business objectives. It is usually visibly manifested by way of branding and the use of trademarks.

_____ comes into being when there is a common ownership of an organisational philosophy that is manifest in a distinct corporate culture -- the corporate personality.

a. Brand orientation
b. Brand recognition
c. Brand ambassador
d. Corporate identity

69. _____ is the act of involvement with various media for the purpose of informing the public of an organization's mission, policies and practices in a positive, consistent and credible manner.

Typically, _____ involve coordinating directly with the people responsible for producing the news and features in the mass media. The goal of _____ is to maximize positive coverage in the mass media without paying for it directly through advertising.

a. 6-3-5 Brainwriting
b. 180SearchAssistant
c. Media relations
d. Power III

Chapter 14. PERSONAL SELLING, SALES MANAGEMENT, AND DIRECT MARKETING

1. _____ is a form of communication that typically attempts to persuade potential customers to purchase or to consume more of a particular brand of product or service. 'While now central to the contemporary global economy and the reproduction of global production networks, it is only quite recently that _____ has been more than a marginal influence on patterns of sales and production. The formation of modern _____ was intimately bound up with the emergence of new forms of monopoly capitalism around the end of the 19th and beginning of the 20th century as one element in corporate strategies to create, organize and where possible control markets, especially for mass produced consumer goods.
   a. ACNielsen
   b. Advertising
   c. ADTECH
   d. AMAX

2. _____ is an unconventional system of promotions that relies on time, energy and imagination rather than a big marketing budget. Typically, _____ tactics are unexpected and unconventional; consumers are targeted in unexpected places, which can make the idea that's being marketed memorable, generate buzz, and even spread virally. The term was coined and defined by Jay Conrad Levinson in his 1984 book _____.
   a. Cause-related Marketing
   b. Diversity marketing
   c. Digital marketing
   d. Guerrilla marketing

3. _____ is defined by the American _____ Association as the activity, set of institutions, and processes for creating, communicating, delivering, and exchanging offerings that have value for customers, clients, partners, and society at large. The term developed from the original meaning which referred literally to going to market, as in shopping, or going to a market to sell goods or services.

   _____ practice tends to be seen as a creative industry, which includes advertising, distribution and selling.

   a. Marketing myopia
   b. Product naming
   c. Customer acquisition management
   d. Marketing

4. _____ is a term commonly used to describe commerce transactions between businesses like the one between a manufacturer and a wholesaler or a wholesaler and a retailer i.e both the buyer and the seller are business entity.This is unlike business-to-consumers (B2C) which involve a business entity and end consumer, or business-to-government (B2G) which involve a business entity and government.

   The volume of B2B transactions is much higher than the volume of B2C transactions. The primary reason for this is that in a typical supply chain there will be many B2B transactions involving subcomponent or raw materials, and only one B2C transaction, specifically sale of the finished product to the end customer.

   a. Social marketing
   b. Business-to-business
   c. Disruptive technology
   d. Customer relationship management

5. A _____ is a plan of action designed to achieve a particular goal.

   _____ is different from tactics. In military terms, tactics is concerned with the conduct of an engagement while _____ is concerned with how different engagements are linked.

   a. Power III
   b. 6-3-5 Brainwriting
   c. 180SearchAssistant
   d. Strategy

Chapter 14. PERSONAL SELLING, SALES MANAGEMENT, AND DIRECT MARKETING

6. The business terms _____ and pull originated in the logistic and supply chain management, but are also widely used in marketing.

A _____-pull-system in business describes the move of a product or information between two subjects. On markets the consumers usually 'pulls' the goods or information they demand for their needs, while the offerers or suppliers '_____es' them toward the consumers.

   a. Manufacturers' representatives
   c. Gold Key Matching Service
   b. Completely randomized designs
   d. Push

7. _____ consists of the processes a company uses to track and organize its contacts with its current and prospective customers. _____ software is used to support these processes; information about customers and customer interactions can be entered, stored and accessed by employees in different company departments. Typical _____ goals are to improve services provided to customers, and to use customer contact information for targeted marketing.
   a. Commercialization
   c. Product bundling
   b. Demand generation
   d. Customer relationship management

8. _____ is a retail channel for the distribution of goods and services. At a basic level it may be defined as marketing and selling products, direct to consumers away from a fixed retail location. Sales are typically made through party plan, one to one demonstrations, and other personal contact arrangements.
   a. Power III
   c. 180SearchAssistant
   b. Direct selling
   d. 6-3-5 Brainwriting

9. _____ is a method of direct marketing in which a salesperson solicits to prospective customers to buy products or services, either over the phone or through a subsequent face to face or Web conferencing appointment scheduled during the call.

_____ can also include recorded sales pitches programmed to be played over the phone via automatic dialing. _____ has come under fire in recent years, being viewed as an annoyance by many.

   a. Joe job
   c. Directory Harvest Attack
   b. Telemarketing
   d. Phishing

10. Customer _____ consists of the processes a company uses to track and organize its contacts with its current and prospective customers. CRelationship management software is used to support these processes; information about customers and customer interactions can be entered, stored and accessed by employees in different company departments. Typical CRelationship management goals are to improve services provided to customers, and to use customer contact information for targeted marketing.
    a. Green marketing
    c. Product bundling
    b. Marketing
    d. Relationship management

11. _____ consists of the sale of goods or merchandise from a fixed location, such as a department store or kiosk in small or individual lots for direct consumption by the purchaser. _____ may include subordinated services, such as delivery. Purchasers may be individuals or businesses.

Chapter 14. PERSONAL SELLING, SALES MANAGEMENT, AND DIRECT MARKETING

a. Thrifting
b. Warehouse store
c. Charity shop
d. Retailing

12. A _____ is a group of employees from various functional areas of the organization - research, engineering, marketing, finance. human resources, and operations, for example - who are all focused on a specific objective and are responsible to work as a team to improve coordination and innovation across divisions and resolve mutual problems.
a. Cross-functional team
b. 180SearchAssistant
c. Job analysis
d. Power III

13. _____ is one of the four aspects of promotional mix. (The other three parts of the promotional mix are advertising, personal selling, and publicity/public relations.) Media and non-media marketing communication are employed for a pre-determined, limited time to increase consumer demand, stimulate market demand or improve product availability.
a. Sales promotion
b. Marketing communication
c. Merchandise
d. New Media Strategies

14. _____ involves disseminating information about a product, product line, brand, or company. It is one of the four key aspects of the marketing mix. (The other three elements are product marketing, pricing, and distribution). P>_____ is generally sub-divided into two parts:

- Above the line _____: Promotion in the media (e.g. TV, radio, newspapers, Internet and Mobile Phones) in which the advertiser pays an advertising agency to place the ad
- Below the line _____: All other _____. Much of this is intended to be subtle enough for the consumer to be unaware that _____ is taking place. E.g. sponsorship, product placement, endorsements, sales _____, merchandising, direct mail, personal selling, public relations, trade shows

a. Bottling lines
b. Davie Brown Index
c. Cashmere Agency
d. Promotion

15. In advertising, a _____ is an advertisement or campaign that uses a more direct, forceful, and overt sales message. This approach works in opposition to a soft sell.

Theorists have examined the value of repetition for _____ versus soft sell messages to determine their relative efficacy.

a. Hard sell
b. GL-70
c. Comparative advertising
d. Rack card

16. In economic models, the _____ time frame assumes no fixed factors of production. Firms can enter or leave the marketplace, and the cost (and availability) of land, labor, raw materials, and capital goods can be assumed to vary. In contrast, in the short-run time frame, certain factors are assumed to be fixed, because there is not sufficient time for them to change.
a. Power III
b. 180SearchAssistant
c. 6-3-5 Brainwriting
d. Long-run

Chapter 14. PERSONAL SELLING, SALES MANAGEMENT, AND DIRECT MARKETING

17. _____ is the process of approaching prospective customers or clients, typically via telephone, who were not expecting such an interaction. The word 'cold' is used because the person receiving the call is not expecting a call or has not specifically asked to be contacted by a sales person.

Within the United Kingdom, the Privacy and Electronic Communications (EC Directive) Regulations 2003 make it unlawful to transmit an automated recorded message for direct marketing purposes via a telephone, without prior consent of the subscriber.

a. Database marketing
b. Cold calling
c. Direct Marketing Associations
d. Power III

18. _____ is the physical search for minerals, fossils, precious metals or mineral specimens, and is also known as fossicking.

_____ is synonymous in some ways with mineral exploration which is an organised, large scale and at least semi-scientific effort undertaken by mineral resource companies to find commercially viable ore deposits. To actually be considered a prospector you must become registered as a professional prospector.

a. 180SearchAssistant
b. 6-3-5 Brainwriting
c. Power III
d. Prospecting

19. A _____ or trade mark, identified by the symbols â„¢ (not yet registered) and Â® (registered) business organization or other legal entity to identify that the products and/or services to consumers with which the _____ appears originate from a unique source of origin, and to distinguish its products or services from those of other entities. A _____ is a type of intellectual property, and typically a name, word, phrase, logo, symbol, design, image, or a combination of these elements. There is also a range of non-conventional _____s comprising marks which do not fall into these standard categories.

a. 180SearchAssistant
b. Trademark
c. Power III
d. Risk management

20. In environmental modeling and especially in hydrology, a _____ model means a model that is acceptably consistent with observed natural processes, i.e. that simulates well, for example, observed river discharge. It is a key concept of the so-called Generalized Likelihood Uncertainty Estimation (GLUE) methodology to quantify how uncertain environmental predictions are.

a. Behavioral
b. 180SearchAssistant
c. 6-3-5 Brainwriting
d. Power III

21. Importance of _____ is critical for any commercial organization. Expanding business is not possible without increasing sales volumes, and effective _____ goal is to organize sales team work in such a manner that ensures a growing flow of regular customers and increasing amount of sales.

Chapter 14. PERSONAL SELLING, SALES MANAGEMENT, AND DIRECT MARKETING

The four phase-model of Management Process

1. Conception
2. Planning
3. Execution
4. Control

This model is cyclical, so it is a constant/continuous process.

=== _____ is attainment of sales force goals in a effective ' efficient manner through planning, staffing, training, leading ' controlling organizational resources.

a. Sales process
c. Request for proposal
b. Hit rate
d. Sales management

22. _____ is the study of the Earth and its lands, features, inhabitants, and phenomena. A literal translation would be 'to describe or write about the Earth'. The first person to use the word '_____' was Eratosthenes .

a. Power III
c. 6-3-5 Brainwriting
b. 180SearchAssistant
d. Geography

23. An _____ is the manufacturing of a good or service within a category. Although _____ is a broad term for any kind of economic production, in economics and urban planning _____ is a synonym for the secondary sector, which is a type of economic activity involved in the manufacturing of raw materials into goods and products.

There are four key industrial economic sectors: the primary sector, largely raw material extraction industries such as mining and farming; the secondary sector, involving refining, construction, and manufacturing; the tertiary sector, which deals with services (such as law and medicine) and distribution of manufactured goods; and the quaternary sector, a relatively new type of knowledge _____ focusing on technological research, design and development such as computer programming, and biochemistry.

a. ACNielsen
c. AMAX
b. ADTECH
d. Industry

24. _____ is one of the four elements of marketing mix. An organization or set of organizations (go-betweens) involved in the process of making a product or service available for use or consumption by a consumer or business user.

The other three parts of the marketing mix are product, pricing, and promotion.

a. Distribution
c. Better Living Through Chemistry
b. Comparison-Shopping agent
d. Japan Advertising Photographers' Association

25. In accounting, _____ has a very specific meaning. It is an outflow of cash or other valuable assets from a person or company to another person or company. This outflow of cash is generally one side of a trade for products or services that have equal or better current or future value to the buyer than to the seller.

a. ACNielsen
b. AMAX
c. ADTECH
d. Expense

26. _____ is a sub-discipline and type of marketing. There are two main definitional characteristics which distinguish it from other types of marketing. The first is that it attempts to send its messages directly to consumers, without the use of intervening media.
   a. Direct Marketing Associations
   b. Database marketing
   c. Power III
   d. Direct marketing

27. Advertising mail junk mail is the delivery of advertising material to recipients of postal mail. The delivery of advertising mail forms a large and growing service for many postal services, and _____ marketing forms a significant portion of the direct marketing industry. Some organizations attempt to help people opt-out of receiving advertising mail, in many cases motivated by a concern over its negative environmental impact.
   a. Phishing
   b. Direct mail
   c. Directory Harvest Attack
   d. Telemarketing

28. The _____ is an independent agency of the United States government, established in 1914 by the _____ Act. Its principal mission is the promotion of 'consumer protection' and the elimination and prevention of what regulators perceive to be harmfully 'anti-competitive' business practices, such as coercive monopoly.

The _____ Act was one of President Wilson's major acts against trusts.

   a. Power III
   b. Federal Trade Commission
   c. 180SearchAssistant
   d. 6-3-5 Brainwriting

29. The _____ of 1914 (15 U.S.C §§ 41-58, as amended) established the Federal Trade Commission (FTC), a bipartisan body of five members appointed by the President of the United States for seven year terms. This Commission was authorized to issue Cease and Desist orders to large corporations to curb unfair trade practices. This Act also gave more flexibility to the US congress for judicial matters.
   a. Gripe site
   b. Federal Trade Commission Act
   c. Comparative negligence
   d. Product liability

30. _____ or advertising-supported software is any software package which automatically plays, displays, or downloads advertisements to a computer after the software is installed on it or while the application is being used. Some types of _____ are also spyware and can be classified as privacy-invasive software.

Advertising functions are integrated into or bundled with the software, which is often designed to note what Internet sites the user visits and to present advertising pertinent to the types of goods or services featured there.

   a. ADTECH
   b. Isearch
   c. ACNielsen
   d. Adware

31. _____ are long-format television commercials, typically five minutes or longer.. _____ are also known as paid programming (or teleshopping in Europe.) Originally, they were a phenomenon that started in the United States where they were typically shown overnight (usually 2:00 a.m. to 6:00 a.m.)

a. ACNielsen
b. ADTECH
c. AMAX
d. Infomercials

Chapter 15. DELIVERING VALUE THROUGH SUPPLY CHAIN MANAGEMENT

1. Competitiveness is a comparative concept of the ability and performance of a firm, sub-sector or country to sell and supply goods and/or services in a given market. Although widely used in economics and business management, the usefulness of the concept, particularly in the context of national competitiveness, is vigorously disputed by economists, such as Paul Krugman .

The term may also be applied to markets, where it is used to refer to the extent to which the market structure may be regarded as perfectly _____.

a. Free trade zone
b. Geographical pricing
c. Competitive
d. Customs union

2. _____ is, in very basic words, a position a firm occupies against its competitors.

According to Michael Porter, the three methods for creating a sustainable _____ are through:

1. Cost leadership - Cost advantage occurs when a firm delivers the same services as its competitors but at a lower cost;

2.

a. 180SearchAssistant
b. Power III
c. 6-3-5 Brainwriting
d. Competitive advantage

3. _____ is one of the four elements of marketing mix. An organization or set of organizations (go-betweens) involved in the process of making a product or service available for use or consumption by a consumer or business user.

The other three parts of the marketing mix are product, pricing, and promotion.

a. Comparison-Shopping agent
b. Distribution
c. Japan Advertising Photographers' Association
d. Better Living Through Chemistry

4. The Oxford University Press defines _____ as 'marketing on a worldwide scale reconciling or taking commercial advantage of global operational differences, similarities and opportunities in order to meet global objectives.' Oxford University Press' Glossary of Marketing Terms.

Here are three reasons for the shift from domestic to _____ as given by the authors of the textbook, _____ Management--3rd Edition by Masaaki Kotabe and Kristiaan Helsen, 2004.

One of the product categories in which global competition has been easy to track is in U.S. automotive sales.

a. Guerrilla Marketing
b. Global marketing
c. Digital marketing
d. Diversity marketing

Chapter 15. DELIVERING VALUE THROUGH SUPPLY CHAIN MANAGEMENT 147

5. _____ is defined by the American _____ Association as the activity, set of institutions, and processes for creating, communicating, delivering, and exchanging offerings that have value for customers, clients, partners, and society at large. The term developed from the original meaning which referred literally to going to market, as in shopping, or going to a market to sell goods or services.

_____ practice tends to be seen as a creative industry, which includes advertising, distribution and selling.

a. Marketing myopia
c. Marketing
b. Customer acquisition management
d. Product naming

6. _____ is the management of the flow of goods, information and other resources, including energy and people, between the point of origin and the point of consumption in order to meet the requirements of consumers (frequently, and originally, military organizations.) _____ involves the integration of information, transportation, inventory, warehousing, material-handling, and packaging. _____ is a channel of the supply chain which adds the value of time and place utility.

a. Power III
c. 6-3-5 Brainwriting
b. Logistics
d. 180SearchAssistant

7. A _____ or logistics network is the system of organizations, people, technology, activities, information and resources involved in moving a product or service from supplier to customer. _____ activities transform natural resources, raw materials and components into a finished product that is delivered to the end customer. In sophisticated _____ systems, used products may re-enter the _____ at any point where residual value is recyclable.

a. Supply chain
c. Supply chain network
b. Purchasing
d. Demand chain management

8. A personal and cultural _____ is a relative ethic _____, an assumption upon which implementation can be extrapolated. A _____ system is a set of consistent _____s and measures that is soo not true. A principle _____ is a foundation upon which other _____s and measures of integrity are based.

a. Package-on-Package
c. Perceptual maps
b. Supreme Court of the United States
d. Value

9. The _____ is a concept from business management that was first described and popularized by Michael Porter in his 1985 best-seller, Competitive Advantage: Creating and Sustaining Superior Performance.

A _____ is a chain of activities. Products pass through all activities of the chain in order and at each activity the product gains some value.

a. Relationship management
c. Mass marketing
b. Business-to-business
d. Value chain

10. _____ is an advertisement in which a particular product specifically mentions a competitor by name for the express purpose of showing why the competitor is inferior to the product naming it.

This should not be confused with parody advertisements, where a fictional product is being advertised for the purpose of poking fun at the particular advertisement, nor should it be confused with the use of a coined brand name for the purpose of comparing the product without actually naming an actual competitor. ('Wikipedia tastes better and is less filling than the Encyclopedia Galactica.')

Chapter 15. DELIVERING VALUE THROUGH SUPPLY CHAIN MANAGEMENT

In the 1980s, during what has been referred to as the cola wars, soft-drink manufacturer Pepsi ran a series of advertisements where people, caught on hidden camera, in a blind taste test, chose Pepsi over rival Coca-Cola.

a. GL-70
b. Heavy-up
c. Comparative advertising
d. Cost per conversion

11. _____ is a broad label that refers to any individuals or households that use goods and services generated within the economy. The concept of a _____ is used in different contexts, so that the usage and significance of the term may vary.

A _____ is a person who uses any product or service.

a. 6-3-5 Brainwriting
b. Power III
c. Consumer
d. 180SearchAssistant

12. _____ is subcontracting a process, such as product design or manufacturing, to a third-party company. The decision to outsource is often made in the interest of lowering cost or making better use of time and energy costs, redirecting or conserving energy directed at the competencies of a particular business, or to make more efficient use of land, labor, capital, (information) technology and resources. _____ became part of the business lexicon during the 1980s.

a. ACNielsen
b. Intangible assets
c. In-house
d. Outsourcing

13. A _____ is a list of the general tasks and responsibilities of a position. Typically, it also includes to whom the position reports, specifications such as the qualifications needed by the person in the job, salary range for the position, etc. A _____ is usually developed by conducting a job analysis, which includes examining the tasks and sequences of tasks necessary to perform the job.

a. 180SearchAssistant
b. 6-3-5 Brainwriting
c. Job description
d. Power III

14. _____ is a sub-discipline and type of marketing. There are two main definitional characteristics which distinguish it from other types of marketing. The first is that it attempts to send its messages directly to consumers, without the use of intervening media.

a. Direct marketing
b. Power III
c. Direct Marketing Associations
d. Database marketing

15. Importance of _____ is critical for any commercial organization. Expanding business is not possible without increasing sales volumes, and effective _____ goal is to organize sales team work in such a manner that ensures a growing flow of regular customers and increasing amount of sales.

Chapter 15. DELIVERING VALUE THROUGH SUPPLY CHAIN MANAGEMENT

The four phase-model of Management Process

1. Conception
2. Planning
3. Execution
4. Control

This model is cyclical, so it is a constant/continuous process.

===_____ is attainment of sales force goals in a effective ' efficient manner through planning, staffing, training, leading ' controlling organizational resources.

a. Request for proposal
c. Sales process
b. Hit rate
d. Sales management

16. _____ generally refers to a list of all planned expenses and revenues. It is a plan for saving and spending. A _____ is an important concept in microeconomics, which uses a _____ line to illustrate the trade-offs between two or more goods.
   a. 6-3-5 Brainwriting
   c. Power III
   b. 180SearchAssistant
   d. Budget

17. In economics, _____ is the removal of intermediaries in a supply chain: 'cutting out the middleman'. Instead of going through traditional distribution channels, which had some type of intermediate (such as a distributor, wholesaler, broker, or agent), companies may now deal with every customer directly, for example via the Internet. One important factor is a drop in the cost of servicing customers directly.
   a. Social shopping
   c. Consumer-to-consumer
   b. Spamvertising
   d. Disintermediation

18. _____ comprises a range of practices used in an organisation to identify, create, represent, distribute and enable adoption of insights and experiences. Such insights and experiences comprise knowledge, either embodied in individuals or embedded in organisational processes or practice. An established discipline since 1991 , _____ includes courses taught in the fields of business administration, information systems, management, and library and information sciences .
   a. Knowledge management
   c. 6-3-5 Brainwriting
   b. 180SearchAssistant
   d. Power III

Chapter 15. DELIVERING VALUE THROUGH SUPPLY CHAIN MANAGEMENT

19. _____ wholesale represents a type of operation within the wholesale sector. Its main features are summarized best by the following definitions:

- _____ is a form of trade in which goods are sold from a wholesale warehouse operated either on a self-service basis, or on the basis of samples (with the customer selecting from specimen articles using a manual or computerized ordering system but not serving himself) or a combination of the two. Customers (retailers, professional users, caterers, institutional buyers, etc.) settle the invoice on the spot and in cash, and carry the goods away themselves.

- Though wholesalers buy primarily from manufacturers and sell mostly to retailers, industrial users and other wholesalers, they also perform many value added functions. The wholesaler, an intermediary, is used based on principles of specialisation and division of labour as well as contractual efficiency. (OECD -Organisation for Economic Cooperation and Development.)

a. Self branding
c. Containerization
b. Davie Brown Index
d. Cash and carry

20. _____s function as professionals who deal with trade, dealing in commodities that they do not produce themselves, in order to produce profit.

_____s can be of two types:

1. A wholesale _____ operates in the chain between producer and retail _____. Some wholesale _____s only organize the movement of goods rather than move the goods themselves.
2. A retail _____ or retailer, sells commodities to consumers (including businesses.) A shop owner is a retail _____.

A _____ class characterizes many pre-modern societies. Its status can range from high (even achieving titles like that of _____ prince or nabob) to low, such as in Chinese culture, due to the soiling capabilities of profiting from 'mere' trade, rather than from the labor of others reflected in agricultural produce, craftsmanship, and tribute.

In the United States, '_____' is defined (under the Uniform Commercial Code) as any person while engaged in a business or profession or a seller who deals regularly in the type of goods sold.

a. Merchant
c. RFM
b. Trade credit
d. Retail loss prevention

21. Merchandising refers to the methods, practices and operations conducted to promote and sustain certain categories of commercial activity. The term is understood to have different specific meanings depending on the context. _____ is a sale goods at a store

In marketing, one of the definitions of merchandising is the practice in which the brand or image from one product or service is used to sell another.

Chapter 15. DELIVERING VALUE THROUGH SUPPLY CHAIN MANAGEMENT

a. Sales promotion
b. New Media Strategies
c. Merchandising
d. Merchandise

22. _____ is the act of consigning, which is placing a person or thing in the hand of another, but retaining ownership until the goods are sold or person is transferred. This may be done for shipping, transfer of prisoners, or for sale in a store (i.e. a _____ shop.)

Features of _____ are as follows: 1)The Relation between the two parties is that of consignor and consignee and not that of buyer and seller 2)The consignor is entitled to receive all the expenses in connection with _____ 3)The consignee is not responsible for damage of goods during transport or any other procedure.

a. History of pawnbroking
b. Garage sale
c. Consignment
d. Self service

23. A _____ is a party that mediates between a buyer and a seller. A _____ who also acts as a seller or as a buyer becomes a principal party to the deal. Distinguish agent: one who acts on behalf of a principal.
a. Power III
b. Broker
c. 180SearchAssistant
d. Spokesperson

24. _____ is a term commonly used to describe commerce transactions between businesses like the one between a manufacturer and a wholesaler or a wholesaler and a retailer i.e both the buyer and the seller are business entity.This is unlike business-to-consumers (B2C) which involve a business entity and end consumer, or business-to-government (B2G) which involve a business entity and government.

The volume of B2B transactions is much higher than the volume of B2C transactions. The primary reason for this is that in a typical supply chain there will be many B2B transactions involving subcomponent or raw materials, and only one B2C transaction, specifically sale of the finished product to the end customer.

a. Social marketing
b. Customer relationship management
c. Business-to-business
d. Disruptive technology

25. _____ is an organization's process of defining its strategy and making decisions on allocating its resources to pursue this strategy, including its capital and people. Various business analysis techniques can be used in _____, including SWOT analysis (Strengths, Weaknesses, Opportunities, and Threats) and PEST analysis (Political, Economic, Social, and Technological analysis) or STEER analysis involving Socio-cultural, Technological, Economic, Ecological, and Regulatory factors and EPISTEL (Environment, Political, Informatic, Social, Technological, Economic and Legal)

_____ is the formal consideration of an organization's future course. All _____ deals with at least one of three key questions:

1. 'What do we do?'
2. 'For whom do we do it?'
3. 'How do we excel?'

In business _____, the third question is better phrased 'How can we beat or avoid competition?'. (Bradford and Duncan, page 1.)

   a. 180SearchAssistant
   b. 6-3-5 Brainwriting
   c. Power III
   d. Strategic planning

26. _____ in organizations and public policy is both the organizational process of creating and maintaining a plan; and the psychological process of thinking about the activities required to create a desired goal on some scale. As such, it is a fundamental property of intelligent behavior. This thought process is essential to the creation and refinement of a plan, or integration of it with other plans, that is, it combines forecasting of developments with the preparation of scenarios of how to react to them.
   a. Power III
   b. 6-3-5 Brainwriting
   c. Planning
   d. 180SearchAssistant

27. A _____ is a plan of action designed to achieve a particular goal.

_____ is different from tactics. In military terms, tactics is concerned with the conduct of an engagement while _____ is concerned with how different engagements are linked.

   a. Power III
   b. 180SearchAssistant
   c. Strategy
   d. 6-3-5 Brainwriting

28. _____ is a rivalry between individuals, groups, nations for territory, a niche, or allocation of resources. It arises whenever two or more parties strive for a goal which cannot be shared. _____ occurs naturally between living organisms which co-exist in the same environment.
   a. Non-price competition
   b. Competition
   c. Price competition
   d. Price fixing

29. In economics, an externality or spillover of an economic transaction is an impact on a party that is not directly involved in the transaction. In such a case, prices do not reflect the full costs or benefits in production or consumption of a product or service. A positive impact is called an _____ benefit, while a negative impact is called an _____ cost.
   a. ACNielsen
   b. ADTECH
   c. AMAX
   d. External

30. The most important feature of a contract is that one party makes an _____ for an arrangement that another accepts. This can be called a 'concurrence of wills' or 'ad idem' (meeting of the minds) of two or more parties. The concept is somewhat contested.
   a. Offer
   b. ADTECH
   c. ACNielsen
   d. AMAX

31. A _____ is defined by the International Co-operative Alliance's Statement on the Co-operative Identity as an autonomous association of persons united voluntarily to meet their common economic, social, and cultural needs and aspirations through a jointly-owned and democratically-controlled enterprise. It is a business organization owned and operated by a group of individuals for their mutual benefit. A _____ may also be defined as a business owned and controlled equally by the people who use its services or who work at it.

Chapter 15. DELIVERING VALUE THROUGH SUPPLY CHAIN MANAGEMENT 153

    a. Power III
    b. 6-3-5 Brainwriting
    c. Cooperative
    d. 180SearchAssistant

32. _____ is the practice of individuals including commercial businesses, governments and institutions, facilitating the sale of their products or services to other companies or organizations that in turn resell them, use them as components in products or services they offer _____ is also called business-to-_____ for short. (Note that while marketing to government entities shares some of the same dynamics of organizational marketing, B2G Marketing is meaningfully different.)
    a. Law of disruption
    b. Mass marketing
    c. Disruptive technology
    d. Business marketing

33. _____ is the examining of goods or services from retailers with the intent to purchase at that time. _____ is an activity of selection and/or purchase. In some contexts it is considered a leisure activity as well as an economic one.
    a. Hawkers
    b. Khodebshchik
    c. Discount store
    d. Shopping

34. _____s is the social science that studies the production, distribution, and consumption of goods and services. The term _____s comes from the Ancient Greek oá¼°κονομῖα from oá¼¶κος (oikos, 'house') + vÏŒμος (nomos, 'custom' or 'law'), hence 'rules of the house(hold)'. Current _____ models developed out of the broader field of political economy in the late 19th century, owing to a desire to use an empirical approach more akin to the physical sciences.
    a. Industrial organization
    b. ADTECH
    c. ACNielsen
    d. Economic

35. _____ occurs when manufacturers (brands) disintermediate their channel partners, such as distributors, retailers, dealers, and sales representatives, by selling their products direct to consumers through general marketing methods and/or over the internet through eCommerce.

Some manufacturers want their brands to capture the power of the internet but do not want to create conflict with their other distribution channels, as these partners are necessary and viable for any manufacturer to maintain and gain success. The Census Bureau of the U.S. Department of Commerce reported that online sales in 2005 grew 24.6 percent over 2004 to reach 86.3 billion dollars.

    a. Trade Symbols
    b. Store brand
    c. Retail design
    d. Channel conflict

36. _____ is the realization of an application idea, model, design, specification, standard, algorithm an _____ is a realization of a technical specification or algorithm as a program, software component, or other computer system. Many _____s may exist for a given specification or standard.
    a. ACNielsen
    b. ADTECH
    c. AMAX
    d. Implementation

37. The _____ is generally accepted as the use and specification of the four p's describing the strategic position of a product in the marketplace. One version of the origins of the _____ starts in 1948 when James Culliton said that a marketing decision should be a result of something similar to a recipe. This version continued in 1953 when Neil Borden, in his American Marketing Association presidential address, took the recipe idea one step further and coined the term 'Marketing-Mix'.

a. Marketing mix
c. 6-3-5 Brainwriting
b. Power III
d. 180SearchAssistant

38. _____ operations or facilities are commonly called 'distribution centers'. '_____' is the term generally used to describe the process or the work flow associated with the picking, packing and delivery of the packed item(s) to a shipping carrier.
    a. ADTECH
    c. Order processing
    b. AMAX
    d. ACNielsen

39. In economics, business, retail, and accounting, a _____ is the value of money that has been used up to produce something, and hence is not available for use anymore. In economics, a _____ is an alternative that is given up as a result of a decision. In business, the _____ may be one of acquisition, in which case the amount of money expended to acquire it is counted as _____.
    a. Fixed costs
    c. Variable cost
    b. Transaction cost
    d. Cost

40. _____ is a value showing the reliability of a person to others because of his/her integrity, truthfulness, and trustfulness, traits that can encourage someone to depend on him/her.

The wider use of this noun is in Systems engineering.

_____ as applied to a computer system is defined by the IFIP 10.4 Working Group on Dependable Computing and Fault Tolerance as:

'[..] the trustworthiness of a computing system which allows reliance to be justifiably placed on the service it delivers [..]'

an alternative and broader definition is provided by IEC IEV 191-02-03:

'_____ the collective term used to describe the availability performance and its influencing factors : reliability performance, maintainability performance and maintenance support performance'

This concept can be further extended to encompass mechanisms to increase and maintain the _____ of a system.

a. 6-3-5 Brainwriting
c. Dependability
b. Power III
d. 180SearchAssistant

41. A _____ for a set of products is a warehouse or other specialized building, often with refrigeration or air conditioning, which is stocked with products (goods) to be re-distributed to retailers, wholesalers or directly to consumers. A _____ is a principle part, the 'order processing' element, of the entire 'order fulfillment' process. _____s are usually thought of as being 'demand driven'.
    a. Power III
    c. 180SearchAssistant
    b. 6-3-5 Brainwriting
    d. Distribution center

Chapter 15. DELIVERING VALUE THROUGH SUPPLY CHAIN MANAGEMENT

42. A _____ is a commercial building for storage of goods. _____s are used by manufacturers, importers, exporters, wholesalers, transport businesses, customs, etc. They are usually large plain buildings in industrial areas of cities and towns.
    a. 6-3-5 Brainwriting
    b. Warehouse
    c. Power III
    d. 180SearchAssistant

43. _____ is a list for goods and materials held available in stock by a business. It is also used for a list of the contents of a household and for a list for testamentary purposes of the possessions of someone who has died. In accounting _____ is considered an asset.
    a. Ending Inventory
    b. ADTECH
    c. ACNielsen
    d. Inventory

44. Radio-frequency identification (_____) is the use of an object (typically referred to as an _____ tag) applied to or incorporated into a product, animal, or person for the purpose of identification and tracking using radio waves. Some tags can be read from several meters away and beyond the line of sight of the reader.

    Most _____ tags contain at least two parts.

    a. 180SearchAssistant
    b. RFID
    c. 6-3-5 Brainwriting
    d. Power III

45. _____ is the use of an object (typically referred to as an RFID tag) applied to or incorporated into a product, animal, or person for the purpose of identification and tracking using radio waves. Some tags can be read from several meters away and beyond the line of sight of the reader.

    Most RFID tags contain at least two parts.

    a. Radio-frequency identification
    b. 6-3-5 Brainwriting
    c. Power III
    d. 180SearchAssistant

Chapter 16. RETAILING: Bricks and Clicks

1. _____ consists of the sale of goods or merchandise from a fixed location, such as a department store or kiosk in small or individual lots for direct consumption by the purchaser. _____ may include subordinated services, such as delivery. Purchasers may be individuals or businesses.
   - a. Charity shop
   - b. Thrifting
   - c. Warehouse store
   - d. Retailing

2. A personal and cultural _____ is a relative ethic _____, an assumption upon which implementation can be extrapolated. A _____ system is a set of consistent _____s and measures that is soo not true. A principle _____ is a foundation upon which other _____s and measures of integrity are based.
   - a. Package-on-Package
   - b. Supreme Court of the United States
   - c. Perceptual maps
   - d. Value

3. The _____ is a concept from business management that was first described and popularized by Michael Porter in his 1985 best-seller, Competitive Advantage: Creating and Sustaining Superior Performance.

   A _____ is a chain of activities. Products pass through all activities of the chain in order and at each activity the product gains some value.
   - a. Relationship management
   - b. Business-to-business
   - c. Mass marketing
   - d. Value chain

4. _____ is anything that is intended to save time, energy or frustration. A _____ store at a petrol station, for example, sells items that have nothing to do with gasoline/petrol, but it saves the consumer from having to go to a grocery store. '_____' is a very relative term and its meaning tends to change over time.
   - a. MaxDiff
   - b. Convenience
   - c. Demographic profile
   - d. Marketing buzz

5. _____ or _____ data refers to selected population characteristics as used in government, marketing or opinion research, or the _____ profiles used in such research. Note the distinction from the term 'demography' Commonly-used _____ include race, age, income, disabilities, mobility (in terms of travel time to work or number of vehicles available), educational attainment, home ownership, employment status, and even location.
   - a. Demographic
   - b. African Americans
   - c. AStore
   - d. Albert Einstein

6. _____ are a form of online advertising on the World Wide Web intended to attract web traffic or capture email addresses. It works when certain web sites open a new web browser window to display advertisements. The pop-up window containing an advertisement is usually generated by JavaScript, but can be generated by other means as well.
   - a. Power III
   - b. Customer intelligence
   - c. Project Portfolio Management
   - d. Pop-up ads

7. _____ is a broad label that refers to any individuals or households that use goods and services generated within the economy. The concept of a _____ is used in different contexts, so that the usage and significance of the term may vary.

   A _____ is a person who uses any product or service.

Chapter 16. RETAILING: Bricks and Clicks 157

a. 6-3-5 Brainwriting
c. 180SearchAssistant
b. Power III
d. Consumer

8. Radio-frequency identification (_____) is the use of an object (typically referred to as an _____ tag) applied to or incorporated into a product, animal, or person for the purpose of identification and tracking using radio waves. Some tags can be read from several meters away and beyond the line of sight of the reader.

Most _____ tags contain at least two parts.

a. 6-3-5 Brainwriting
c. 180SearchAssistant
b. Power III
d. RFID

9. _____ is the use of an object (typically referred to as an RFID tag) applied to or incorporated into a product, animal, or person for the purpose of identification and tracking using radio waves. Some tags can be read from several meters away and beyond the line of sight of the reader.

Most RFID tags contain at least two parts.

a. 6-3-5 Brainwriting
c. Power III
b. 180SearchAssistant
d. Radio-frequency identification

10. _____ is the examining of goods or services from retailers with the intent to purchase at that time. _____ is an activity of selection and/or purchase. In some contexts it is considered a leisure activity as well as an economic one.
a. Discount store
c. Hawkers
b. Khodebshchik
d. Shopping

11. _____ in its literal sense is the process of transformation of local or regional phenomena into global ones. It can be described as a process by which the people of the world are unified into a single society and function together.

This process is a combination of economic, technological, sociocultural and political forces.

a. Power III
c. 6-3-5 Brainwriting
b. 180SearchAssistant
d. Globalization

12. Merchandising refers to the methods, practices and operations conducted to promote and sustain certain categories of commercial activity. The term is understood to have different specific meanings depending on the context. _____ is a sale goods at a store

In marketing, one of the definitions of merchandising is the practice in which the brand or image from one product or service is used to sell another.

a. Merchandising
c. Sales promotion
b. New Media Strategies
d. Merchandise

13. An _____ is the manufacturing of a good or service within a category. Although _____ is a broad term for any kind of economic production, in economics and urban planning _____ is a synonym for the secondary sector, which is a type of economic activity involved in the manufacturing of raw materials into goods and products.

There are four key industrial economic sectors: the primary sector, largely raw material extraction industries such as mining and farming; the secondary sector, involving refining, construction, and manufacturing; the tertiary sector, which deals with services (such as law and medicine) and distribution of manufactured goods; and the quaternary sector, a relatively new type of knowledge _____ focusing on technological research, design and development such as computer programming, and biochemistry.

a. ADTECH
b. ACNielsen
c. AMAX
d. Industry

14. The _____ or _____ is used by business and government to classify and measure economic activity in Canada, Mexico and the United States. It has largely replaced the older Standard Industrial Classification system; however, certain government departments and agencies, such as the U.S. Securities and Exchange Commission (SEC), still use the SIC codes.

The _____ numbering system is a six-digit code.

a. Power III
b. 6-3-5 Brainwriting
c. 180SearchAssistant
d. North American Industry Classification System

15. There are many important decisions about product and service development and marketing. In the process of product development and marketing we should focus on strategic decisions about product attributes, product branding, product packaging, product labeling and product support services. But product strategy also calls for building a _____.

a. Technology acceptance model
b. Macromarketing
c. Product line
d. Pinstorm

16. _____ is an advertisement in which a particular product specifically mentions a competitor by name for the express purpose of showing why the competitor is inferior to the product naming it.

This should not be confused with parody advertisements, where a fictional product is being advertised for the purpose of poking fun at the particular advertisement, nor should it be confused with the use of a coined brand name for the purpose of comparing the product without actually naming an actual competitor. ('Wikipedia tastes better and is less filling than the Encyclopedia Galactica.')

In the 1980s, during what has been referred to as the cola wars, soft-drink manufacturer Pepsi ran a series of advertisements where people, caught on hidden camera, in a blind taste test, chose Pepsi over rival Coca-Cola.

a. Heavy-up
b. GL-70
c. Comparative advertising
d. Cost per conversion

Chapter 16. RETAILING: Bricks and Clicks

17. A _____ is a small store or shop that sells candy, ice-cream, soft drinks, lottery tickets, newspapers and magazines, along with a small selection of food and grocery supplies. Stores that are part of gas stations may also sell motor oil, windshield washer fluid, radiator fluid, and maps. Often toiletries and other hygiene products are stocked, and some of these stores also offer money orders and wire transfer services or liquor products.
   a. Power III
   b. Convenience store
   c. 6-3-5 Brainwriting
   d. 180SearchAssistant

18. A _____ is a retail establishment which specializes in selling a wide range of products without a single predominant merchandise line. _____s usually sell products including apparel, furniture, appliances, electronics, and additionally select other lines of products such as paint, hardware, toiletries, cosmetics, photographic equipment, jewelery, toys, and sporting goods. Certain _____s are further classified as discount _____s.
   a. Power III
   b. 180SearchAssistant
   c. 6-3-5 Brainwriting
   d. Department store

19. A _____ is a type of department store, which sell products at prices lower than those asked by traditional retail outlets. Most discount department stores offer wide assortments of goods; others specialize in such merchandise as jewelry, electronic equipment, or electrical appliances. _____s are not dollar stores, which sell goods at a dollar or less.
   a. Strip mall
   b. Sales per unit area
   c. Gruen transfer
   d. Discount store

20. A _____ is a commercial building for storage of goods. _____s are used by manufacturers, importers, exporters, wholesalers, transport businesses, customs, etc. They are usually large plain buildings in industrial areas of cities and towns.
   a. Power III
   b. 6-3-5 Brainwriting
   c. 180SearchAssistant
   d. Warehouse

21. A _____ is a retail store, usually selling a wide variety of merchandise, in which customers pay annual membership fees in order to shop. The clubs are able to keep prices low due to the no-frills format of the stores. In addition, customers are required to buy large, wholesale quantities of the store's products, which makes these clubs attractive to both bargain hunters and small business owners.
   a. Power centre
   b. Consignment
   c. Self service
   d. Warehouse club

22. An _____ or factory outlet or 'Best Saving Outlet' is a retail store in which manufacturers sell their stock directly to the public through their own branded stores. The stores can be brick and mortar or online. Traditionally, a factory outlet was a store, attached to a factory or warehouse.
   a. Online ticket brokering
   b. Endcap
   c. Electronic Shelf Label
   d. Outlet store

23. _____ is a retail channel for the distribution of goods and services. At a basic level it may be defined as marketing and selling products, direct to consumers away from a fixed retail location. Sales are typically made through party plan, one to one demonstrations, and other personal contact arrangements.
   a. Direct Selling
   b. Power III
   c. 180SearchAssistant
   d. 6-3-5 Brainwriting

Chapter 16. RETAILING: Bricks and Clicks

24. The _____ is the name of several similar trade associations in the United States, United Kingdom, Australia, Malaysia, Singapore, and New Zealand that represent direct selling companies.

The American _____ is the national trade association of leading firms that manufacture and distribute goods and services sold directly to consumers typically through in-home or person-to-person sales.

Founded in Binghamton, New York in 1910, the association was originally called the Agents Credit Association.

a. 180SearchAssistant
b. Power III
c. 6-3-5 Brainwriting
d. Direct Selling Association

25. _____ is a sales technique in which a salesperson walks from one door of a house to another trying to sell a product or service to the general public. A variant of this involves cold calling first, when another sales representative attempts to gain agreement that a salesperson should visit. _____ selling is usually conducted in the afternoon hours, when the majority of people are at home.

a. Marketing management
b. Performance-based advertising
c. Fast moving consumer goods
d. Door-to-door

26. In commerce, a _____ is a superstore which combines a supermarket and a department store. The result is a very large retail facility which carries an enormous range of products under one roof, including full lines of groceries and general merchandise. In theory, _____s allow customers to satisfy all their routine weekly shopping needs in one trip.

a. 180SearchAssistant
b. Hypermarket
c. Power III
d. 6-3-5 Brainwriting

27. A _____ is a plan of action designed to achieve a particular goal.

_____ is different from tactics. In military terms, tactics is concerned with the conduct of an engagement while _____ is concerned with how different engagements are linked.

a. 6-3-5 Brainwriting
b. Power III
c. Strategy
d. 180SearchAssistant

28. _____ is defined by the American _____ Association as the activity, set of institutions, and processes for creating, communicating, delivering, and exchanging offerings that have value for customers, clients, partners, and society at large. The term developed from the original meaning which referred literally to going to market, as in shopping, or going to a market to sell goods or services.

_____ practice tends to be seen as a creative industry, which includes advertising, distribution and selling.

a. Marketing myopia
b. Product naming
c. Customer acquisition management
d. Marketing

29. _____, is a form of Network Marketing (however the terms are often used interchangeably.) It is a marketing strategy that compensates promoters of direct selling companies not only for product sales they personally generate, but also for the sales of others they introduced to the company. The products and company are usually marketed directly to consumers and potential business partners by means of relationship referrals and word of mouth marketing.

Chapter 16. RETAILING: Bricks and Clicks 161

a. Cross-selling
b. Pay to surf
c. Service provider
d. Multi-level marketing

30. A _____ is a non-sustainable business model that involves the exchange of money primarily for enrolling other people into the scheme, often without any product or service being delivered.

_____s are illegal in many countries, including the United States, the United Kingdom, France, Germany, Canada, Romania, Colombia, Malaysia, Poland, Norway, Bulgaria, Australia, New Zealand, Japan, Italy, Nepal, Philippines, South Africa Sri Lanka, Thailand, Iran, the People's Republic of China, Mexico, Portugal and The Netherlands. These types of schemes have existed for at least a century.

a. Pyramid scheme
b. 6-3-5 Brainwriting
c. Power III
d. 180SearchAssistant

31. _____ is a term commonly used to describe commerce transactions between businesses like the one between a manufacturer and a wholesaler or a wholesaler and a retailer i.e both the buyer and the seller are business entity.This is unlike business-to-consumers (B2C) which involve a business entity and end consumer, or business-to-government (B2G) which involve a business entity and government.

The volume of B2B transactions is much higher than the volume of B2C transactions. The primary reason for this is that in a typical supply chain there will be many B2B transactions involving subcomponent or raw materials, and only one B2C transaction, specifically sale of the finished product to the end customer.

a. Customer relationship management
b. Social marketing
c. Disruptive technology
d. Business-to-business

32. _____ is one of the four elements of marketing mix. An organization or set of organizations (go-betweens) involved in the process of making a product or service available for use or consumption by a consumer or business user.

The other three parts of the marketing mix are product, pricing, and promotion.

a. Comparison-Shopping agent
b. Distribution
c. Better Living Through Chemistry
d. Japan Advertising Photographers' Association

33. In the Mediterranean Basin and the Near East, a _____ is a small, separated garden pavilion open on some or all sides. _____s were common in Persia, India, Pakistan, and in the Ottoman Empire from the 13th century onward. Today, there are many _____s in and around the Topkapı Palace in Istanbul, and they are still a relatively common sight in Greece.

a. 6-3-5 Brainwriting
b. Kiosk
c. Power III
d. 180SearchAssistant

34. _____ describes activities of businesses serving end consumers with products and/or services.

An example of a B2C transaction would be a person buying a pair of shoes from a retailer. The transactions that led to the shoes being available for purchase, that is the purchase of the leather, laces, rubber, etc.

Chapter 16. RETAILING: Bricks and Clicks

a. Societal marketing
c. Demand generation
b. Corporate capabilities package
d. Business-to-consumer

35. Electronic commerce, commonly known as _____ or eCommerce, consists of the buying and selling of products or services over electronic systems such as the Internet and other computer networks. The amount of trade conducted electronically has grown extraordinarily with wide-spread Internet usage. A wide variety of commerce is conducted in this way, spurring and drawing on innovations in electronic funds transfer, supply chain management, Internet marketing, online transaction processing, electronic data interchange (EDI), inventory management systems, and automated data collection systems.
a. E-commerce
c. AMAX
b. ADTECH
d. ACNielsen

36. In economics, business, retail, and accounting, a _____ is the value of money that has been used up to produce something, and hence is not available for use anymore. In economics, a _____ is an alternative that is given up as a result of a decision. In business, the _____ may be one of acquisition, in which case the amount of money expended to acquire it is counted as _____.
a. Variable cost
c. Fixed costs
b. Transaction cost
d. Cost

37. _____ is a crime used to refer to fraud that involves someone pretending to be someone else in order to steal money or get other benefits. The term is relatively new and is actually a misnomer, since it is not inherently possible to steal an identity, only to use it. The person whose identity is used can suffer various consequences when he or she is held responsible for the perpetrator's actions.
a. AMAX
c. ADTECH
b. Identity theft
d. ACNielsen

38. _____ in economics and business is the result of an exchange and from that trade we assign a numerical monetary value to a good, service or asset. If I trade 4 apples for an orange, the _____ of an orange is 4 - apples. Inversely, the _____ of an apple is 1/4 oranges.
a. Pricing
c. Price
b. Contribution margin-based pricing
d. Discounts and allowances

39. _____s are Web-based intelligent software applications that can help online shoppers find lower price for commodities or services. Price comparison services was the earliest service a _____ provides. To search the price of a particular item, a _____ would search multiple online stores based on the keyword the online shopper provides.
a. Distribution
c. Net Promoter^R score
b. Comparison-Shopping agent
d. Book of business

40. _____ refer to a collection of facts usually collected as the result of experience, observation or experiment or a set of premises. This may consist of numbers, words particularly as measurements or observations of a set of variables. _____ are often viewed as a lowest level of abstraction from which information and knowledge are derived.
a. Data
c. Mean
b. Sample size
d. Pearson product-moment correlation coefficient

41. In marketing and strategy, _____ refers to a reduction in the sales volume, sales revenue, or market share of one product as a result of the introduction of a new product by the same producer.

Chapter 16. RETAILING: Bricks and Clicks

For example, if Coca Cola were to introduce a similar product (say, Diet Coke or Cherry Coke), this new product could take some of the sales away from the original Coke. _____ is a key consideration in product portfolio analysis.

a. Co-marketing
c. Business-to-consumer

b. Marketing
d. Cannibalization

42. In marketing, _____ has come to mean the process by which marketers try to create an image or identity in the minds of their target market for its product, brand, or organization. It is the 'relative competitive comparison' their product occupies in a given market as perceived by the target market.

Re-_____ involves changing the identity of a product, relative to the identity of competing products, in the collective minds of the target market.

a. GE matrix
c. Moratorium

b. Containerization
d. Positioning

43. _____ is the provision of service to customers before, during and after a purchase.

According to Turban et al., '_____ is a series of activities designed to enhance the level of customer satisfaction - that is, the feeling that a product or service has met the customer expectation.'

Its importance varies by product, industry and customer.

a. COPC Inc.
c. Facing

b. Customer experience
d. Customer service

44. _____ is a super-regional shopping mall located in the Twin Cities suburb of Bloomington, Minnesota. The mall is located southeast of the junction of Interstate 494 and Minnesota State Highway 77, north of the Minnesota River and is across the interstate from the Minneapolis-St. Paul International Airport. In the United States, it is the second largest enclosed mall in terms of retail space but is largest in terms of total enclosed floor area.

a. Mall of America
c. 6-3-5 Brainwriting

b. Power III
d. 180SearchAssistant

45. A _____ is the space, actual or metaphorical, in which a market operates. The term is also used in a trademark law context to denote the actual consumer environment, ie. the 'real world' in which products and services are provided and consumed.

a. 180SearchAssistant
c. 6-3-5 Brainwriting

b. Power III
d. Marketplace

46. _____ are prices at which demand is relatively high. In introductory microeconomics, a demand curve is downward sloping to the right and either linear or gently convex to the origin. The first is usually true, but the second is only piecewise true, as price surveys indicate that demand for a product is not a linear function of its price and not even a smooth function.

a. Fee
b. Price points
c. Relationship based pricing
d. Price markdown

47. _____ is one of the four Ps of the marketing mix. The other three aspects are product, promotion, and place. It is also a key variable in microeconomic price allocation theory.
   a. Price
   b. Relationship based pricing
   c. Competitor indexing
   d. Pricing

48. In retail an _____, draw tenant, anchor tenant is one of the larger stores in a shopping mall, usually a department store or a major retail chain.

When the planned shopping mall format was developed by Victor Gruen in the mid-1950s, signing larger department stores was necessary for the financial stability of the projects, and to draw retail traffic that would result in visits to the smaller stores in the mall as well. Anchors generally have their rents heavily discounted, and may even receive cash inducements from the mall to remain open.

   a. Endcap
   b. Online ticket brokering
   c. Outlet store
   d. Anchor store

49. _____ is systematic determination of merit, worth, and significance of something or someone using criteria against a set of standards. _____ often is used to characterize and appraise subjects of interest in a wide range of human enterprises, including the arts, criminal justice, foundations and non-profit organizations, government, health care, and other human services.

Depending on the topic of interest, there are professional groups which look to the quality and rigor of the _____ process.

   a. ADTECH
   b. AMAX
   c. ACNielsen
   d. Evaluation

50. _____ is the realization of an application idea, model, design, specification, standard, algorithm an _____ is a realization of a technical specification or algorithm as a program, software component, or other computer system. Many _____s may exist for a given specification or standard.
   a. AMAX
   b. Implementation
   c. ACNielsen
   d. ADTECH

51. A _____ is a written document that details the necessary actions to achieve one or more marketing objectives. It can be for a product or service, a brand, or a product line. _____s cover between one and five years.
   a. Marketing strategy
   b. Marketing plan
   c. Disruptive technology
   d. Prosumer

52. _____ in organizations and public policy is both the organizational process of creating and maintaining a plan; and the psychological process of thinking about the activities required to create a desired goal on some scale. As such, it is a fundamental property of intelligent behavior. This thought process is essential to the creation and refinement of a plan, or integration of it with other plans, that is, it combines forecasting of developments with the preparation of scenarios of how to react to them.

a. 180SearchAssistant	b. Planning
c. 6-3-5 Brainwriting	d. Power III

53. _____ is an organization's process of defining its strategy and making decisions on allocating its resources to pursue this strategy, including its capital and people. Various business analysis techniques can be used in _____, including SWOT analysis (Strengths, Weaknesses, Opportunities, and Threats) and PEST analysis (Political, Economic, Social, and Technological analysis) or STEER analysis involving Socio-cultural, Technological, Economic, Ecological, and Regulatory factors and EPISTEL (Environment, Political, Informatic, Social, Technological, Economic and Legal)

_____ is the formal consideration of an organization's future course. All _____ deals with at least one of three key questions:

1. 'What do we do?'
2. 'For whom do we do it?'
3. 'How do we excel?'

In business _____, the third question is better phrased 'How can we beat or avoid competition?'. (Bradford and Duncan, page 1.)

a. Strategic planning	b. 180SearchAssistant
c. Power III	d. 6-3-5 Brainwriting

54. _____ is a business term meaning the market segment to which a particular good or service is marketed. It is mainly defined by age, gender, geography, socio-economic grouping, technographic, or any other combination of demographics. It is generally studied and mapped by an organization through lists and reports containing demographic information that may have an effect on the marketing of key products or services.

a. Category Development Index	b. Distribution
c. Brando	d. Market specialization

55. _____ is the process by which a new idea or new product is accepted by the market. The rate of _____ is the speed that the new idea spreads from one consumer to the next. Adoption is similar to _____ except that it deals with the psychological processes an individual goes through, rather than an aggregate market process.

a. Kano model	b. Market development
c. Perceptual maps	d. Diffusion

56. _____ is a theory of how, why, and at what rate new ideas and technology spread through cultures. Everett Rogers introduced it in his 1962 book, _____s, writing that 'Diffusion is the process by which an innovation is communicated through certain channels over time among the members of a social system.' The adoption curve becomes an s-curve when cumulative adoption is used.

Rogers theorized that innovations would spread through a community in an S curve, as the early adopters select the innovation (which may be a technology) first, followed by the majority, until a technology or innovation has reached its saturation point in a community.

According to Rogers, diffusion research centers on the conditions which increase or decrease the likelihood that a new idea, product, or practice will be adopted by members of a given culture.

a. 6-3-5 Brainwriting
c. Power III
b. 180SearchAssistant
d. Diffusion of Innovation

57. The _____ is generally accepted as the use and specification of the four p's describing the strategic position of a product in the marketplace. One version of the origins of the _____ starts in 1948 when James Culliton said that a marketing decision should be a result of something similar to a recipe. This version continued in 1953 when Neil Borden, in his American Marketing Association presidential address, took the recipe idea one step further and coined the term 'Marketing-Mix'.

a. 6-3-5 Brainwriting
c. Power III
b. 180SearchAssistant
d. Marketing mix

58. _____ is a marketing term, and involves evaluating the situation and trends in a particular company's market. _____ is often called the 'three c's', which refers to the three major elements that must be studied:

- Customers
- Costs
- Competition

The number of 'c's' is sometimes extended to four, five, or even six, with 'Collaboration', 'Company', and 'Competitive advantage'.

- Marketing mix
- SWOT analysis

a. 180SearchAssistant
c. 6-3-5 Brainwriting
b. Power III
d. Situation analysis

59. _____ is a branch of philosophy which seeks to address questions about morality, such as how a moral outcome can be achieved in a specific situation (applied _____), how moral values should be determined (normative _____), what moral values people actually abide by (descriptive _____), what the fundamental semantic, ontological, and epistemic nature of _____ or morality is (meta-_____), and how moral capacity or moral agency develops and what its nature is (moral psychology.)

Socrates was one of the first Greek philosophers to encourage both scholars and the common citizen to turn their attention from the outside world to the condition of man. In this view, Knowledge having a bearing on human life was placed highest, all other knowledge being secondary.

a. ACNielsen
c. ADTECH
b. Ethics
d. AMAX

60. A _____ is a process that can allow an organization to concentrate its limited resources on the greatest opportunities to increase sales and achieve a sustainable competitive advantage. A _____ should be centered around the key concept that customer satisfaction is the main goal.

A _____ is most effective when it is an integral component of corporate strategy, defining how the organization will successfully engage customers, prospects, and competitors in the market arena.

a. Cyberdoc
b. Psychographic
c. Societal marketing
d. Marketing strategy

61. A _____ is a brief statement of the purpose of a company, organization. It is ideally used to guide the actions of the organization.

_____s often contain the following:

- Purpose of the organization
- The organization's primary stakeholders: clients, stockholders, etc.
- Responsibilities of the organization towards these stockholders
- Products and services offered

Generally shorter _____s are more effective than longer ones.

In developing a _____:

- Encourage input as feasible from employees, volunteers, and other stakeholders
- Publicize it broadly

The _____ can be used to resolve differences between business stakeholders. Stakeholders include: employees including managers and executives, stockholders, board of directors, customers, suppliers, distributors, creditors, governments (local, state, federal, etc.), unions, competitors, NGO's, and the general public.

a. 6-3-5 Brainwriting
b. Power III
c. 180SearchAssistant
d. Mission statement

62. Organizational culture is not the same as _____. It is wider and deeper concepts, something that an organization 'is' rather than what it 'has' (according to Buchanan and Huczynski.)

_____ is the total sum of the values, customs, traditions and meanings that make a company unique.

a. Corporate culture
b. 180SearchAssistant
c. Cross-functional team
d. Power III

Chapter 16. RETAILING: Bricks and Clicks

63. _____ is difficult to define. For example, in 1952, Alfred Kroeber and Clyde Kluckhohn compiled a list of 164 definitions of '_____' in _____: A Critical Review of Concepts and Definitions. However, the word '_____' is most commonly used in three basic senses:

- excellence of taste in the fine arts and humanities
- an integrated pattern of human knowledge, belief, and behavior that depends upon the capacity for symbolic thought and social learning
- the set of shared attitudes, values, goals, and practices that characterizes an institution, organization or group.

When the concept first emerged in eighteenth- and nineteenth-century Europe, it connoted a process of cultivation or improvement, as in agriculture or horticulture. In the nineteenth century, it came to refer first to the betterment or refinement of the individual, especially through education, and then to the fulfillment of national aspirations or ideals.

a. Albert Einstein
b. AStore
c. African Americans
d. Culture

64. Competitiveness is a comparative concept of the ability and performance of a firm, sub-sector or country to sell and supply goods and/or services in a given market. Although widely used in economics and business management, the usefulness of the concept, particularly in the context of national competitiveness, is vigorously disputed by economists, such as Paul Krugman .

The term may also be applied to markets, where it is used to refer to the extent to which the market structure may be regarded as perfectly _____.

a. Geographical pricing
b. Customs union
c. Free trade zone
d. Competitive

65. In economics, an externality or spillover of an economic transaction is an impact on a party that is not directly involved in the transaction. In such a case, prices do not reflect the full costs or benefits in production or consumption of a product or service. A positive impact is called an _____ benefit, while a negative impact is called an _____ cost.
a. ADTECH
b. External
c. AMAX
d. ACNielsen

66. _____s is the social science that studies the production, distribution, and consumption of goods and services. The term _____s comes from the Ancient Greek οἰκονομία from οἶκος (oikos, 'house') + νόμος (nomos, 'custom' or 'law'), hence 'rules of the house(hold)'. Current _____ models developed out of the broader field of political economy in the late 19th century, owing to a desire to use an empirical approach more akin to the physical sciences.
a. Industrial organization
b. ACNielsen
c. ADTECH
d. Economic

67. _____ is a strategic planning method used to evaluate the Strengths, Weaknesses, Opportunities, and Threats involved in a project or in a business venture. It involves specifying the objective of the business venture or project and identifying the internal and external factors that are favorable and unfavorable to achieving that objective. The technique is credited to Albert Humphrey, who led a research project at Stanford University in the 1960s and 1970s using data from Fortune 500 companies.

Chapter 16. RETAILING: Bricks and Clicks 169

a. SWOT analysis
c. Market environment

b. Lead scoring
d. Product differentiation

68. In operant conditioning, _____ occurs when an event following a response causes an increase in the probability of that response occurring in the future. Response strength can be assessed by measures such as the frequency with which the response is made (for example, a pigeon may peck a key more times in the session), or the speed with which it is made (for example, a rat may run a maze faster.) The environment change contingent upon the response is called a reinforcer.
  a. Relationship Management Application
  c. Generic brands
  b. Completely randomized designs
  d. Reinforcement

69. A _____ or logistics network is the system of organizations, people, technology, activities, information and resources involved in moving a product or service from supplier to customer. _____ activities transform natural resources, raw materials and components into a finished product that is delivered to the end customer. In sophisticated _____ systems, used products may re-enter the _____ at any point where residual value is recyclable.
  a. Purchasing
  c. Supply chain network
  b. Supply chain
  d. Demand chain management

70. Consumer market research is a form of applied sociology that concentrates on understanding the behaviours, whims and preferences, of consumers in a market-based economy, and aims to understand the effects and comparative success of marketing campaigns. The field of consumer _____ as a statistical science was pioneered by Arthur Nielsen with the founding of the ACNielsen Company in 1923.

Thus _____ is the systematic and objective identification, collection, analysis, and dissemination of information for the purpose of assisting management in decision making related to the identification and solution of problems and opportunities in marketing.

  a. Logit analysis
  c. Marketing research process
  b. Focus group
  d. Marketing research

71. The general definition of an _____ is an evaluation of a person, organization, system, process, project or product. _____s are performed to ascertain the validity and reliability of information; also to provide an assessment of a system's internal control. The goal of an _____ is to express an opinion on the person/organization/system (etc) in question, under evaluation based on work done on a test basis.
  a. ACNielsen
  c. AMAX
  b. ADTECH
  d. Audit

72. In financial accounting, _____ or cost of sales includes the direct costs attributable to the production of the goods sold by a company. This amount includes the materials cost used in creating the goods along with the direct labor costs used to produce the good. It excludes indirect expenses such as distribution costs and sales force costs.
  a. Cost of goods sold
  c. Stock obsolescence
  b. FIFO and LIFO accounting
  d. Stock demands

73. _____, Gross profit margin or Gross Profit Rate can be defined as the amount of contribution to the business enterprise, after paying for direct-fixed and direct-variable unit costs, required to cover overheads (fixed commitments) and provide a buffer for unknown items. It expresses the relationship between gross profit and sales revenue.

It can be expressed in absolute terms:

Gross Profit = Revenue − Cost of Goods Sold

or as the ratio of gross profit to sales revenue, usually in the form of a percentage:

_____ Percentage = (Revenue-Cost of Goods Sold)/Revenue

Cost of goods sold includes variable costs and fixed costs directly linked to the product, such as material and labor.

a. 180SearchAssistant
b. Power III
c. Gross margin
d. Profit maximization

74. An _____, operating expenditure, operational expense, operational expenditure or OPEX is an on-going cost for running a product, business, or system. Its counterpart, a capital expenditure (CAPEX), is the cost of developing or providing non-consumable parts for the product or system. For example, the purchase of a photocopier is the CAPEX, and the annual paper and toner cost is the OPEX.

a. AMAX
b. ADTECH
c. ACNielsen
d. Operating expense

75. In accounting, _____ has a very specific meaning. It is an outflow of cash or other valuable assets from a person or company to another person or company. This outflow of cash is generally one side of a trade for products or services that have equal or better current or future value to the buyer than to the seller.

a. Expense
b. ACNielsen
c. ADTECH
d. AMAX

76. In economic models, the _____ time frame assumes no fixed factors of production. Firms can enter or leave the marketplace, and the cost (and availability) of land, labor, raw materials, and capital goods can be assumed to vary. In contrast, in the short-run time frame, certain factors are assumed to be fixed, because there is not sufficient time for them to change.

a. Power III
b. 6-3-5 Brainwriting
c. 180SearchAssistant
d. Long-run

77. _____ is a list for goods and materials held available in stock by a business. It is also used for a list of the contents of a household and for a list for testamentary purposes of the possessions of someone who has died. In accounting _____ is considered an asset.

a. ADTECH
b. Inventory
c. Ending Inventory
d. ACNielsen

78. The _____ is an equation that equals the cost of goods sold divided by the average inventory. Average inventory equals beginning inventory plus ending inventory divided by 2.

Chapter 16. RETAILING: Bricks and Clicks

The formula for _____ :

$$\text{Inventory Turnover} = \frac{\text{Cost of Goods Sold}}{\text{Average Inventory}}$$

The formula for average inventory:

$$\text{Average Inventory} = \frac{\text{Beginning inventory} + \text{Ending inventory}}{2}$$

A low turnover rate may point to overstocking, obsolescence, or deficiencies in the product line or marketing effort.

a. ACNielsen
c. ADTECH
b. AMAX
d. Inventory turnover

79. In economics, _____ is the desire to own something and the ability to pay for it. The term _____ signifies the ability or the willingness to buy a particular commodity at a given point of time .

a. Discretionary spending
c. Market dominance
b. Market system
d. Demand

80. In economics, _____ is the ratio of the percent change in one variable to the percent change in another variable. It is a tool for measuring the responsiveness of a function to changes in parameters in a relative way. Commonly analyzed are _____ of substitution, price and wealth.

a. Opinion leadership
c. Intellectual property
b. Elasticity
d. ACNielsen

81. Price _____ is defined as the measure of responsiveness in the quantity demanded for a commodity as a result of change in price of the same commodity. It is a measure of how consumers react to a change in price. In other words, it is percentage change in quantity demanded as per the percentage change in price of the same commodity.

a. ACNielsen
c. Elasticity of demand
b. AMAX
d. ADTECH

82. _____ is defined as the measure of responsiveness in the quantity demanded for a commodity as a result of change in price of the same commodity. It is a measure of how consumers react to a change in price. In other words, it is percentage change in quantity demanded as per the percentage change in price of the same commodity.

a. Power III
c. 6-3-5 Brainwriting
b. Price elasticity of demand
d. 180SearchAssistant

83. _____ is a pricing method used by companies. It is used primarily because it is easy to calculate and requires little information. There are several varieties, but the common thread in all of them is that one first calculates the cost of the product, then includes an additional amount to represent profit.
   a. Relationship based pricing
   b. Break even analysis
   c. Loss leader
   d. Cost-plus pricing

84. _____ is the level of inventory that minimizes the total inventory holding costs and ordering costs. The framework used to determine this order quantity is also known as Wilson _____ Model. The model was developed by F. W. Harris in 1913.
   a. Economic order quantity
   b. ACNielsen
   c. AMAX
   d. ADTECH

85. _____ operations or facilities are commonly called 'distribution centers'. '_____' is the term generally used to describe the process or the work flow associated with the picking, packing and delivery of the packed item(s) to a shipping carrier.
   a. ACNielsen
   b. ADTECH
   c. Order processing
   d. AMAX

86. In marketing, _____ refers to the total cost of holding inventory. This includes warehousing costs such as rent, utilities and salaries, financial costs such as opportunity cost, and inventory costs related to perishibility, shrinkage and insurance.

When there are no transaction costs for shipment, _____s are minimized when no excess inventory is held at all, as in a Just In Time production system.

   a. Merchandise management system
   b. Vendor Managed Inventory
   c. Reverse auction
   d. Carrying cost

ANSWER KEY

Chapter 1

1. c	2. d	3. d	4. c	5. c	6. d	7. d	8. a	9. d	10. c
11. c	12. d	13. d	14. b	15. a	16. d	17. d	18. d	19. c	20. d
21. d	22. d	23. b	24. d	25. d	26. a	27. c	28. a	29. b	30. c
31. d	32. a	33. a	34. d	35. d	36. b	37. d	38. c	39. b	40. b
41. c	42. d	43. c	44. a	45. d	46. d	47. b	48. d	49. d	50. d
51. d	52. d	53. d							

Chapter 2

1. d	2. a	3. b	4. a	5. d	6. d	7. d	8. d	9. d	10. b
11. b	12. d	13. d	14. d	15. d	16. d	17. d	18. d	19. d	20. d
21. d	22. d	23. d	24. d	25. c	26. a	27. d	28. d	29. d	30. d
31. d	32. b	33. d	34. d	35. d	36. b	37. b	38. b	39. a	40. b

Chapter 3

1. b	2. d	3. d	4. a	5. c	6. d	7. d	8. b	9. d	10. d
11. d	12. a	13. a	14. a	15. d	16. b	17. a	18. c	19. c	20. c
21. c	22. c	23. c	24. a	25. a	26. b	27. d	28. b	29. d	30. d
31. c	32. a	33. b	34. a	35. d	36. d	37. d	38. d	39. d	40. c
41. a	42. d	43. b	44. d	45. c	46. d	47. a	48. c	49. c	50. a
51. d	52. a	53. a	54. d	55. d	56. d	57. d	58. a	59. a	60. d
61. a	62. c	63. d	64. c	65. d	66. b	67. b	68. d	69. c	70. d
71. a	72. d	73. d	74. d	75. a	76. d	77. d	78. d	79. c	80. d
81. d	82. d								

Chapter 4

1. a	2. b	3. d	4. c	5. d	6. b	7. d	8. c	9. a	10. d
11. b	12. a	13. d	14. d	15. d	16. c	17. d	18. d	19. d	20. d
21. c	22. d	23. c	24. b	25. d	26. c	27. d	28. d	29. d	30. d
31. d	32. d	33. d	34. d	35. d	36. d	37. d	38. d	39. b	40. b
41. a	42. b	43. d	44. d	45. a	46. d	47. b	48. d	49. d	50. c
51. d									

Chapter 5

1. d	2. d	3. d	4. b	5. c	6. b	7. d	8. d	9. c	10. b
11. a	12. d	13. d	14. d	15. b	16. d	17. c	18. d	19. a	20. d
21. c	22. c	23. b	24. b	25. c	26. b	27. d	28. b	29. c	30. d
31. d	32. d	33. d	34. a	35. c	36. c	37. a	38. b	39. d	40. c
41. d	42. d	43. c	44. d	45. c					

Chapter 6

1. d	2. d	3. d	4. d	5. d	6. b	7. d	8. d	9. b	10. d
11. c	12. d	13. d	14. c	15. b	16. a	17. d	18. d	19. d	20. d
21. d	22. b	23. c	24. d	25. c	26. d	27. d	28. a		

Chapter 7

1. b	2. d	3. d	4. c	5. d	6. d	7. a	8. c	9. d	10. c
11. d	12. a	13. d	14. d	15. d	16. a	17. d	18. d	19. d	20. a
21. b	22. a	23. d	24. a	25. d	26. d	27. d	28. d	29. d	30. a
31. d	32. a	33. d	34. b	35. b	36. d	37. d	38. b	39. d	40. d
41. d	42. d	43. d	44. d	45. b	46. a	47. c			

Chapter 8

1. a	2. b	3. b	4. d	5. d	6. a	7. d	8. d	9. d	10. d
11. a	12. d	13. d	14. d	15. c	16. a	17. a	18. b	19. d	20. a
21. d	22. d	23. a	24. d	25. d	26. a	27. b	28. b	29. d	30. d
31. a	32. b	33. b	34. d	35. b	36. d	37. d	38. b	39. a	40. d
41. d									

Chapter 9

1. b	2. d	3. d	4. c	5. c	6. d	7. d	8. d	9. b	10. b
11. b	12. a	13. d	14. b	15. d	16. d	17. d	18. c	19. b	20. d
21. d	22. d	23. d	24. a	25. d	26. d	27. d	28. d	29. c	30. d
31. c	32. d	33. b	34. c	35. d	36. c	37. a	38. b	39. d	

Chapter 10

1. c	2. d	3. c	4. b	5. a	6. c	7. d	8. d	9. a	10. b
11. d	12. b	13. a	14. d	15. c	16. d	17. d	18. d	19. a	20. b
21. d	22. c	23. d	24. d	25. a	26. c	27. d	28. d	29. c	30. c
31. d	32. d	33. d	34. a	35. c	36. c				

Chapter 11

1. d	2. d	3. b	4. d	5. a	6. d	7. a	8. d	9. d	10. b
11. d	12. a	13. c	14. b	15. c	16. d	17. b	18. a	19. d	20. d
21. a	22. c	23. d	24. a	25. b	26. a	27. d	28. d	29. d	30. a
31. d	32. c	33. a	34. b	35. b	36. b	37. c	38. d	39. b	40. a
41. d	42. d	43. d	44. d	45. a	46. d	47. d	48. d	49. c	50. b
51. d	52. d	53. d	54. d	55. d	56. b	57. a	58. c	59. a	60. d
61. c	62. d	63. d	64. d	65. d	66. d	67. a	68. a	69. b	70. b
71. b	72. b	73. d	74. d	75. d	76. b	77. a			

Chapter 12

1. c	2. d	3. d	4. d	5. d	6. d	7. a	8. c	9. d	10. b
11. d	12. c	13. d	14. a	15. b	16. d	17. d	18. a	19. b	20. a
21. d	22. d	23. d	24. b	25. c	26. d	27. a	28. d	29. b	30. b
31. d	32. d	33. d	34. b	35. b	36. b	37. c	38. a	39. d	40. b
41. c	42. d	43. c							

ANSWER KEY

Chapter 13

1. d	2. a	3. a	4. d	5. d	6. b	7. a	8. d	9. d	10. a
11. a	12. b	13. d	14. d	15. d	16. a	17. a	18. b	19. d	20. d
21. d	22. c	23. a	24. d	25. d	26. d	27. d	28. c	29. d	30. b
31. d	32. d	33. d	34. a	35. d	36. d	37. a	38. d	39. d	40. d
41. a	42. b	43. d	44. c	45. c	46. a	47. d	48. c	49. d	50. d
51. d	52. d	53. b	54. d	55. c	56. b	57. d	58. d	59. d	60. c
61. b	62. c	63. c	64. d	65. d	66. d	67. d	68. d	69. c	

Chapter 14

1. b	2. d	3. d	4. b	5. d	6. d	7. d	8. b	9. b	10. d
11. d	12. a	13. a	14. d	15. a	16. d	17. b	18. d	19. b	20. a
21. d	22. d	23. d	24. a	25. d	26. d	27. b	28. b	29. b	30. d
31. d									

Chapter 15

1. c	2. d	3. b	4. b	5. c	6. b	7. a	8. d	9. d	10. c
11. c	12. d	13. c	14. a	15. d	16. d	17. d	18. a	19. d	20. a
21. d	22. c	23. b	24. c	25. d	26. c	27. c	28. b	29. d	30. a
31. c	32. d	33. d	34. d	35. d	36. d	37. a	38. c	39. d	40. c
41. d	42. b	43. d	44. b	45. a					

Chapter 16

1. d	2. d	3. d	4. b	5. a	6. d	7. d	8. d	9. d	10. d
11. d	12. d	13. d	14. d	15. c	16. c	17. b	18. d	19. d	20. d
21. d	22. d	23. a	24. d	25. d	26. b	27. c	28. d	29. d	30. a
31. d	32. b	33. b	34. d	35. a	36. d	37. b	38. c	39. b	40. a
41. d	42. d	43. d	44. a	45. d	46. b	47. d	48. d	49. d	50. b
51. b	52. b	53. a	54. d	55. d	56. d	57. d	58. d	59. b	60. d
61. d	62. a	63. d	64. d	65. b	66. d	67. a	68. d	69. b	70. d
71. d	72. a	73. c	74. d	75. a	76. d	77. b	78. d	79. d	80. b
81. c	82. b	83. d	84. a	85. c	86. d				

www.ingramcontent.com/pod-product-compliance
Lightning Source LLC
Chambersburg PA
CBHW082203230426
43672CB00015B/2882